For my friend
of old, John

July 2004

HISTORY OUT OF CONTROL

HISTORY OUT OF CONTROL

Confronting Global Anarchy

PETER CRUTTWELL

A RESURGENCE BOOK

A Resurgence Book
published in 1995 by
Green Books Ltd
Foxhole, Dartington
Totnes, Devon TQ9 6EB, UK

Composed in 11½ on 14 Adobe Bembo
by Chris Fayers, Soldon, Devon EX22 7PF

Printed on acid-free paper
by Biddles Ltd
Guildford, Surrey, UK

A catalogue record for this book
is available from The British Library

ISBN 1 870098 60 9 (hardback)

Contents

List of Illustrations

List of Tables, Graphs & Charts

To the memory of
Timothy William Pugh

It is customary for an author to attribute some of the virtues a book may have to the advice and vigilance of those friends upon whom successive drafts of the manuscript had been inflicted; and to absolve them from censure where authorial obstinacy prevailed and permitted its vices to survive. I see no reason to depart from such prudent practice.

I wish to thank John Elford for maintaining an enthusiastic watching-brief during the last few months of editing; and both Maurice Ash and John for their invaluable comments concerning the logic, argument and structure of the later parts of the book.

Writing is a dark and lonely business, and it's probably better that way: it is tempting fate to express satisfaction when the words flow easily, and pointless to complain when they don't. What really does help are the encouragement and interest of others, and in that respect I would like to thank:

Sarah Bruce, for her quiet patience; John Blackwell, for his strictures on precision of style and tone; David Cosserat, whose implacable disagreement with much of what I wrote has been a source of great confidence that I was right; Duncan Hamilton, whose reaction to the conception of the book was so positive; Roger Jackling, for his astute comments on some of the political content; Mark Lomas, for his usual sage counsel; Andrew Place, who read the earliest draft; George Pulver, whose skill with statistics on a 486 PC is unique; Ann and Phil Thomas, staunch and enlightened supporters; and, not least and probably to his surprise, my father John Cruttwell who insisted with old-fashioned novelistic orthodoxy that the book should have not only a beginning and a middle—which were the easy bits—but an ending as well.

Finally, my thanks to Elizabeth Smith for her delightful sketch on page 167, and to James Gardiner of East Devon Technical College for his graphics wizardry.

'So long as histories are written of separate individuals, whether Caesars, Alexanders, Luthers, or Voltaires, and not the histories of *all*, absolutely *all*, those who take part in an event, it is quite impossible to describe the movement of humanity without the conception of a force compelling men to direct their activity towards a certain end. And the only such conception known to historians is that of power.'

Leo Tolstoy: *War and Peace (Second Epilogue)*

'There are those who wish our concern for environment might prove a passing fad. This development is happening at a time... when it had seemed materialism was set to triumph over all opposition and science was but a short step away from penetrating the mind of God. Just when it had begun to seem we could with impunity exploit the earth indefinitely, environmental concerns have arisen that threaten to overwhelm humankind and, as with global warming, themselves are the product of this knowledge.'

Maurice Ash: *The Fabric of the World*

Prologue

IN THE INTRODUCTION TO THIS BOOK, I say that I am writing about the future of history. I also say that it is not a book about the 'environment' as such, although environmental matters, and discussion of them, form one of the book's three interlocking themes. What, then, is the connexion between the future of history and the condition of the environment at the threshold of the third millennium and how does it provide the basis for the subsequent two hundred pages?

Environmental issues are now never far from the front pages of any serious newspaper and, if it should seem that they are now being elbowed out of the headlines—perhaps partly through public apathy or fatigue—it must be in part also the result of the extraordinary international political developments in these dying days of the very late twentieth century. That is, in fact, the connexion: there is wide and intense debate on the environment and, in separate forums, on the direction and very meaning of history itself as this catastrophic century stumbles to a close. At the same time, there are fewer political and economic certitudes, even as economic growth seems to have displaced all other measures of the historical progress of humanity; and politics and politicians the world over are held in abjectly low esteem for both their ethics and their ineffectiveness in managing our affairs. I believe that there is now an urgent need to view all of these products of human activity through linked lenses.

The purely *personal* origin of my book, however, lies in the savannah and jungles of the Brazilian Amazon, the slums of Colombia, the Bolivian and Peruvian altiplano and the concrete canyons of Wall Street many years ago. This was where my nascent career took me after I had falteringly followed in the footsteps of Bacon and Macaulay at Trinity College, Cambridge, without significantly advancing the sum of human knowledge.

But part of the luggage I took to the Western Hemisphere was an intense and longstanding interest in a theory of history and it was there in the West, it seemed, that great slabs of it were happening with whole continents and peoples being convulsed and propelled in uncharted directions as the dominance of what I shall call the *economic imperative*— the new secular theology created by the twentieth century—reached into the remotest geographical recesses to touch people who, until recently, had had no history. It wasn't the *detail* of the events which was interesting so much as the sense simply that history was *happening*—and for some people, indeed, just starting or perhaps about to end. What was happening? Why? Was there direction and purpose? What of those peoples for whom there was no history? It was as if, for me, Europe had had *its* history and certainly what I was seeing and being a part of was an awful lot more exciting than studying the proceedings of the Council of Trent or trying to understand why the Albigensian heretics should have even bothered.

My first 'historical' experience in the New World was unreal. New York was immobilised by a combined dock- and newspaper strike and a savagely cold winter, which made job-hunting extremely difficult. But my funds were running out and I had to find work just to survive to the spring and the end of the strikes. I signed on at a typing agency and was promptly sent round to a dingy office on lower Park Avenue where I was to spend several weeks typing mailshot envelopes for what the foxed sign on the frosted glass door declared—without, it seemed, great confidence—was the 'World Peace Council'. The door was opened by a tall thin stooped old man who mumbled that his name was Norman Thomas and that he was founder of the Council. Mr Thomas showed me to the typewriter whereupon I proceeded to type all morning until he shuffled up and suggested we go out to get a sandwich at a nearby deli.

At the lunch counter he politely quizzed me, and I then asked him how he had come to found the Council and what it did. Its purpose seemed to be about as harmless as it was ineffectual judging by my mailing list, and it had been founded by Mr Thomas after a lifetime in politics. Having read American history in my second year, I suddenly realised who he was. He was the great dean of American socialists, Norman Matoon Thomas, born in 1884 and the successor to Eugene Debs. He was the perennial candidate for the first US socialist presidency and had first run against Franklin Roosevelt in 1932.

We had lunch almost every day for the next few weeks, in the same deli, and talked endlessly about politics and history. It was a wonderful experience for me, who had never before met an 'historical' figure. I remember once asking Norman how deep was his regret that none of his six presidential campaigns had yielded him the key to the White House. No, he said, he was not disappointed because almost all the things he had fought for, like safety in the coal mines of West Virginia and the rights of grape-pickers in California, had come to pass since they were *historically inevitable*. But he admitted sadly that his innate historical optimism had not reckoned with the atomic bomb, and that it was now the World Peace Council's mission to ensure that the Bomb would not mark the end of history.

I survived the winter and the strikes and finished typing against the Bomb.

Years later and I had graduated from the typing pool, and from another university, to become finance director of an international mining company. I used to spend weeks on end running around in obscure but generally beautiful parts of the world (odd and perverse of God—is it not?—to have tended to dump a high percentage of His mineral bounty in beauty spots) seeking to ensure that our operations conformed to that year's budget and to some distantly prescribed standards of financial accountability.

A few hours from New York—where enormous movements of people were still taking place, in a country which had just come out the other side of the Cuban Missile Crisis (good history, that one, in every respect), and where I would shortly live through the assassination of John Fitzgerald Kennedy and watch Jack Ruby shoot down Lee Harvey Oswald on my kitchen television in real-time history one Sunday morning—and I was driving a Chevrolet pick-up truck along a road cut without compromise through the Brazilian rain-forest just weeks before by a logging company, and making my way north from the Amazon to a base-camp after spending the night on an almost empty island the size of Switzerland that lay in the mouth of the river.

The scale of those operations, mining or logging, was stupendous and—frankly—thrilling. But I was soon to join the Sierra Club—one of the pioneer conservationist groups in the United States—and I began to find it increasingly difficult to reconcile the excitement—the buzz— I undoubtedly derived from watching the heroic feats of the earth-movers and crawling drag-lines with the aftermath lying beneath their tracks. (I joined the Sierra Club after seeing an advertisement in an airline magazine extolling to the pioneers amongst its passengers the superior virtues of shooting caribou in Alaska with semi-automatics from a circling helicopter—'every hunter gets a free champagne breakfast on board and no risk of frost-bite!', as I recall the text. Some hunter). This is where for me there first began to emerge the glimmer of a connexion between human history and our now shifting environment, and the notion that both might be heading for oblivion at about the same time as each succumbed to the economic imperative.

I remember once flying over the estuary of the São Francisco River in north-eastern Brazil and out into the South Atlantic. We were on a geophysical reconnaissance mission: the experts can spot tell-tale signs of mineral deposits from the air. All I could see, as far the eye could range over the ocean, was a rust-red soup, only highly non-nutritious. It came from iron-mine tailings hundreds of miles back up the river and, for all I know, it's even bigger today.

I remember stopping the truck for a rest at a camp of sutlers following the road-builders on the Mato Grosso-Para stateline in the middle of the wilderness. The place was full of whores, and ruffians from all over, many of them armed, and I don't suppose that the native hunting people and animals in the newly 'reached' forest had ever seen a white man— certainly none of this ilk—until the economic imperative reached *them*. Some of the ruffians had captured a beautiful dove-like bird, had hung it by one leg from the hurricane-lamp with a piece of string and were lobbing empty beer bottles at it. It was alive. Adrenalin picked me up, marched me over to the lamp, guided my Swiss Army knife through the twine, tucked the bird into my bush-jacket and got me back in the truck and away before I—and, I have to believe, the speechless audience— even realised what was happening.

Those native peoples had lived there for ever, history-free. Now, suddenly, they'd really caught up and that would soon be the end of history for them. They used to eat birds like the one I rescued: but it was okay for me that they ate birds—they always had, and the birds knew it too.

I remember the Tequendama Hotel in Bogotá. There was an attempted military coup or civil insurrection of some sort once when I was staying there. We were holed up, probably securely enough, in the well-victualled basement where we played cards and table-tennis while the tanks clanked overhead to a small-arms counterpoint. After a day or so I got bored. One night, fortified with some of the best Scotch smoked salmon I've ever eaten plus a bottle of Chablis, I managed to clamber out through some kind of cellar skylight and up into the unlit street and unaccountably soon found myself in the *barrios*—the slums which ranked, in every sense of the word, with anything the *favelas* of Rio or São Paolo had to offer.

Looking back, I think that this slum was probably relatively safe, even for someone born in St Pancras, and given the bizarre circumstances: I was almost invisible, and anyway the inhabitants of this particular neigh-bourhood seemed without exception to be grotesquely down-trodden and dispirited Chibcha Indians from the mountains—recent brief migrants into history. At the time, I thought: what, in God's name, had brought them down? The answer was partly the despoliation of their land, and partly the meretricious demand of burgeoning cities all over Latin America for labour to power the new economics.

They were all smoking something and drinking something else and were huddled round—wait for it—US-made Zenith television sets! Where did the electricity come from? Who paid for it? Those few who did bother to look up at me had opaque eyes of, it seemed to me, unfathomable depth and apartness. What *could* they be watching—or understanding?

Next day the putsch had failed—or succeeded. I can't remember and it wasn't too clear, or important. Anyway, before getting the plane out to Miami, I went over and visited the beautiful Spanish colonial two-storey building—a national monument—where the declaration of independence was promulgated in about 1818. I took a photograph of it—in case it too was to go the way of so many others and into history, as its ugly new neighbours seemed to portend.

Oh yes! the Chibchas were watching 'I dream of Jeannie' with Larry Hagman and Barbara Eden mouthing Spanish out of Burbank, California. But no Indian subtitles for the Chibchas: that's when their history started. Briefly.

This is when history went out of control.

Introduction

THIS IS A BOOK about the future of human history. It is an idiosyncratic exploration of the condition of the world and of the way that history has worked to bring us to the threshold of the third millennium. I am curious about the prospects for humankind as the millennium approaches; and I was driven to write it because of uncertainty where I stood in it. Nobody seems more likely than I to enlighten myself even though at this point, as 1995 approaches, I have absolutely no idea where the exploration will take me.

It seeks to explore the possibility that there has been a single force or a set of related forces which have driven history from prehistoric times to the end of the second millennium of the Common Era—the view of the so-called historicists and of certain contemporary political writers. It takes a look at various theories of Universal History which have been floated in the last two centuries, and assesses their relevance to our present conjuncture, where it suggests that there is now present an historically quite unique and murderous panoply of threats to human survival—at least, to a survival in any historically and culturally recognisable form—in the early third millennium. The scale and nature of these threats are no longer matters of dispute; and they have now become so monstrous as to have overturned all our comfortable theories of history. They are presented and analysed in terms of the scale and speed with which they have managed to deflect human history from what had, for many centuries, appeared to be a broadly steady pattern of progress through successive levels of spiritual and material enlightenment. I then show that these stresses are both cause and effect of the now-global obsession with economic growth and production as virtually the sole measures of human activity towards some never-defined goal. Political power and its proper exercise have been forfeited to this mindless process; and I proceed to advocate a reassertion of local and national social and political power as the basis necessary for the solution to the environmental and social catastrophes which humankind now contemplates. I conclude by assessing the challenges which both the catastrophes and the strategies necessary to avert them will offer to today's all-conquering and unquestioned commitment to liberal economic democracy; and how our present political, economic and social institutions may respond to this challenge. The book is not yet another addition to the environment bibliography: it just so happens that the state of today's environment is a major part of the murderous panoply and has now become, alongside the future of liberal economic democracy, one of the two main elements in the design of the history to come.

My starting-point is the unsurprising verdict that the world in 1995 would have appeared absolutely unchanged from recent ice ages in every particular—except as a result of natural causes—had it not been for the emergence into prehistory of *homo sapiens* some scores of millennia ago. Mine is necessarily a highly anthropocentric view: it is, after all, only human beings who are conscious of history, conscious of the passage of time and of the piling-up of events into a great historical midden of fact and fantasy, hope and despair; only human beings who perceive the way in which the past is formed out of the future and who seek to record the process through systematic historical analysis. It is also unashamedly ethnocentric in viewing the world from a Western observation point since it is incontestable that it is the impact of the West which is, for better or worse, most firmly imprinted in the most literal sense on the face of the third millennium world.

Prehistory is defined in the technical sense as the period before surviving written or engraved records of the most elementary nature begin to appear—say in Sumeria around 3500 BC with cuneiform writing. Up to that date, and indeed for some thousands of years to come, humans existed in such small numbers that their impact on all but the micro-environments in which tentative tribal groupings gathered, was minimal. Consequently, there were no forces making for disequilibrium.

The resulting thesis cannot be separated from my prejudice (my present inclination to suspect) that the original emergence and current dominance of *homo sapiens* are entirely random—purely biological—and that history is, equally, a random walk in the sense that, although we shall be looking for connective drives which link history, my guess is that history may prove not to have what philosophers call a 'teleological' foundation—that is to say a direction, even a destination, which is based upon some original design or purpose. Quite to the contrary, I expect to find that my prejudice will readily promote itself to a conviction that history has no ultimate meaning, no purpose, no higher sanction, whether or not we find persuasive connexions and drives. But it just may have a mechanism, and one which has now malfunctioned.

Equally, the thesis postulates that humans are the only sentient beings on Earth, and that their impact on it through economic motivation—

the matter of a nanosecond in geological time—has now become so massive and exponential in the rate and scale of its consequences that earlier academic or theosophical theories of history have now become largely irrelevant in helping us to come to terms with the year 2001 and further out.

The very word 'history' has at least two useful and commonly understood meanings and both appear in the first sentence of this book. One meaning is simply the aggregate of past events and facts of whose reality we can be more or less certain. We 'know' that there was a Roman general, statesman and historian named Julius Caesar who died in 44 BC; we know that Christopher Columbus 'discovered' the New World in 1492 AD; and we know that the atomic bomb was first used in anger on 6 August 1945 on the Japanese city of Hiroshima.

Another meaning is literary, analytical and descriptive and it has to do with the treatment of these events and facts by historians. This is 'historiography'—literally the writing of history. The historian gathers facts and makes conjectures where evidence is inconclusive; he evaluates the data and relates it to external factors and, through comparison and analysis, seeks to identify causes and, perhaps, goes on to assess the impact of these events, and the conclusions drawn from them, for the future.

The influence of the historian's work may extend well beyond the subjects he treats and the audience for whom his work is written. Those who have read Edward Gibbon's *Decline & Fall of the Roman Empire* (1766-88) number far fewer than those who are subconsciously influenced by it two hundred years later; nobody, it seems, nowadays reads Oswald Spengler's magnificent *The Decline of the West* (1918-1922), and yet the title and the image it conjures survive in odd contrast with the neglect of the book today; and I suspect that Alexis de Tocqueville's *Democracy in America* (1835) continues to present an authentic profile or an idealised vision of the Great Republic despite the corrosion of one hundred and sixty years.

H.G. Wells, Karl Marx, Winston Churchill, Frederick Jackson Turner, R.H. Tawney, Thomas Carlyle, G.F. Hegel, Arnold Toynbee, Oswald Spengler, Edward Gibbon—all these and many others have left a subtle imprint on the *popular* perception of the historical time and space we inhabit, even amongst those who have never turned a page of their books. Philosophers and politicians, social psychologists and educators, journalists and scientists, economists and jurists—even businessmen and soldiers—all are influenced by the history they read and—far more significantly—by the theories of history which their reading of history will lead them—often subconsciously—to construct. And it follows that their lay reading of history assumes great social importance in influencing the wider population which may have little direct contact with professional historians.

I have great admiration for Francis Fukuyama and his recent book *The End of History and the Last Man* where he concludes that there now is a Universal History valid for the 1990s and seemingly forever henceforth: that, through the triumphal and irreversible march of natural sciences over the past 400 years, combined with the rather more arcane Hegelian notion of 'recognition'—let us paraphrase it as a concept of human worth, dignity, self-respect and socially accorded honour—Western-style liberal economic democracy has now finally emerged incontestably as man's preferred form of social, political and economic organisation as evidenced in its final vanquishing of communism. It may well be that this is true—at least, that this is what we would all like—but I fear that history will not deliver.

My book has a background, three themes and a resolution: the Background is the 125 years stretching back to 1875 and forward to the third millennium—a symbolic, but nevertheless resonant and conveniently mind-concentrating beacon date. My birthdate is half way through—1937—and I shall be looking back a lifetime from then at the first half of the period to about 1875, and examining a list, a sort of economic and cultural *dramatis personae*, of industrial and economic and related developments which have been defining elements in colouring our world roughly up to Los Alamos in July 1945 when we exploded a bomb called 'Trinity'. But, of course, the list doesn't stop there—in the desert—and I shall then go on to look at the second half, at the subsequent lifetime to 2001.

Technological, social, political and—supremely—economic developments in the second half of this century have continued to accumulate with unabated and accelerating speed and insidiousness to the point where the estrangement of humanity from a world with any meaningful resemblance to even 1937, let alone 1875, is almost total.

Theme One is that the motor of history has been the human drive to control all aspects of our environment, in the very broadest sense of the term; that this drive for control has been spectacularly successful; but that its very success has contained a self-immolating gene. It is now quite clear that End-of-History theory cannot cope with the third millennium.

Theme Two is that there has now erupted, from immediate origins somewhere in the last half of the nineteenth century, an exponentially exploding and intertwined virus of mindlessly-used technology, industrialisation, and population growth which will 'go critical' in the early part of the new millennium.

Theme Three is that the dominance of the economic motive the world over, insupportable levels of consumption, rising and quite unsatisfiable 'consumer' expectations, and the manifest inability and unwillingness of all governments to face these issues now collude to pose a unique and immediate threat to the planet and our occupation of it; and that there are not available—yet, at any rate, or in prospect—any tried, tested and democratically acceptable means of responding with any confidence to these defiant challenges.

The three Themes have to do with a loss of *stability*, *balance* and *continuity*. All are mere tributaries of indeterminate length to some purposeless yet apparently irreversible historical process.

Finally, there is a Resolution in the form of a single precondition for the survival of humanity in and beyond the twenty-first century.

Chapter 1

Theories of Universal History:
the view from 1995

'Back there, centuries ago, at the turning of the worlds, the African had the labor, the Indian had the land, and the European had a plan—and the necessary fire-power.' Lerone Bennett: *The Shaping of Black America*.

Prologue

I DON'T BELIEVE the 'Europeans' did have a plan: they don't have one even now, four or five hundred years later. And I don't believe that the Pilgrim Fathers thought further ahead than the prospect of a damn good Thanksgiving dinner with the Wampanoags in 1621.

Lerone Bennett is wrong and yet I get his point. In an ironic sense, an observer viewing the fallen years from the eve of the Third Millennium might be forgiven for concluding that virtually every aspect of the world around him was prima facie evidence that Leif Ericson and Christopher Columbus, Captain John Smith and Amerigo Vespucci were indeed commanders of advance parties charged with getting the European Plan off the ground, and carrying out that particular piece of history.

Oswald Spengler published the first volume of *The Decline of the West* in Munich in 1918. This magnificent and now sadly neglected masterpiece is the first of two heroic twentieth-century ventures into territory previously trodden perhaps only by G.F. Hegel, whose *The Philosophy of History* was published after his death in 1831. Arnold Toynbee followed Spengler with the publication in 1934 of the first volume of *A Study of History*, which was completed with the appearance of the tenth volume in 1955. All three men—Spengler was a mathematician, Hegel a philosopher, Toynbee the only professional historian—sought to construct not so much global chronological histories, but principally a *universal theory of history*, a system almost which would show that 'history' could be dissected and presented as a dynamic process rather than a random succession of causes and effects. Indeed, Spengler explicitly disavows the cause-and-effect approach to history and certainly *The*

Decline of the West, at least, is not the ideal place to look for a phalanx of historical artifacts neatly strung together in a persuasive causal chain.

In this chapter I am going to be looking at these theories; but I shall first come to grips with the issue posed in the quotation and first few lines written above: that is, from what observation platform am I to view history? I have done a few miles, and I now find myself living in the corner of a large damp island—tethered somewhat unenthusiastically to the northwest coast of Europe—after half a lifetime in a hundred and more countries around the world. Must I have—can I have?—a disinterested global view of history, untainted by what I am and—above all—by what has been making all that history? Oswald Spengler does us a useful service by pointing out that subdividing history into 'Ancient, Medieval and Modern' is 'incredibly meaningless and… what is worse, it rigs the stage.' What stage? He says 'The ground of Western Europe is treated as a steady pole… for no better reason than because we live on it… and great histories of millennial duration and mighty far-away Cultures are made to revolve around this pole… in a quaintly conceived system of sun and planets.' It is in our West-European conceit that this 'phantom world-history' is acted out; indeed, 'The word "Europe" ought to be struck out of history.'[1]

And so Spengler resolves to replace this Ptolemaic system of history with a suitably modern Copernican system which gives equal time on the steady pole to Indians, Babylonians, Chinese, Egyptians, Arabs, Mexicans, Greeks and Romans. Well, I'm all for that except that it really *does not work*. Throughout *The Decline of the West* there is an abiding whiff with every page you turn of what Spengler calls the 'West-European-American' culture, like incense in even the remotest crypts and alcoves of a cathedral. Whiff or leitmotiv, *West-Europe-America* is what Spengler is all about as he proceeds to formulate his world-history. In a kind of historical *trompe l'oeil*, he constructs ingenious 'contemporary' matrices of six epochs—Western, Classical, Indian, Arabian, Egyptian and Chinese; and he analyzes the 'present' and 'imminent' ills of each Culture and eulogises its 'past' glories. But neither the West's ills nor its glories are ever truly replicated wholly or even largely in the other Cultures he assesses. I shall return to Spengler and his method of 'contemporary epochs', but now I am brought back to what proves so powerfully to be my chosen (Spengler's covert) observation platform: West-Europe-America and, as I said earlier, to what has been making all the history for the past several hundred years.

This is not a triumphalist Eurocentrist value-judgement. Nor is it a piece of ethnocentric prejudice; it is a statement of incontrovertible and, in the opinion of many people, disagreeable fact. The West and all its works—for good and ill—are footprinted all over the world from Nordkyn Cape to Tierra del Fuego, from Cape Verde to the Kamchatka Peninsula. A global economy is emerging and it has now become impossible to proffer the example of a single country which is not connected, however tenuously but certainly with thickening bonds, to the system. And that system is the West-European-American industrial consumer economy, understood for these purposes to include Japan. Exceptions to it—Burkina Faso, North Korea, any others?—merely prove the rule. I do not suggest that the footprint is everywhere welcome—Islamic Fundamentalism is not the only example of a churlish reception; but I shall show that it is a phenomenon of unprecedented historical power and that it is reversible only in a disagreeable realisation of Spengler's vision. We shall come to that later but I shall first conclude this prologue with an ultra-compressed and simplified view of the historical train which has made the the West-European-American way the way of the world. This is an exception to the rule that knowing where you've come from will be helpful in getting you to where you want to be.

The West-European-American Colossus: 1450 to date

I SHALL ESCHEW the relativistic, reductionist clutter of so many of today's commentators, nail my historical colours firmly and without hesitation to the West-European-American 'steady pole'; and describe how the world looked five centuries or so ago on the eve of Columbus' sure-footed departure for... India, and trace what has filled the years since. We'll start in the Western hemisphere and move westwards.

There were highly developed but, in today's terms, 'reactionary' or static civilizations, empires even, in central America: the Mayan and Aztec centred on Mexico, and in Andean south America, the Inca. North America was peopled largely by hunters and gatherers although there is recent evidence of earlier and much more 'advanced' cultures in what is now the American southwest. Neither horse nor gunpowder nor iron nor serious ocean-going vessels were known throughout the two continents.

Across an empty Pacific and there floated an insular Japan which was to wait another four hundred years until 1853 before being prised open by Commodore Perry; while China was prospering artistically after a century of the Ming Dynasty. Tamburlane had earlier ravished the Punjab and massacred the citizens of Delhi, but by the middle of the sixteenth century the Turkoman Baber and his grandson Akbar had subjugated India and established the Mogul Empire which built the Taj Mahal and survived until the British Raj three hundred years later. Further west, the Ottoman Turks under Muhammad II captured Constantinople in 1453 and brought the Byzantine rump of the Roman Empire to an end. Mehmet II had attacked from the west and, with the great city safely tucked up, the way was open to press on and up into central Europe.

In Muscovy in 1480, Ivan the Great had defied the Mongol Khan of the Golden Horde by refusing to pay tribute; he called himself 'tsar', derived with etymological sanction from 'Caesar', and had then set about establishing the future Russian Empire to the north and east. Here, somewhere between the Vistula and Moscow, was to be Europe's eastern frontier. Arab Islam, from the Atlantic across North Africa to the edges of the Ottoman Empire was comatose, and the Fifth and last Crusade had ended ignominiously in defeat at Domazlice. Finally, sub-Saharan Africa would scrape by for those same four hundred years with the benefit of neither brutish borders nor meddling missionaries.

But what of Europe? By 1450 its population had probably recovered in both numbers and spirit from the Black Death which had struck in 1348. The Hundred Years' War would shortly finish and England and France would then, with minor interruptions, keep away from each other's throats until La Hogue and Blenheim two centuries and more later. Western Europe began to get on with the business of building dynastic nation states, and to creating the internal political and economic structures which would enable human and material resources to be marshalled and eventually projected across the oceans in a way never seen since the most expansive and aggressive days of the Roman Empire, but far exceeding its impact. For many Europeans perched on the edge of a vulnerable continent with Islam pressing from the east and the Mediterranean a closed and contested lake, the Atlantic beckoned. The Portuguese were already inching their way down the west African coast in the earlier years of the fifteenth century with the support of Henry the Navigator, son of João I, in a strange crusade in quest of both gold and convertible pagans. Bartolomeo Diaz rounded the Cape of Good Hope in 1487, and by 1499 Vasco da Gama had established a route to India, outgunning Arab opposition with his heavily-armed ships and imposing a Portuguese trading empire which would extend to China and Japan.

The first books were printed, probably at Haarlem by Coster in about 1446 and by Gutenberg in Mainz at about the same time. 1250 years after his death, Ptolemy was brought to Renaissance Florence and translated into Latin so that, by the last quarter of the century, printed editions were available to politicians and seafarers alike. Great strides were made in the development of bigger and more reliable fire-arms and artillery. Huge swathes of oak were felled to build the new generation of jumbo warships which Toynbee says remained essentially unchanged and unsurpassed right up until Nelson's time over three hundred years later; but it was at the head of a very modest flotilla of three far smaller versions—the flagship 'Santa Maria', and two tiny caravels, 'Nina' and 'Pinta'—that Cristoforo Colon sailed out of Cadiz in 1492 on his way to history.

That Columbus, his brother Vicente and their crew of eighty-eight, *chose* to embark on such an audacious voyage was the result of a piece of proto-mercantilism by Ferdinand of Aragon and Isabella of Castile, who were busy ethnically cleansing Spain, so as to complete the Christian reconquest of Spain and were eager to shorten the voyage to the East. That they, and undoubtedly later explorers, were *able* to do so was probably the indirect result of a serendipitous partnership between a physician and an architect eleven hundred miles away in Florence. Paolo del Pozzo Toscanelli was also a mathematician and his new friend Filippo Brunelleschi was also a builder. They had collaborated in the design and construction of the Duomo and other Florentine buildings of the early-fifteenth century and used methods which incorporated quite novel and unique mathematical calculation, in place of the frequently disastrous rule-of-thumb approach to construction. One of the discoveries was *perspective* and the focal point.

Later, Toscanelli was to engage in some early lateral thinking and apply these principles to map-making, applying geometry to the measurement of distances—of straight lines converging on Ptolemy's graph-paper concept of the sphere, and thereby supplementing navigational arts which had until then been literally a matter of star-gazing: steering by the Pole Star became progressively more difficult as the navigator approached the Equator, and downright impossible once past it when the Pole Star sank beneath the waves astern. It is almost beyond doubt that the skipper of the 'Santa Maria' weighed anchor with the benefit of this new knowledge, and that he profited also from advances made during the century in the construction of more accurate time-pieces, compasses and sextants.

This voyage and its sequels were of the most profound significance and they reverberate to this very day. Sixteenth-century Europe, viewed on a great global weather report, would have exhibited closely-serried ranks of expansionary isobars—a local high-pressure system in a low-pressure world. During the sixteenth century most of Europe's nation states, and some of the Papal, got in on the act—the Dutch, Spanish, French, Portuguese and latterly the English. Most spectacular was Hernan Cortes' expedition from Cuba in 1519 which, consisting of a mere 600 men, some horses and a handful of ships' cannon, led within twelve months to the death of Montezuma and the destruction of an Aztec empire which had been as many centuries in the making. A decade later and Francisco Pizarro terminated the Inca ruler Atahuallpa with an even smaller party of men. South and central America—named for the Italian Amerigo di Vespucci—California and the American southwest came under Spanish and Portuguese sway.

Europe itself had secured its own backyard by breaking the Turkish siege of Vienna in 1683 with a multinational European army, thus finally stemming the penetration of Islam from the south-east, to complement the exploits of Charles Martell who had turned it back 950 years earlier in the west at the battle of Poitiers.

In early seventeenth-century America, England, her energies refocussing after the Armada, was busy setting up colonies—originally trading posts—in a huge necklace stretching from St Kitts in the Caribbean and Bermuda through Virginia and Massachusetts and up towards Nova Scotia. Both the English and the Dutch had established an 'East India Company'; while the Hudson's Bay Company was founded in 1670 in a wave of state-sponsored mercantilism canonised in 1664 with the publication of Thomas Mun's *England's Treasure by fforaign Trade*. By 1674 Dutch colonists and explorers—no longer able to call New Amsterdam 'home'—had joined the Portuguese and switched their attention east of the Cape of Good Hope. At the same time, in 1688, William Dampier was speculating that a wild shore he had just visited '...joynes neither to Asia, Africa nor America'. It was Australia, and exactly one hundred years later Sydney was founded.

Meanwhile the Russians had not been idle. Peter the Great had acquired ship-building technology from the English and Dutch in 1697; and in 1703 he once again tapped West European technology by commissioning an Italian-Swiss architect, Domenico Trazzini, to work on newly-founded St Petersburg—Russia's window on the West. Russian Imperial bonds were floated on the London and Paris money exchanges in the late nineteenth century to finance the Trans-Siberian railway and by 1905 you could book a sleeper through from Moscow to Vladivostok.

The early nineteenth-century collapse of the Spanish Empire in Latin America, and later the conversion of Brazil from the the seat of the Portuguese Empire to a republic, in no way detract from this picture of European global domination: to the contrary, in almost all cases the republican governments which emerged from empire comprised men of European ancestry and often education, and it was British and American money which built the railways, developed the mines and created the *estancias* of Argentina.

The Mogul Empire was formally wound up with the Sepoy Mutiny in 1858, and Queen Victoria added 'Empress of India' to the coinage in 1876.

The Germans and the Italians were late entrants to the game, largely through tardiness in fusing their component parts into unitary states which could formulate national policies and project them across the oceans—a process delayed by the bickering of princes and Popes alike. But by the turn of the nineteenth century German acquisition of Tanganyika and southwest Africa and Belgian seizure of the Congo had completed the Europeans' carve-up of the continent. Even the United States indulged a latent imperial taste and, borne on a wave of jingoistic support, had by 1898 added the Philippines, Cuba and Porto Rico to its portfolio. The French, Dutch and British held all of southeast Asia—but for Siam, even though this was a British client state. As for China, although partial conquest would wait until the Japanese puppet state of Manchukuo and the rape of Nanking in 1937, it was already humiliated under the feeble Manchu Empire of the late nineteenth century by a string of British, American, German and Japanese enclaves, Treaty Ports, post-offices and extra-territorial concessions. Indeed, Sir Robert Hart served as Inspector-General of the Chinese Imperial Maritime Customs Service from 1864 to 1906. Finally, all of the Pacific was in British, French and American hands by 1900, and even Antarctica was shared out, largely among members of the West-European-American club.

To complete this account of West-European-American *territorial* conquest of the earth, it remains to record the collapse of the Ottoman Empire in 1917, and the engulfing by France and Great Britain of the residue, including effective British partitioning of Persia with Russia; and, last of all, Italian seizure of Libya and most of the Horn of Africa, in which whole huge continent only Abyssinia and part of Morocco remained independent; and, of course, tiny Liberia, but even it was founded by the United States and still uses US dollars, or at least a few of them.

A chronicle of inter-European rivalries for trade and territory is not relevant to this cameo of empire-building: what matters is the overall extent of European penetration. By 1937, West-European-American domination of land and sea was complete and I really am one of those whose grandmother taught me how to colour the map. It should not be imagined from this account that the entire rest of the world was inactive during the period: of course it was not, but there is no doubt that it was on the receiving end of a history being radiated out of the West.

This has been a description of the geography—what the maps looked like in 1450 and how they changed from mono- to multi-chrome in five hundred years, and on to today's kaleidoscopic range of hues. It isn't necessary to go through the same exercise to describe the accompanying political, economic, military, social, commercial and cultural consequences of European expansion from fifteenth-century sea-faring to twentieth-century world economic empire. It is not necessary to recite the endless roll-call of scientists and inventors, artists and thinkers from Galileo and Newton, Leonardo and Bach, Jefferson and Watt, to Beethoven and Pasteur, Einstein and Picasso, Planck and Sibelius to underline the predominantly one-way nature of the West-European-American traffic with the rest of the world. The geography itself is a proxy for everything else—for the thesis that the condition and evolution of today's world can be understood only via this historical iteration and from this West-European-American vantage point—the steady pole which Spengler so wanted to share with the 'rest of the world' and whose members he was so careful to identify for enrolment in the 'world-history' adventure.

I reiterate that this vantage point is not, in addition, a value judgement; nor do I advance any claims of West-European-American moral or cultural superiority: there are other forums for that debate. I have merely presented the evidence that—for better or worse—today's and tomorrow's world as a whole reflects in every nook and cranny the domination of the West-European-American irruption which began five hundred years ago; and it is largely this phenomenon which preoccupies our three world-historians, even if none of them was able to perceive fully how that domination was to become transmuted into a global obsession with production and consumption.

There is a delicious paradox: partisans of Spengler along with those bitterly opposed to this domination by the West, have little choice but to subscribe to this same West-European-American orientation of history, for the precise reason that they are themselves the *theoretical* antithesis to it. To be sure, most of the map is not coloured the same way as it was in 1937; but most of the trappings of the politico-industrial culture which subsisted then throughout the world, courtesy of the West, are not only still here, but still here and pasted all over it with a vengeance. The antithesis is decolonisation. And the synthesis, the resolution, the ultimate irony? It is quite simply (and tragically for those addicted to diversity in all its forms) that the decolonised—free, at last, to divert to alternative life-ways or, for that matter, to revert to the old ones—what have they done? The most highly motivated amongst them have consciously, aggressively and unashamedly opted to sign up for membership, if not right away then as soon as 'development' permits, of the West-European-American system, the club.

Of course, large areas of the world *will* remain aloof, through either conscious choice or because their natural condition and endowments do not permit them the option. This must be so of much of Africa and Andean Latin America, for example; and the future direction and evolution of China and India, to take just two obvious and massive examples, must remain a matter of most uncertain conjecture. But what is now beyond speculation is that the entire world has long been compromised by and into the West-European-American system; and that will remain my vantage-point as I now turn to consider the principle and purpose of a theory of universal history, and to assess the achievements of those who have constructed them.

The Search for a Universal History

'Real history is heavy with fate but free of laws.' Oswald Spengler: *The Decline of the West*.

The notion of a 'theory of history' is very seductive and, like seduction itself, both pleasurable and dangerous. At the one innocent extreme, it would be surprising if the professional historian, after trawling through a million historical artifacts, should not begin to detect parallels and similarities which, through refinement and enhancement, allow—perhaps persuade—him to clean up the scatter-diagram of history and replace it with a broad, strong, elegant curve which slices through the central evidence, by-passes random and distant observations—noise—and thereby fashions for him a kind of historiographical template.

This is a perfectly respectable exercise of the historian's art. Indeed, we have every right to expect professional historians to do more than generate catalogues of facts to support a verdict or conclusion about a particular historical episode. Should they not also synthesize the results of their studies into a coherent view of history as a natural phenomenon in its own right? May it not therefore have its own dynamic, its own direction, its own meaning—if not quite its own purpose—for the better guidance of the politicians and others whose duty requires them to deal with the consequences of history and respond courageously to their impact on the future?

In fact, historians, philosophers, economists and sociologists have made a sufficient number of attempts to construct a general theory of history for us to refer to the objective as a 'Universal History'. Kant and Nietzsche were both aware of the possibility of history as a process in its own right, while Hegel and Marx proceeded to construct elaborate theories of the 'directionality' of history starting from the same base, and using similar techniques—the dialectic process—but arriving at very different destinations. Earlier thinkers, such as Hobbes and Locke, pioneered in the formulation of integrated political, social and economic theories of history which found practical expression in the constitution and form of government framed by the Founding Fathers of the United States.

There is of course the other, less innocent, extreme where a theory of history may be either deliberately fabricated or highjacked so that history may then be re-created through eclectic manipulation of the evidence to yield a presentation which demonstrates progress towards some ineluctable historical truth.

Marx and Engels published their *Manifesto of the Communist Party* in 1848. The Manifesto set out a theory of history viewed from the pinnacle of Western industrial civilisation. All of human history, ran the theory, had contributed inexorably and cognitively to the achievements of the West. At the heart of this dynamic process lay a nexus of social, political, cultural and intellectual factors driven by over-riding economic imperatives. Set-backs there might be, but this progress would continue, onwards and upwards, to ever higher peaks and in an unswerving direction through the iron laws of Economic Determinism, Dialectical Materialism and Scientific Socialism.

Confirmation seemed to arrive, and from an unexpected quarter, in the writing of Herbert Spencer and, in 1859, with the publication of Charles Darwin's 'Origin of the Species'. Anthropology was littered with biological dead-ends and pot holes but it was beyond doubt that the fittest had survived and would continue to displace inferior strains; and this, together with Wagner, was powerful support for Nietzsche and for many of Hegel's disciples.

The Communist revolution was scheduled to break out simultaneously in England, France, Germany and America, although it would need a helping hand in the trigger nation—England—because, according to Marx, 'The English possess all the necessary material preconditions of the social revolution [but] what they lack is the spirit of revolutionary passion.'

Through the perverseness of history, however, it was to be the Russia of 1917 rather than nineteenth-century England where the Communist millennium would arrive. It therefore fell to Soviet historians, apparatchiks and apologists to respond to the challenge posed by the persistent and increasingly embarrassing refusal of the Soviet system to deliver what had clearly been ordained in the Manifesto.

After seventy-five years, the results were devastating. If nature does, indeed, copy art, then we can also state with confidence that the distortions and perversions of Soviet historiography were themselves agents in helping to create—in the most literal sense—the economic and social chaos in the Soviet Union from which Scientific Socialism was to have spared humanity: one lie needed two to support it, four more to support these two and so on. Sir Walter Scott had it right with his 'tangled web'.

It is a perfectly proper part, then, of the historian's mission to distil from his research an objective theory of history which he may then test in subsequent historical analysis. The simpler the theory and the less frequently and radically it has to be modified, the more persuasive it will become and the greater will be its social and political usefulness. Applying Occam's Razor, 'It is vain to do with more what can be done with fewer.'

In this respect, I touched briefly on the Marxist 'teleological', almost visionary, view of history, which seeks to construct a cosmic blueprint of human activity somehow self-directed rationally and irresistibly towards a predetermined socialist world. Although Marxism had lost some of its founders' exuberance by October 1917, the faith in the inevitability of socialism persisted despite the stubborn refusal of capitalism to conform to the Marxist prognosis, and it was mightily aided by a systematic editing—sometimes subtle, sometimes crude—of the news before it became 'history'.

Now that the Soviet Union has imploded, and the West finds itself without a jousting-partner, where does this leave history and our understanding of it? Does it change it at all? And is it possible, or even necessary, to attempt a post-mortem, or is it better to abandon the effort in favour of the search for a new theory of history—one which might combine the pragmatism of the reactive, 'Western' approach to history on the one hand, with the mechanistic and self-fulfilling interpretation applied to it by Marxism, on the other? Let us now introduce our world-historians and see whether they can help us to understand how we have arrived at where we are in 1995.

I. Oswald Spengler

Oswald Spengler was born in 1880 at Blankenburg in the Harz mountains into an unremarkable family. He read philosophy, history and mathematics and took his PhD at Halle in 1904. He became an Oberlehrer, a high-school teacher of maths at Munich, until 1911 when an inheritance enabled him to concentrate fulltime on his life's work: he published Volume I of *The Decline of the West* in Munich in December 1918, and then a revision plus Volume II in 1922. His name was unknown to the unsuspecting world on which he was to launch his weighty tome with all the impact of one of the Kaiser's howitzers which were still, in Vernon Scannell's memorable phrase, 'guffawing away' in Flanders a few hundred miles to the west.

His objective was nothing if not ambitious and unique, and it is worth quoting in full: 'In this book is attempted for the first time the venture of *predetermining* history, of following the still *untravelled* stages in the history of a Culture, and specifically of the only Culture of our time and on our planet which is *actually in the phase of fulfilment*—the West-European-American.'[2] The italics are mine. Spengler tells us that when he conceived the book in 1911, 'the World-War appeared to me both as imminent... and inevitable'[3] and, a page later, he advances the extraordinary claim that 'the approaching World-War... was a historical change of phase occurring within a great historical organism of definable compass at the point *preordained for it hundreds of years ago*.'[4] The latter italics are also mine.

Although, in the words of Spengler's translator, 'this severe and diffi-cult philosophy of history' rapidly sold over 90,000 copies, the recep-tion was nevertheless frequently hostile, partly because it may not have had the imprimatur of quite all of the German academic establishment, partly because it was regarded as anti-democratic and a glorification of war, and partly because it was perceived—and still is, for that matter—as a work of profound pessimism. Furthermore, Spengler seems anti-Christian. Whether this is true, let alone whether it is relevant, the reader may judge from the following pages. Suffice it to say for now that there is no room for anything other than dispassion in intellectual or scien-tific endeavour: if a proper interpretation of the facts used in Spengler's analysis should have led the good doctor to a 'disagreeable' conclusion of the kind for which he has been indicted, then what would the critics have preferred? A contrived conclusion? No—Spengler was loyal to the convictions which emerged from his work and we should plead for the life of the messenger.

Spengler's claim, then, is quite unequivocal: a correct theory of universal history will enable practitioners of the theory *actually to fore-cast events*, and this in contrast to the professional historian's view of his-tory as 'a sort of tapeworm industriously adding on to itself one epoch after the other.'[5] The key to Spengler's theory lies in his viewing history as an organic process: 'The means whereby to identify dead forms is Mathematical Law. The means whereby to understand living forms is Analogy.'[6] This is Spengler's *morphology* of world history—drawing an analogy between historical happenings and the life-cycle of living forms.

Spengler was a disciple of Goethe (1749-1832), a polymath of Renaissance breadth who was one of the foundations of a new Euro-pean respect for German scholarship. Spengler describes Goethe as a 'naturalist... who hated Mathematics... who followed out the develop-ment of the plant-form from the leaf—the Destiny in nature and not the Causality [so as to reveal the] organic logic out of the profusion of all the challenging details [of history].'[7] In a violent reaction to the rampant influence of Darwin ('There is no more conclusive refutation of Darwinism than that furnished by palaeontology.', i.e. fossils.[8]), Spen-gler says that Darwinism is 'the megalopolitan-intellectual product of the most abstract of Civilizations [which] kills all that is organic and fateful' in history.[9] That Civilization was England and it is England, and her American extension, which represented for Spengler a great deal of what had gone wrong with the West since the heyday of Napoleon. Civilization suppresses the spirit of Culture.

Spengler's concept of a Universal History is, therefore, almost biological; and it is also three-dimensional. The first of these dimensions is the *organic*: cultures are born—they are organisms—they grow, mature and decay. These are the epochs of history which he derives from Goethe's 'Geistesepochen'; they are variously Spring, Summer, Autumn and Winter, or Pre-cultural, Early Period, Late Period and, finally, Civilization. It is this last one which the West currently occupies and Spengler doesn't care for it one little bit. Indeed, he cares for nothing about the twentieth century and has cared for very little since Napoleon Bonaparte. 'For Western existence the distinction between... Culture and Civilization—the living body of a soul and the mummy of it... lies at about the year 1800—on the one side of that frontier life in fullness and sureness of itself formed... in one great uninterrupted evolution from Gothic childhood to Goethe and Napoleon, and on the other the autumnal, artificial, rootless life of our great cities.'[10] For instance, 'What is practised as art today—be it music after Wagner or painting after Cezanne, Leibl and Monet—is impotence and falsehood... [and in place of artists we] find only industrious cobblers and fools.'[11] He tells us that Western megalopolitan man will be 'inwardly finished' from about the year 2000, just as the Roman age finished off the Classical age.

Spengler's loathing of what Civilization, the last of his Epochs, had brought to world history does not, however, prevent him from adoring some of its artifacts born of the nineteenth century and certain to obtrude into the twentieth, and they make for a fascinating digression into Spengler's personality. 'We have descended [in the age of Civilization] from the perspective of the bird to that of the frog... far better to construct an aero-engine than a new theory of apperception that is not wanted... I would sooner have the fine mind-begotten forms of a fast steamer, a steel structure, a precision-lathe, the subtlety of many chemical and optical processes, than all the pickings and stealings of present-day 'arts and crafts', architecture and painting included.'[12] Perverse or not, this is a view which will undoubtedly command broad support in 1995.

And Spengler's ambivalence about modernity is compounded in the special contempt he reserves for today's 'type of scholar whose clarity of vision comes under some irresistible spell when it turns from a frock-coat to a toga, from a British football-ground to a Byzantine circus, from a transcontinental railway to a Roman road in the Alps, from a thirty-knot destroyer to a trireme, from Prussian bayonets to Roman spears—nowadays, even from a modern engineer's Suez Canal to that of a Pharoah. He would admit a steam-engine as a symbol of human passion and an expression of intellectual force if it were Hero of Alexandria who invented it, not otherwise.'[13]

A second dimension is Spengler's superimposition on world-history's four Epochs of three so-called 'contemporary' Spiritual, Culture and Political vantage points, which enables him to view by analogy a number of otherwise disparate historical periods, for want of a better word, according to the precise position of each in its passage through the inescapable cycle of birth to decay.

These periods, the third dimension, are nine in number and represent a type of sum of human historical societal experience: Indian, Classical, Arabian, Western, Egyptian and Chinese, Byzantine, Mayan and Aztec.

This is, therefore, the three-dimensional matrix which summarises the world-history to the 'present day', although Spengler would probably reject this notion of 'history having reached', as it were, any date, as such; and it is thus perfectly possible for him to draw broadly—but, of course, only theoretically—*synchronous* analogies (hence the use of the word 'contemporary') between, for example, in the Political Epoch, the imminent decline of Egypt in the Hyskos period of the Middle Kingdom (1680-1580 BC), the flourishing of Beethoven and Delacroix in the Culture Epoch (ca. 1800 AD), and, in the Spiritual Epoch, the lives of Plato and Aristotle in the 4th century BC. Not only that but—tantalisingly—he can bring in also the transition from Napoleon to 'The System of the Great Powers' in 2000 AD. Since we are about to cross this latter threshold, it will be as well to understand in some detail what Spengler means by his four Epochs; but I want first to touch briefly on Spengler's style, his language and prejudice, bearing in mind my earlier comment that his book is not a narration of history.

Charles Francis Atkinson's translation is itself an heroic accomplishment, and I say that only partly in recognition of my own imperfect command of the German language. Spengler is a dreamer, a visionary, and his language and personality draw on the roots of a kind of mysticism which is no more than remotely accessible to the late twentieth-century reader not steeped in the deepest psychological complexity and symbolism of the German forest. Consider these examples of his language: my book, he writes, 'addresses itself solely to readers who are capable of living themselves into the word-sounds and pictures as they read. Difficult this undoubtedly is, particularly as our awe in face of mystery—the respect that Goethe felt—denies us the satisfaction of thinking that dissections are the same as penetrations [into history].'[14] Or, 'The nineteenth and twentieth centuries, hitherto looked on as the highest point of an ascending straight line of world-history, are in reality a stage of life... characterized by a civilized spirituality', followed (comfortingly) by 'This high plane of contemplation once attained, *the rest is easy.*' [my emphasis] 'Trained to regard world-historical evolution as an *organic unit seen backwards* from our standpoint in the present, we are enabled [by my theory] to follow the broad lines into the future—a privilege of dream-calculation till now permitted only to the physicist.'[15] [my emphasis]

And finally, 'There is a wondrous music of the spheres which wills to be heard and which a few of our deepest spirits will hear... the last Faustian philosophy.'[16] It would be pretentious to deny that there are wide expanses of Spengler territory, and hidden chasms, which we simply can neither cross nor penetrate. In the last analysis, Spengler was on balance right but ultimately for the wrong reasons. His language and personality are unique and frequently obscure; but equally, there are passages of quite extraordinarly passion and even, I find, of humour. And I shall be quoting some of them, particularly from Volume II, not least because they make for eerily beautiful and poignant prophesy.

Spengler was not of the twentieth century; he was a man who—to employ his own notion of contemporaneity mentioned earlier—lived, or would like to have lived, back in the Summer or early Autumn, in the late pre-Civilization Epoch whether Western or Egyptian, Classical or Chinese, Arabian or Indian: at almost any time, that is, before Goethe's Faust made his compact with Mephistopheles and the barbarian reached the city walls.

And so to our discussion of the Epochs, and their unique linkage of contemporary events and peoples separated by millennia.

Spring and the Pre-Cultural Period spawn Homer and Dante, Mycenae and the coronation of Charlemagne; Francis of Assisi and the Talmud, the Shang dynasty in China, Tower of Babylon and the New Testament. But there is no culture, no art, no science, no religion or political form of a stature adequate to constitute a society—there is, in a sense, no history: they are years of infancy.

Summer and the Early Period of Culture, bring the Old Kingdom of Egypt alongside the English Wars of the Roses, Mohammed and Martin Luther, the Pyramids, Doric column and flying buttress of Gothic cathedrals, Michelangelo and Galileo, mosaics and algebra, Francis Bacon and the Spartan aristocracy. Pythagoras and Descartes were thinking like thoughts, the politics are feudal and the economy rural. There was Chivalry about, and the city was on its way.

Autumn and the Late Period of Culture: the City has arrived. Spengler says that 'The town… is a plant-like being'—the organic analogy once again—and that 'world-history is the history of civic man. Peoples, states, politics, religion, the arts, and all sciences rest upon one prime phenomenon of human being, the town.'[17] What else is happening? The Indians invent 'zero' and Goethe is thinking about Faust; Plato and Aristotle, Goya and Beethoven are stretching our minds; Oliver Cromwell chooses Corinthian instead of Doric columns; and Aya Sophia was converted into a mosque during the presidency of George Washington. The Middle Kingdom of Egypt was decaying just as Voltaire had put the final touches to *Candide*.

And along with these more conventionally 'historical' events there were now emerging more subtle, powerful and insidious forces which were to project us into the final Epoch: money becomes pre-eminent and the intelligentsia elbows out tradition; the City conquers the countryside and the bourgeoisie replace the privileged classes who had previously conducted the affairs of government.

And now today—Winter and Civilization. For Spengler, this era began with the eclipse of Napoleon and there are three separate phases. Faust has signed up with Mephistopheles, and Marx is busy writing *Das Kapital* in a front-row seat of the newly completed Colosseum in Rome. In China, the two-hundred year 'Period of the Contending States' has begun while in Europe there will be World War and the 'System of the Great Powers'. Archimedes has just finished taking an inspirational bath while over in New York City the Woolworth Building now pierces the skyline of Broadway. Buddhism is secure in India, Caesar is uttering immortal dying words already written by Shakespeare, and Wagner and Manet are Europe's answer to the temples at Luxor. Islam has seen 800 years of 'practical fatalism' and Socialism is on the march in Europe while Jenghis Khan terrorises central Asia.

Spengler says that 'The future of the West is not a limitless tending upwards and onwards towards our present ideals, but a single phenomenon of history, strictly limited and defined as to form and duration, which covers a few centuries and can be viewed and, in essentials, *calculated from available precedents*.' [my italics][18] So there we have it. The West's future will last a few hundred years from the start of the period of Civilization around 1800.

In the first phase, Winter is on its way and the Megalopolitan Civilization has dawned: religion and spiritually creative forces are being extinguished and life itself becomes problematical. Money and Democracy are dominant and economics permeate political forms and authorities; we would call it consumerism. 'In all Civilizations alike, these cities aim at the chessboard form, which is the symbol of soullessness', and 'I see, long after AD 2000, cities laid out for ten to twenty million inhabitants, spread over enormous areas of countryside, with buildings... and notions of traffic and communication that we should regard as fantastic to the point of madness.'[19]

It is the age of gigantism and wars of annihilation: 'With this enters the age of gigantic conflicts, in which we find ourselves today. The Chinese call it Shan-Kwo, the "Period of the Contending States".'[20] It was to last until the third millennium, and perhaps we've seen it. Spengler then produces some inspired prophecy for the twentieth century: 'If the nineteenth century has been relatively poor [sic] in great wars— and revolutions—and has overcome its worst crises by means of congresses, this has been due precisely to the continuous and terrific war-preparedness which has made disputants substitute chess-moves for war', and 'In these wars of theirs for the heritage of the whole world, continents will be staked, India, China, South Africa, Russia, Islam called out, new tactics and technics played and counterplayed.'[21]

It is now the the second phase and we have breached the third millennium. 'In the form of democracy, money [had] won, but as soon as it has destroyed the old orders of the Culture, the Chaos gives forth a new and overpowering factor [Caesarism before which] the money collapses. The Imperial Age, in every Culture alike, signifies the end of the politics of mind and money. The powers of the blood... resume their ancient lordship.'[22] It is the age of the strongman: nation states decline into a formless population and reform themselves as an 'Imperium'— into empires of 'gradually-increasing crudity of despotism'—and 'Force-politics triumph over money.'[23] Ideals like the *Contrat Social* and the *Communist Manifesto* scarcely extend beyond 'the two centuries that belong to party politics, and their end comes not from refutation, but from boredom—which has killed Rousseau long since and will shortly kill Marx.'[24] There is a single world power or leader and wars have ceased.

And so to the third phase 'calculated from available precedents' to start after 2200. It is deepest winter and there is a reversion to feuding baronies and border wars. The Imperium has imploded and has been replaced with the power of individuals and patrician groups. Now, 'With the formed state, high history also lays itself down weary to sleep. Man becomes a plant again, adhering to the soil, dumb and enduring… a busy, not inadequate swarm, over which the tempest of soldier-emperors passingly blows. In the midst of the land lie the old world-cities, empty receptacles of an extinguished soul, in which a historyless mankind slowly nests itself. It is a drama noble in its aimlessness, noble and aimless as the course of the stars, the rotation of the earth, and alternance of land and sea, of ice and virgin forest upon its face. We may marvel at it, or we may lament it—but it is there.'[25]

★ ★ ★ ★

In the course of conveying a precis of Spengler's philosophy of history I have made liberal use of some of the finest representative quotations, and a few more will follow. His language is powerfully depictive and I, for one, will readily swallow the more obscurantist passages for the pleasure of the poetry and the pictures which peep through. But, beyond the literary and philosophical niceties, how does his performance now rate seventy and eighty years after the manuscripts were completed?

We shall not forget that although Spengler set out to construct a *universal* theory of history—what he calls 'world-history'—the vehicle he uses is, as I showed at the outset, the *West-European-American* because it is 'specifically the only Culture of our time and on our planet which is actually in the phase of fulfilment.' Now, we may be a little uncertain what he means by 'fulfilment': after all, he cannot have been suggesting that all the other Cultures had closed down for a bit of a breather while the West got on with its preordained act. (As we shall see later, Toynbee maintains that there are still seven cultures surviving—just—out of his primal total of twenty-eight.)

Did Spengler perhaps mean that the end-state of his cycle—Civilization—had already been reached by the entire rest of the world, and that the West is only now having its innings? Either way—the West on its own or the rest already home and dry—Spengler would certainly have been mistaken if he was implying that the West-European-Americans could carry out their fulfilment closeted off from the rest of the world, and without having any impact on it.

There is, in fact, a third interpretation and it is this one which we must pin to Spengler's theory of world-history and the place of the West within it. We have already seen it in the Prologue: it is 'beyond speculation that the entire world has long been compromised by and into the West-European-American system.' I believe that this is also Spengler's conclusion and that, as a consequence, it is the subtext of his entire work. The West has become over the last 400 years or so the locomotive of the world's economy and, therefore, of its history. Let us, then, now go on to consider Spengler's achievements on two counts: first, his performance as a soothsayer and, second, as an historical theorist.

Spengler has been praised for his prophetic vision: for example, in foretelling the outbreak of the (first) World War and of total wars of annihilation; of the rise of the superstate and of superpower confrontation; and of the advent of the mega-cities of ten and twenty million souls, of gigantic machines and of speed and scale. We should not conclude that the first two were examples of anybody's clairvoyance, let alone the peculiar province of Spengler. We have already seen that in 1911 the imminence of the World War was clear to him, but his vision— of an horizon only three years away—was certainly not especially rare: one does not have to scan contemporary issues of *The Times* and *Hansard*, or assess the Royal Navy's battleship building programme in the early 1900s for evidence of what many people must have been thinking even though King George V and Kaiser Wilhelm II were cousins. I am reminded of a much earlier piece of popular foreboding:

'Germany is a thundering great nation', he said; 'Do you think we'll ever fight her?' Erskine Childers: *The Riddle of the Sands* (1903)

No. Here Spengler was not notably prophetic. He says of the American Civil War that 'even in the numbers of troops it involved [it] far surpassed the order of magnitude of the Napoleonic Wars' and that, for the first time, war resorted to the telegraph, the railway, armoured ships, torpedoes, rifled weapons and monster artillery. He is even more enthusiastic in his praise of the ingenuity shown during the Russo-Japanese War, when submarines and aircraft as well as speed of invention were so effective.[26] This war would have contrasted impressively with even 1870 when 'The Prussian-German people [had one of their] three great moments.'[27] These facts were not classified and it would have been neither difficult nor enterprising for any interested observer to extrapolate such experiments in 'total war' forward into a scenario for the technological Aladdin's Cave of the twentieth century.

It is a truism of history writing that, leaving aside its purely literary qualities, it *should* get better with the passage of years, partly because the modern historian cannot plead that he doesn't have the facts, and partly because he can take the recent recorded past and 'bolt it on' to its more distant predecessor and so construct a more persuasive ordering of cause-and-effect—much as a mathematician uses regression analysis to retro-construct an algorithmic chain which leads to some present mathematical observation. In this respect, there is a risk of underrating the work of earlier historians (and, in this case, of undervaluing Spengler's prophecy) precisely because we are spoiled by the advantages of 'knowing how it all ended'.

Nevertheless, it must be said that his forecasts of superstates and superpower collision were made against a background where such things were already set fair, and for all to see, to become a feature of the new century, and that Spengler was only one observer amongst many to speculate on 'gigantism' in North America and to recognise a new order of mega-imperialism in the guise of the British Empire: 'Leibniz [and Goethe] laid down the principle that Napoleon grasped... after Wagram... that the neck of Suez [rather than European tinkering] would one day be the key to world dominance.'[28]

Even Germany herself, though about to be defeated, was a clear example of how a remote agrarian state in north-central Europe could be metamorphosed in a generation or so into a global power, and Spengler was well aware that Japan had done the same trick over a comparable period of time, 'and probably with still greater success'.[29]

As for his observations that London and Paris had become 'world-cities', this is not exactly a statistical *aperçu* of the first order. Much more significant, as a portent of things to come, was this remark: 'The rise of New York to the position of world-city during the Civil War... may perhaps prove to have been the most pregnant event of the nineteenth century.'[30] Because I believe that what Spengler had to say about *cities* and *machines*, about *gigantism*, *speed* and *scale*, was truly prophetic and probably the most important legacy of his work, I am going to defer discussion of it till the conclusion of this section and proceed now to a consideration of Spengler as historical theorist.

Let us rehearse his view of history as an organic process—of birth, growth, maturity and decay—and his unequivocal assertion that this approach now permitted for the first time the *forecasting of history* through precise pathological analogy with past cultures. Most lay-people will have little trouble grasping the organic concept: after all, evidence of it abounds in the most physical and visible forms which

Westerners revere, preserve (or come to regret having destroyed), visit, touch, and consign to VCR, from the Parthenon to the Olde Curiosity Shoppe and from Angkor Wat to Williamstown. The past and its transition to the present fill hundreds of millions of paperbacks and hundreds of thousands of miles of celluloid. There can be few people in Europe who are not conscious that they have come through an atrocious century of uncontrollable and accelerating change, from the slow certainties of 1900 to the Future Shock of 2001 and that, however much greater may now be their material wellbeing, Europe and its component parts have aged: that is history on the hoof. And this perception cannot but be shared—with appropriate variations—across the Atlantic and around the world. We may dispute the exact position we currently occupy on his organic cycle and the rate at which we're travelling it, but one of Spengler's supreme achievements is to have articulated, although not to have patented, an historical mechanism which is somehow now widely familiar and persuasive; and it is ironically this very familiarity which has served to relegate him to his relative obscurity in 1995.

By contrast, however, we can now see that his notion of history as *preordained* and *predetermined* and therefore *forecastable*—is simply untenable, not least for a mild-mannered agnostic and especially not for an atheist. And since he advocates the parallel doctrine of historical destiny, it would appear that the notion is *not* available to serve as a device for the deliberate *management* of history, that is to say as a means whereby we can either tinker with the short-term future or formulate galactic strategies for the much longer term—which would anyway be quite inconsistent with Spengler's view of our powerlessness.

We shall now conclude with his thoughts about cities and machines—things which may be of greater concern to most people than an organic view of history. Spengler knew that the history of the world was the history of the city; for him, the 'very problem that we are living through today with hardly the remotest conception of its immensity'[31] is the tension between the 'soul' of Athens and the 'intellect' of Rome; between the province and the world-city, between Florence and New York, between man and machine. Spengler adored machinery and great functional buildings like Roman aqueducts and the Colosseum which he favoured over 'rows of statuary... friezes... and overloaded architraves'[32] but he knew it was all part of the Faustian trap and that, one day, it would begin to unravel. Here, in some of his finest writing, are his City and his Machine, Gigantism, Speed and Scale:

'There stands the miracle of the Cosmopolis, the great petrifact, a

symbol of the formless—vast, splendid, spreading in insolence. It draws
within itself [from] the now impotent countryside, human masses that
are wafted as dunes from one to another or flow like loose sand into the
chinks of stone. Here money and intellect celebrate their greatest and
their last triumphs. It is the most artificial, the cleverest phenomenon
manifested in the light-world of human eyes—uncanny, 'too good to be
true,' standing already almost beyond the possibilities of cosmic forma-
tion.'[33]

'The discovery of the steam-engine... upset everything and transformed economic life. Till then nature had rendered services, but now
she was tied to the yoke as a slave, and her work was as though in
contempt measured by a standard of horse-power. We advanced from
the muscle-force of the Negro... to the organic reserves of the Earth's
crust, where the life-forces of millennia lay stored as coal... and water-
forces are already being brought in to supplement coal. As the horse-
powers run to millions and milliards, the numbers of the population
increase and increase, on a scale that no other Culture ever thought
possible... Work becomes the great word of ethical thinking.... The
machine works and forces the man to co-operate. The entire Culture
reaches a degree of activity such that the earth trembles under it.'[34]

And finally, 'Hence the fantastic traffic that crosses the continents in
a few days, that puts itself across oceans in floating cities, that bores
through mountains, rushes about in subterranean labyrinths, uses the
steam-engine till its last possibilities have been exhausted, and then
passes on to the gas-engine, and finally raises itself above the roads and
railways and flies in the air; hence it is that the spoken word is sent in
one moment over all the oceans; hence comes the ambition to break all
records and beat all dimensions, to build giant halls for giant machines,
vast ships and bridge-spans, buildings that deliriously scrape the clouds,
fabulous forces pressed together to a focus to obey the hand of a child,
stamping and quivering and droning works of steel and glass in which
tiny man moves as unlimited monarch and, at the last, feels nature as
beneath him.'[35]

II. Georg Wilhelm Friedrich Hegel

I thought long and hard before deciding in what order to present our
three world-historians. I finally chose to subpoena Spengler first: this
was partly because he happens to be my preferred choice of the three—

simply as a writer and an extraordinary thinker and personality; and partly because he probably best exemplifies for the uninitiated the search for a 'universal' or 'world' history, as distinct from a history of the world. Also his concept is intuitively obvious to a great many people, to the point of having become, in fact, the way that many of us now view the world, and this regardless of whether we pay any attention to the mindless charge that he is 'pessimistic'. Thus, my decision to present Spengler first does not reflect any view concerning the superiority or otherwise of his Universal History.

The decision to call Hegel next lies to some extent in his being a foil to Spengler, and he offers some relief in wearing his erudition more lightly although far less entertainingly. He is also an *historian of the world* in a sense which Spengler is not. In vain will you look for any connected narrative of the history of the world in *The Decline of the West*, whereas Hegel, in *A Philosophy of History*, gives it to us in a familiar and uncomplicated sequence: Introduction (where his thesis is set out), the Orientals, the Greeks, the Romans and, finally, the Germans—and no index. Of course, he does not *ignore* other historical currents, but they are either treated as important incidental themes, for example the United States of North [sic] America as a European extension: 'America is therefore the land of the future... where the burden of the World's History shall reveal itself'[1] or dismissed, at considerable length, as is Africa: 'At this point we leave Africa, not to mention it again. For it is no historical part of the World; it has no movement or development to exhibit. Historical movements... belong to the Asiatic or European World.'[2]

Unfortunately, Hegel doesn't get himself across without obliging his readers to put in a hard day's work at the coal-face of mysticism. He is both a passionate Protestant and a pragmatic metaphysicist—unusual marriages of epithet and adjective. In the latter respect, he is more than a match for Spengler and his text abounds in references to *Geist*, *Weltgeist* (cf. Spengler's *Geistesepochen* and *Spirit*), *Reason* and the *Idea* as literally tangible forces in driving history. This recurrent mysticism in the German Idealist philosophers is impenetrable to many English and American readers, although it must be said that even Toynbee's history is, as we shall see, shot through with a religiosity which only vigilance by the reader prevents from completely destroying the objectivity of his work; and I am naggingly reminded that Hegel was certainly deeply impressed by Hobbes—hardly a noted mystic in the German mould— not least for his role in supporting Charles II while in exile, and in furthering the cause of English imperial expansionism. It is almost as if

Hegel, landlocked inwardly in the forest fastnesses of German mysticism, envied Hobbes and others their outward, Atlantic-oriented outlook. Somehow, Hobbes—and, for that matter, English and American thinkers of a stature the equal of the German Romantics, from Francis Bacon to Edward Gibbon, John Locke to Thomas Jefferson, John Stuart Mill and Herbert Spencer—have managed to formulate and transmit their theories without recourse to a mysticism which, for many of us, does nothing to clarify the thinking of some of their German cousins: in fact, it may only obscure.

(On the matter of forests, Hegel says at one point that 'Had the woods of Germany been in existence, the French Revolution would not have occurred.'[3] This is not, in fact, a suggestion that the Jacobins were frustrated mystics who would have as lief laid aside the tools of terrorism and become sylvan Quietists had the French forests survived the shipbuilders. It is, rather, an extraordinary piece of historical perception: of post-colonial America he says 'a real State and a real Government arise only after a distinction of classes has arisen, when wealth and poverty become extreme… America is hitherto exempt from this pressure, for it has the outlet of colonization constantly and widely open, and multitudes are continually streaming into the plains of the Mississippi… and by this means the chief source of discontent is removed.'[4] This perception anticipated Frederick Jackson Turner's frontier theory by seventy years).

What, then, of Hegel the militant Protestant? And does his religious passion help or hinder the formulation and transmission of *his* theory of history?

Hegel was born in 1770 and would have had a keen appreciation of the Seven Years'War between England and France, which had ended a few years earlier in 1763 with the defeat of the French (of whom Hegel was also a great admirer), and which finally sealed the fate of North America as an outpost of English political culture—at least, for the time being. He was also strongly influenced by two later events: the American War of Independence of 1776 and the French Revolution of 1789. Both revolutions brought about an extension, or rather the attainment, of a great measure of Freedom, the striving for which is the motive power for Hegel's world history, and on whose account Hegel's writing is garlanded with a great deal of mystical and metaphysical baggage. In fact, his philosophy of history is very nearly—but not perfectly—comprehensible without it. Unfortunately, the divine element which he invokes and incorporates into his system makes it intellectually incomplete and not entirely accessible to those unacquainted with Hegel's history-steering deity.

Hegel was a theologian and, in his earlier years, a disciple of Immanuel Kant. Belief in the power of *Reason*, inculcated by Kant, was to permeate Hegel's entire later formulation of a system which would integrate philosophy, law, history, art and religion into one single, cohesive rational structure to embrace all of human experience, and by which human purpose would be explicated. For Hegel there was no dichotomy between Reason and the working out of God's purpose: Kant's intolerance of metaphysics was too austere for Hegel, who believed not only that a metaphysical understanding of the absolute and universal was possible but also that it was entirely compatible with the exercise of Reason; in fact, that they were indivisible. 'in beginning the study of Universal History, we should... have the firm, unconquerable *faith* [my emphasis] that Reason does exist there; and that the World of intelligent and conscious volition is not abandoned to chance, but must show itself in the light of the self-cognizant Idea.'[5]

What, then, is or what motivates Reason? 'The time must eventually come for understanding that rich product of active Reason, which the History of the World offers to us. It was for awhile the fashion to profess admiration for the wisdom of God, as displayed in animals... and plants. But, if it be allowed that Providence manifests itself in such objects... why not also in Universal History? But Divine Wisdom, i.e., Reason, is one and the same... and we must not imagine God to be too weak to exercise his wisdom on a grand scale', i.e. to guide history.[6] And later, 'it may be said of Universal History, that it is the exhibition of Spirit in the process of working out the knowledge of what it is potentially. And as the germ bears in itself the whole nature of the tree, and the taste and the form of its fruits, so do the first traces of Spirit virtually contain the whole of that History.'[7]

So there we have it. I have read variously that *Geist* or *Weltgeist* are too abstract for non-Germans to fathom. Unfortunately, I find that neither of the following two wordy synonyms propels me very far down the path to a better understanding of what Hegel had in mind: according to Fukuyama, 'Spirit = collective human consciousness' while Talcott Parsons really scores with '*Geist*, or, as we would now be inclined to say, the *component of cultural orientation*.' [my emphasis][8] Perhaps we should give Hegel the benefit of the doubt: I don't believe that he would have understood *either* of these so-called definitions of *Geist* since the quotations in the previous paragraph make it perfectly clear that, for

Hegel, history was a non-random process mapped out by a God who knew what he was up to and had enlisted human beings to be the agents by which the process would be implemented. I personally don't believe a word of it, but I am convinced that this was, indeed, Hegel's *Weltanschauung* and that it can be held up to sympathetic scrutiny late in the twentieth century and evaluated by purely secular refraction.

Hegel proposed to formulate a Philosophical History of the World by which he meant *not* 'a collection of general observations respecting it, suggested by the study of its records, and proposed to be illustrated by its facts, but *Universal History* itself.'[9] In this respect, his purpose was identical to Spengler's although he stopped short of emulating Spengler's claim that his method would enable predetermined history to be forecast, and thus he avoids the blasphemy of suggesting that his Universal History would reveal God's will. Hegel says that the first type of history is *Original*, where authors such as Thucydides and Herodotus simply set down facts of which they were aware as contemporaries and that even where they clearly ghosted speeches by, say, Pericles, 'it must yet be maintained that they were not foreign to the character of the speaker.'[10] A second multi-type is *Reflective*, where the historian attempts to portray a view of an entire people or country; or he seeks to infer pragmatical lessons even though 'Experience and history teach... that peoples and governments never have learned anything from history, or acted on principles deduced from it.'[11] This historian may also be a critic or interpreter of other historical narratives; or he may seek to establish abstractions from history which then lead to Hegel's third approach, which is the *Philosophical History of the World*.

Hegel explains: 'The only Thought which Philosophy brings... to the contemplation of History, is the simple conception of Reason; that Reason is the Sovereign of the World; that the history of the world, therefore, presents us with a rational process... Reason is the substance of the Universe.'[12] And, 'The truth, then, [is] that a Providence (that of God) presides over the events of the World... for *Divine Providence* is Wisdom, endowed with an infinite Power, which realizes its aim, viz., the absolute rational design of the World.'[13] Finally, lest there be any lingering doubt of Hegel's confidence in his method—even *after* he has effectively claimed that it has divine authority—he says 'what I shall have further to say... is not to be regarded as hypothetical; the *result of the investigation* we are about to pursue... happens to be known to me, because I have traversed the entire field.'[14] No academic modesty there.

This is how Hegel can be at once the passionate Protestant *and* the pragmatic metaphysicist: his religiosity dominates his philosophy—it throbs within it—whilst, even in the midst of his metaphysics, his method seems almost to emulate the mechanistic calculations of an astronomer in his search for cosmic self-reinforcing truths—a system to encompass man's relationship to man, and to the constraints of law, power, history, art and religion which he allows to be imposed upon him by the State. Let us now look, then, at the system Hegel created, but shorn of the theological baggage, except where the burden is beneficial to an understanding of Hegel, at least.

'The History of the World is nothing but the development of the Idea of Freedom'[15], and it is this drive for freedom which powers Hegel's system. Freedom is attainable only with the development of the State to which individuals voluntarily submit because they perceive the compact to be in their and their neighbours' greater interest. There are parallels between Hegel's view of the State and its life-cycle—almost its pathology—and the organic process which we encounter in Spengler. 'What traveller among the ruins of Carthage, of Palmyra, Persepolis, or Rome, has not been stimulated to reflections on the transiency of kingdoms and men, and to sadness at the thought of a vigorous and rich life now departed.'[16] But, as I have said earlier, Hegel does not claim predictive qualities for his system, and his momentary sadness soon turns into redemptive joy 'at the rise of a *new* life—that while death is the issue of life, life is also the issue of death.'[17]

This notion of rebirth should not be summarily rejected as being too obviously a theosophical device—a prop—because it shades quite effortlessly into another key tenet of Hegel's system, and one which was to have such a profound impact on a student of Hegel, who was not content merely to interpret history but resolutely set about creating a path for its preordained future: this was the *dialectical method* and the student was Karl Marx. The dialectical method—whether it has to do with Christian theology, logic, or Marxist economics—rests on the perception that tensions, inconsistencies and paradoxes exist in the human condition which are represented in the assertion of a *thesis* and the counterassertion of an *antithesis*, and which are finally resolved by *synthesis*. It is this highly dynamic process whose ratchet-like gearing propels the synthesis forward to the point where it becomes itself the first term—the thesis—in a new tension. Through this procession of resolutions, progress is made irresistibly towards a perfectible objective, which is the State: 'The State is the Idea of Spirit in the external manifestation of human Will and its Freedom. It is to the State, therefore, that change in... History indissolubly attaches itself.'[18]

Hegel then says that the Nation is the vessel of World History and that the Spirit is 'the whole complex of its institutions... that is its work—that is what this particular Nation is.' The Spirit, the Nation become the individual's 'character and capability, enabling him to have a definite place in the world—to be *something*. For he finds the being of the people to which he belongs an already established, firm world... with which he has to incorporate himself. In this its work, therefore— its world—the Spirit of the people enjoys its existence and finds its satisfaction. A Nation is moral—virtuous—vigorous—while it is engaged in realizing its grand objects'. But then (shades of Spengler) 'The Nation can still accomplish much in war and peace at home and abroad... but it lives the same kind of life as the individual when passing from maturity to old-age. This mere *customary life* (the watch wound up and going on of itself) is that which brings on natural death.'[19]

And so the cycle is self-perpetuating. Or, rather, it *can be*. 'A people can only die a violent death when it has become naturally dead in itself, as, e.g., the German Imperial Cities, the German Imperial Constitution' unless the 'Spirit of a People... advance[s] to the adoption of some new purpose.'[20] This is why Hegel and other German Romantics shed few tears at the total victory of Napoleon over the bureaucratically sclerotic Prussians at the battle of Jena in 1806, because the Spirit of the People then did indeed advance to a new purpose. Within a few years Prussia was to re-emerge as a model of the state Hegel advocated, its administration rationalized and its militaristic tradition stiffened with the Spirit of nationalism and—dare it be said?—'a new historical mission'. 1813 and the Liberation of Germany were one of Spengler's 'three great moments' in Prussian history. In 1818 Hegel himself moved to the University of Berlin and became indelibly personified as the philosophical mouthpiece of the new Prussia; and it would not be many years before he would begin one of his lectures with these words: 'The German Spirit is the Spirit of the new World... The destiny of the German peoples is, to be the bearers of the Christian principle.'[21]

There is not much purple prose in Hegel; indeed, his lectures seem not to have been great crowd-pullers and *The Philosophy of History* was cobbled together posthumously by his son from scruffy lecture-notes. However, I do like his aphorism of 'History as the slaughter-bench at which the happiness of peoples, the wisdom of States, and the virtue of individuals have been victimized'[22] and it leads us to introduce another important principle in Hegel's system where, despite his Christian credentials, he feels secure in ignoring the inconvenient verities of Jesus as reported by St Matthew: 'Blessed are the meek; for they shall inherit the earth' and 'Blessed are the merciful; for they shall obtain mercy' (Chapter Five, verses 5 and 7). This reminds me of Spengler's comment on Hegel's historical method that 'he meant to ignore those peoples which did not fit into his scheme of history.'[23]

For Hegel, forgetful of St Matthew, the role of the Hero is indispensable in enabling history to unfold according to the its guiding Idea. Even though they be unconscious of the Idea, the Heroes are 'at the same time... thinking men, who had an insight into the requirements of the time—*what was ripe for development*' and 'Great men have formed purposes to satisfy themselves, not others.'[24] These are Spengler's 'Caesar-Men' for whom there are flexi-rules or no rules at all. Theirs is not, Hegel says, a happy lot: 'When their object is attained they fall off like empty hulls from the kernel. They die early, like Alexander; they are murdered, like Caesar; transported to St Helena, like Napoleon.'[25]

It is clear that for Hegel the ends justify the means, since history is the Enactment of God's Purpose and the distinction between commanding and obeying is absolutely necessary. This was to be convenient for Marx, and for Lenin and Stalin. Here is Hegel's unequivocal licence to the Hero: 'A World-historical individual is not so unwise as to indulge a variety of wishes to divide his regards. He is devoted to the One Aim, regardless of all else. It is even possible that such men may treat other great, even sacred interests, inconsiderately; conduct which is indeed obnoxious to moral reprehension. But so mighty a form must trample down many an innocent flower—crush to pieces many an object in its path.'[26] Hegel's Bible-reading would seem, indeed, to have been eclectic.

This brings us to Hegel's recommended constitution of the State. He regards the Republic as—in theory—the only just and true political constitution; and he says that even high officials in *monarchical* [my emphasis] constitutions actually support the republican ideal, but see that it cannot be realized in the practical world. Therefore 'we must be satisfied with less freedom; the monarchical constitution—under the given circumstances, and the present moral condition of the people— being even regarded as the most advantageous.'[27] This is, of course, a cop-out: a convenient political device which allows Hegel's republican system to be postponed to suit the circumstances. 'The present moral condition of the people' will strike us as a grave and weakly elitist flaw— an escape clause—in Hegel's system because, as we have seen in this century, it is a perfect hostage to the opportunism of latterday 'Heroes' who clearly failed to deliver in the years after Hegel's death; and when his God has equally clearly failed to intercede and bring about the Universal History announced by Hegel as being the object of Divine Providence.

These, then, are the rafters and purlins of the Hegelian edifice: history is inspired by a divine Spirit in its unswervable quest for Freedom through the operation of Reason; that quest—whose ultimate success is never in doubt—is driven by a process in which anomalies are resolved through reconciliation of opposites, new and ever-nobler objectives are set—the new National Spirit—and the whole enterprise is steered by the actions of Supermen striving through the chosen nations of history. The result is the State—for the time being, at least, monarchical—with which the individual lives not in perfect equality with his fellow-man, to be sure, but in the highest attainable level of harmony where the individual has willingly subordinated his 'mere brute emotions and rude instincts' to a common weal. 'The antithesis of Church and State vanishes... and the Spiritual becomes reconnected with the Secular',[28] although 'It must be frankly stated, that with the Catholic Religion no rational constitution is possible.'[29]

Where has history left Hegel a century and three-quarters later? Hegel's school rapidly fragmented after his death and few would deny that Karl Marx then proceeded to carry out a selective highjacking of the Hegelian system with results which were beyond the imagination of either man. But there is more than a whiff of sanctimonious wish-fulfilment in Hegel and although I have said elsewhere that Hegel would have been horrified to see what had become of his vision at the end of the twentieth century, it is difficult to avoid the uneasy feeling that Hegel—and Nietzsche, for that matter—was at the very least an unwitting source and sanction for what Prussianism was to become later in his century and that which followed.

We have seen that Hegel's system is almost perfectly comprehensible and satisfactory once stripped of all the mystical and metaphysical baggage which burdens it. But the problem arises in the system's ultimate dependence on the notion of divine direction and authority. And needless to say, that this indispensable divine element is Christian and, even more restrictively, specifically Protestant: not exactly of an ecumenical compass likely to command wide support. Without this metaphysical mortar, I fear that the whole edifice loses its neatness— loses the astronomical perfection that we talked of earlier. Finally, and before I hand Hegel over to be remarketed in late twentieth-century agnostic clothing, we must ask whether, in promoting the Protestant God to the role of arbiter of Universal History, he lays himself open to charges of extreme religious racism.

Hegel is quite convinced that history moves against the jet-stream: 'The History of the World travels from East to West, for Europe [with, presumably, the American extension of whose future importance he was so certain] is absolutely the end of History, Asia the beginning.'[30] Furthermore, in discussing Freedom, he makes the famous assertion that 'the Eastern nations knew only that *one* is free; the Greek and Roman world only that *some* are free; while *we* know that all men absolutely... are free.'[31], i.e. the transition from despotism to the Western European republican-monarchist system. This schema found later endorsement in Spengler, as we have seen—albeit resolutely *without* all the paraphernalia of divine purpose; and it is for this reason that I chose to present our three universal historians on a *West-European-American* historical stage where the play began around 1450 and is running still. In summary, we must reject Hegel's notion of God's purpose—any god's—being mani-fested in history; but his location of its wellsprings seems much more securely founded, however distasteful we may find the Prussian obsession.

Perhaps we should excuse him and close with his recognition of where history would end up: 'America is therefore the land of the future... It is a land of desire for all those who are weary of the histor-ical lumber-room of Old Europe.'[32]

Hegel re-marketed 1992

Hegel left the end of history in Europe, recuperating somewhere on the north German plain, and poised—as he saw it—to resume one day its relentless and Providentially-guided journey on to the Pacific.

One hundred and sixty years later Francis Fukuyama, an American political scientist, came forward and provided Hegel with the agnostic clothing which would enable him to be re-marketed for use as the world staggers out of the political and economic turmoil of the late twentieth century and into the historylessness of the third millennium. With *The End of History and the Last Man*, Fukuyama re-appraises Hegel both directly, and through the writing of Alexandre Kojève, whom he describes as Hegel's greatest twentieth century interpreter—just as Marx had occupied that position in the nineteenth. His book has there-fore re-opened the 'End of History' debate.

These are Fukuyama's starting-points: 'The twentieth century, it is safe to say, has made all of us into deep historical pessimists.'[33] But, 'The monumental failure of Marxism as a basis for real-world societies—plainly evident 140 years after the *Communist Manifesto*—raises the question of whether Hegel's Universal History was not in the end the more prophetic one.'[34] Fukuyama is far from being a metaphysicist, and he allows not the merest hint of Hegel's theology to limp into this century and to flavour the new relevance he claims for Hegel's Universal History; but he asserts nothing less than that the world has arrived at the brink of the End of History in the form of Hegel's *State*, but now transformed from monarchy to liberal democracy and now rid, at last, of the tensions and contradictions which, as we saw earlier, were resolvable only through the dialectic process.

Fukuyama argues passionately that, over the past 400 years, the development and systematic application of natural sciences in the West have been one of the two major drivers of history. He rejects the idea that history can be cyclical, as Aristotle believed, because the effect of the growth of natural science is cumulative and empirical and, barring a universal obliteration of human memory in some cataclysm, cannot be lost.

For Fukuyama, liberal economic democracy had been germinating for two or three centuries in the West and is now blossoming triumphantly throughout the world as—successful in its own backyard—one illiberal regime after another reels before the onslaught of democracy and the subject people embrace the philosophy as man's preferred form of social and political organisation. There are resonant parallels between this process, undeniably triumphant in the West if lacking firm historical roots elsewhere, and Hegel's view of *Freedom* as the engine of history. Fukuyama even gives us a rather naive league-table of those nations which qualified as of the date of the publication of his book in 1992.

To the dominance of natural science in the modern world, Fukuyama yokes the other major driver of history. This is the need for 'recognition' identified somewhat arcanely by Hegel as the elemental force which actuates all mankind and which accounts for exceptional human achievements of whatever nature—artistic, military, political, philosophical and so forth. Let us paraphrase it as a concept of human worth, dignity, self-respect and socially accorded honour: we saw it earlier in Hegel's reference to the individual's need 'to have a definite place in the world' i.e., the *State*.[35]

Fukuyama postulates that the operation of these historical processes has led to the triumph in the late twentieth century of liberal democracy as humankind's preferred form of social, economic and political organisation which has vanquished monarchy, theocracy, aristocracy, as earlier forms of polity; and in the middle and closing years of this century, has seen off first fascism and latterly communism. This, again, echoes Hegel's progress of history from *despotism* in the East to *democracy* in Greece, and from *aristocracy* in Rome to the 'republican' monarchies of the early nineteenth century.

Fukuyama concludes that the triumph of liberal democracy in its traditional breeding-ground in the West, and its relentless spread through hitherto infertile soil in the rest of the world, have ushered in the End of History in the sense that global armed conflicts will not erupt between liberal democratic states, and that the liberal democratic form of political and economic organisation represents the self-fulfilling pinnacle of human striving.

I could have found a secular reading of Hegel's thesis utterly convincing had I thumbed my way through *The Philosophy of History* in the 1830s. And I might even accept in Fukuyama's persuasive writing a ringing late-twentieth century endorsement of a dusted-off Hegel were it possible to view his conclusions in purely abstract political, social and economic terms—if, that is, I don't have to look out of the window. After all, viewed from the vantage-point of 1995, Marxism can be seen as an ultimately unsuccessful strain of Hegelianism destroyed partly by the surge of liberal democracy and partly by its own rogue genes.

Unfortunately, liberal democracy cannot operate in its own historical isolation ward, where 'political', 'social' and 'economic' are abstractions capable of perfection *there*, at the recently announced End of History, and needing to pay no sideways glance at what else happens most uncooperatively to be going on at the same time *here*, at a quite different fork of history. It is almost as if we are being asked to operate on two time-scales. Fukuyama, in an unwitting citing of Kojève, says that now, at the End of History, with 'no further great political goals to struggle for, [men] could preoccupy themselves with *economic activity* alone.' [my emphasis][36]

Well, maybe. But I shall have much more to say later about this disastrous preoccupation; and, as it is, other things have unfortunately been happening out there in the years since cholera stilled Hegel's pen in 1831 and Fukuyama booted up his word-processor a century-and-a-half later; and we shall see that these comfortable endorsements of Western thought and achievement are going to be stretched as never before if neo-Hegelian man is to come to terms in the third millennium with the very by-products of that success.

The flaw in Hegel's Universal History is sadly matched by an equally fatal one in Fukuyama's otherwise excellent book: there is so much of value and insight, but he cannot be pardoned for his extraordinary feat of insulating what he calls the 'Promised Land' of liberal democracy from what we can all see to be the Real World. He devotes in total a cursory, dismissive half-page to environmental threats, there are but twelve words on 'population', nothing on resource depletion, a ritual nod in the direction of nuclear winters, and there is no integrated treatment whatsoever of the interrelated issues of forms of government, science and technology, and personal freedom which are going to become paramount in the third millennium. Hegel has no need to be defended retroactively for failure to spot portents which were not even on the distant horizon in the 1820s: Fukuyama has no such excuse when the entrails are strewn in reeking piles across the world.

III. Arnold Joseph Toynbee

I have explained why I chose to present Spengler first; and there are good enough reasons why Toynbee might have followed next, since there are certain similarities in the view each man took of history as being a process of birth, growth, maturity and decline. However, on reflection I feel that Hegel will provide a better foil by being sandwiched between them; and there is an advantage in looking at Toynbee last, as the most recent and best-known of the Universal Historians—*A Study of History* having appeared in a series of ten volumes between 1934 and 1955.

Toynbee follows Spengler in formulating a theory of world history through the dissection of a number of 'civilizations', rather than nations. For Toynbee's purposes there are twenty-eight such civilizations or societies, which can be identified and studied as discrete units. These range from the dead civilizations of Egypt and the Andes; through what he calls the 'fossilized relics of certain societies now extinct'[1]; on to the 'death-bed' of the Hellenic Society (to which the West is affiliated); and, finally, to a mere five civilizations which inhabit the twentieth century. These are the Christian orthodox of south-eastern Europe and Russia; Islam, from Morocco to the Great Wall of China; Hindu India; the Far East up to the Pacific; and, last, *Western Christendom* by which he means

Western Europe-America (and Australasia). There is a comfortable reso-
nance here with both Spengler's and Hegel's geocultural units—and also
a close parallel with my Prologue—when Toynbee says of the West that
'on the economic... and political plane [it] is undoubtedly co-extensive
with the whole inhabitable and navigable surface of the Earth'.[2]

(I should note that my views of Toynbee stem largely from some years
of cohabitation with the unabridged ten-volume edition—later
augmented to twelve—of *A Study of History* commended to me by a
splendid and encouraging professor at Cambridge called Jack
Gallagher—a sadly missed and underrated intellect. However, for the
benefit of the general reader I have deliberately restricted my quotations
to the text of the two-volume Somervell abridgement.)

Toynbee divides his civilizations into two groups: fifteen have derived
from earlier civilizations—they are 'affiliated' in the sense of the West's
bond with the Graeco-Roman or Hellenic world; but six have emerged
straight from the primal, historyless swamp. Since primitive societies
which have survived to this day are static, Toynbee claims that they must
at some point have been 'dynamically progressive'. This is something of
a non-sequitur: it is difficult to imagine a time when the Inuits of Arctic
Canada, for example, or the Aborigines of Arnhemland were either
dynamic or progressive, and it is surely more charitable to dispense with
both adjectives and to say simply that both societies had, at least until
recently, made an extremely effective compromise with the conditions
in which they found themselves—static or no.

In any event, the question Toynbee poses is: what makes a static
society flick the switch, slip up a gear and become dynamic? He introduces the notion of imitation or *mimesis*, whereby in primitive, static
societies there is veneration—mimesis—directed towards the older
generation and to ancestors; whilst 'in societies in process of civilization,
mimesis is directed towards creative personalities who command a
following because they are pioneers.'[3] There is, of course, a gap in the
process even here which Toynbee seems to have overlooked: namely,
what is the spark which animated this 'process of civilization' itself in the
first place? The calculus becomes almost infinitesimal. There is, indeed,
a caveat: the difference between primitive and higher societies is surely
not, Toynbee asks, permanent and fundamental. 'We have said that primitive societies are as old as the human race, but we should more properly have said that they are older.'[4] But Toynbee then ventures into some
highly debatable anthropology—both physical and social—when, as
part of his search for this elusive spark, he talks of the 'mutation of sub-

man into man' and says that 'it is clear that mankind could not have become human except in a social environment.'[5]

The spark is to be found in that widthless kerf between Yin and Yang, the static and dynamic of the Chinese formula: that is Toynbee's 'ledge' on which *primitive societies* lie torpid, while *civilizations* are likened to the companions of the torpid 'who have just risen to their feet and have started to climb up the face of the cliff above.'[5] Somewhere, then, is the spark. But first there are two damp squibs in the way of ignition—*race* and *environment*.

Toynbee dismisses both the notion that racial superiority exists as a factor in energizing the move from static to dynamic and, in particular, the association of racial superiority with colour or, rather, the absence of colour. He finds Nietzsche's 'blond beast' to be a Teutonic figment, and points out that the (correct) identification of most European and many west Asian and Indian languages as having a common primeval origin—'Aryan'—had then been misappropriated to fabricate the inference that all those people who spoke Indo-European languages were physically related and therefore part of an enormous master-race 'responsible for practically all the achievements of human civilization'.[6] According to this criterion, even Dante and Jesus Christ had been co-opted as fully paid-up Indo-Germans!

Spengler says somewhere that Darwinism had made 'biology politically effective', and certainly the expansion of the West in the nineteenth century will have provided clear proof of White racial superiority for those who wanted it. But for Toynbee the race squib is, indeed, a dud: he shows that the contributors to at least half his civilizations were nothing if not multiracial although, in an eerie reflection of Hegel's dismissal of Africa cited earlier, he concedes only that 'The Black races alone have not contributed positively to any civilization—as yet.'[7] 'Enough has been said to justify us in dismissing the theory that a superior race has been the cause and author of the transition from Yin to Yang, from static to dynamic, in one part of the world after another since a date some six thousand years ago.'[8]

And so to the environment, i.e. geography and climate. Toynbee cites Hippocrates' amusing theory of the beneficial effect of mountains on the physique and courage of your average *montagnard*; in unfavourable contrast are 'sultry hollows covered with water-meadows', which are not conducive to good physiques, courage and endurance. Toynbee suggests that if modern-day parallels can be found which match the distinction drawn by the ancient Greeks in their admiration of the steppe-living Scythians but their contempt for the lotus-eaters of the Lower Nile Valley, then 'the environment theory will be vindicated.'[9] In a brief fact-finding tour of Eurasia and Afrasia, of North and South America, Australia, India, China and a few outlying geographical suburbs, Toynbee fails to detect any contemporary evidence to support the view of Hippocrates. Thus, *environment* joins *race* as an equally unhelpful factor in identifying the spark of history. That is Toynbee's conclusion and it must, of course, be given proper prominence in our evaluation of his theory of history as it emerges. We are left, however, with the tantalising regret that Toynbee should not have chosen a less naive approach to test the race and environment theories and had experimented with a rather more complex set of simultaneous equations.

Toynbee's path to discovering the spark is 'to shut our eyes, for the moment, to the formulae of science in order to open our ears to the language of mythology... [and to find the spark in an] encounter between two superhuman personalities.'[10] There has to be an external factor which intrudes 'with a stimulus of the kind best calculated to evoke the most potently creative variations.'[11] The reader will probably now have guessed that not only was Toynbee a mystic (so was Spengler, of a kind, and yet this caused no problems of comprehension) but—and this makes for a far higher order of complication—he was a fervent Christian, to boot; and if it was his Christian convictions which not merely helped but were actually dominant in propelling him to a personally satisfying theory of history—utterly consistent with his beliefs and supportive of his God's role in fashioning history—then it must equally be acknowledged that the divine spark will be for many people either an irrelevant distraction or a fatal flaw in Toynbee's system.

Toynbee's energizing factor—my spark—is the tension, the *challenge* and *response* in a host of familiar myths: the Serpent in the Garden, Satan in the Book of Job, Mephistopheles in Faust. I do not propose to spend any time in deconstructing Toynbee's religiosity: it would be not only presumptuous, but also both pointless and beyond the capacity of a simple-minded agnostic. Furthermore, the nature of the energizing agent—divine or, far more probably, genetic and environmental—is not only immaterial, but also does not of itself compromise the *mechanics* of Toynbee's theory. What matters is the incontestable conclusion of both Toynbee and our other two universal historians that it is the role of *extraordinary people* or the *creative minority* to make history, whether they are busy carrying out God's masterplan, as Toynbee (and Hegel, let us recall) would have it; or, as secular historians will insist, when they are simply acting and *reacting* to random events of mindless causality and, in the process, becoming part of that causality in creating new historical wall-paper. Reaction to tensions by the creative minority, imposing their will on the majority, and the succeeding cycle of action and reaction, constitute Toynbee's conception of history as a process of 'challenge-and-response' which have a distinct echo in Hegel's dialectic.

I do not intend to make further examination of the Christian element in Toynbee's system. Let us instead ask the historian himself to describe the role and fate of the extraordinary man, the newly energized history-maker: 'The first stage, then, of the human protagonist's ordeal is a transition from Yin to Yang through a dynamic act—performed by God's creature under temptation from the Adversary—which enables God Himself to resume His creative activity. But this progress has to be paid for; and it is not God but God's servant, the human sower, who pays the price. Finally, after many vicissitudes, the sufferer triumphant becomes the pioneer. The human protagonist in the divine drama not only serves God by enabling Him to renew His creation but also serves his fellow men by pointing the way for others to follow.'[12]

Where have we now reached in our understanding of Toynbee's theory of history? We have seen that he views the sum of human history through a constellation of twenty-eight quite clearly identifiable *societies* or *civilizations*—rather than nations—of which five survive; and, as we remarked of Hegel, if this seems an intuitively obvious approach to us in 1995, we should not underestimate the length of the stride Toynbee took in helping to change historical perceptions. He dismisses *race* and *environment* as factors having any discernible impact on history; and he sees societies making the transition from static to dynamic through *challenges* posed and *responses* to them made by *creative people* and *minorities* acting in the midst and on behalf of a compliant majority. These people are conduits of divine will—their fingertips reaching out to God's in a way reminiscent of Adam on the ceiling of the Sistine Chapel. But the divine nature claimed by Toynbee for their mission is no more vital—in fact, it is an irritating distraction—to an understanding of the role of the creative minority than it was when we examined the role of the superman in Hegel. We can now broaden our understanding by looking at what happens after the society has gone dynamic—has reached its critical mass—and here there are parallels with Spengler.

Toynbee says of Spengler that he 'declares that every civilization passes through the same succession of ages as a human being; but his eloquence on this theme nowhere amounts to proof, and we have already noticed that societies are not in any sense living organisms.'[13] Toynbee goes on to say that while Spengler's biological and Herbert Spencer's psychological analogies of society are at their least harmful as aids to our understanding of *primitive societies*, they are quite incapable of expressing 'the relation in which *growing civilizations* [my emphasis] stand to their individual members'[14]; and he defines a human society as a 'system of relationships between human beings who are not only individuals but are also social animals.'[15] Whilst we can agree with Toynbee that the almost 'pathological' element in Spengler's theory of history pushes the organic analogy too far, he certainly fails to refute Spengler's principle of a cycle of birth, growth, maturity and decline; nor are Toynbee's definitions of society and of the relationship to it of the individual necessarily at variance with Spengler's cycle. In fact, Toynbee is himself a partisan of the cycle theory and—operating within it—his 'challenge-and-response' mechanism performs perfectly convincingly.

Let us, then, see how Toynbee does indeed incorporate *cycle* into his theory. In fact, endorsement of the principle is to be found in the very title headings of the first volumes: *genesis, growth, breakdown* and *disintegration*, and it is more accurate to talk of incorporating challenge-and-response—the underlying formula in the Study—*within* this much longer cyclical process than to imagine it operating *outside* of it. 'In a growing civilization a challenge meets with a successful response which proceeds to generate another and a different challenge which meets with another successful response. There is no term to this process of growth unless and until a challenge arises which the civilization in question fails to meet—a tragic event which means a cessation of growth and... breakdown.'[16] I shall come back with further evidence of the essentially cyclical backdrop to the procees of challenge-and-response but first I present some concrete examples of the process in action.

We recall from Toynbee's discussion of *environment* as a possible key player in history that, because it could not be shown that similar environments have reliably produced similar civilizations (i.e. the correlation eventually breaks down after a few similarities are dredged up), a favourable environment cannot itself be relied upon to offer the challenge necessary to provoke a creative response. Toynbee then jolts our conventional speech-conditioned thoughts about 'the environment being right' or 'where environmental conditions permit', and proceeds to turn the notion completely on its head. It is not *favourable* environments which issue the challenge—it's the *hostile* ones, and it is these which, in Toynbee's neo-Faustian mythology, winnow the soon-to-become dominant creative minorities from the supine majority and elicit the response. So, what does a challenge-and-response look like? Here are a few examples.

Toynbee writes of the *Egyptiac* Civilization which became 'dynamic' after 4000 BC. Why did it? It seems that at this time northern Europe still lay in the frigor of the last ice-age and that ice covered the continent as far south as the Harz mountains (where Spengler was to be born several thousand years later), and that today's parched Sahara enjoyed plentiful rainfall which watered its abundant parklands and savannahs so that they supported a fauna which would not look out of place around today's Zambesi, over three thousand miles further south. Whilst woolly rhinoceros, mammoth and reindeer were grazing in Surrey and around Paris, Egypt would have been thickly populated with palaeolithic hunters and there was every conventional reason to suppose that they would flourish here while torpid Europe continued to freeze. However, as the European ice-shield retreated northwards, the Atlantic cyclone belt went with it and there began a relentless process of desiccation in North Africa.

The hunters—unaware though they undoubtedly were that something was happening, because of its insidiousness—were being *challenged*, and there were only three possible *responses*. 'They might move northward or southward with their prey, following the climatic belt to which they were accustomed; they might remain at home eking out a miserable existence on such game as could withstand the drought; or they might—still without leaving their homeland—emancipate themselves from dependence on the whims of their environment by domesticating animals and taking to agriculture.'[17] Toynbee shows that those that did not respond paid the penalty of extinction; others did respond by changing either their habitat, e.g. following the game south, or their way of life, e.g. becoming the nomads of the Steppes who survive to this day. Yet others obliged Toynbee by doing both, and so went on to create one of his twenty-eight civilizations... 'out of some of the primitive societies of the vanishing Afrasian grasslands.'[18]

We will now turn to the *Mayan* and *Andean* Civilizations. Long before Phidias began work on the Earl of Elgin's Marbles, the luxuriant lowland forests of central America flung down a challenge. In the highlands, land was easily cultivated in conditions of scanty vegetation and simple irrigation. But on the rich coastal lowlands 'great trees had to be felled and fast-growing bushes kept down by untiring energy.' 'The Mayan culture was made possible by the agricultural conquest of the rich lowlands where the exuberance of nature can only be held in check by organized effort.'[19] The challenge found no response on the other side of the Isthmus of Panama.

In the Andes and on the adjoining Pacific coast the challenges were 'a bleak climate and a grudging soil; on the coast… heat and drought of an almost rainless equatorial desert at sea-level'. The coastal pioneers 'conjured their oases out of the desert by husbanding the scanty waters that descended from the western scarp of the plateau and giving life to the plains by irrigation.' Their fellow *creative minorities* on the plateau 'transformed their mountain-sides into fields by husbanding the scanty soil on terraces preserved by a ubiquitous system of laboriously constructed retaining walls.'[20]

For the third example of challenge-and-response theory, I will switch away from the specific examples drawn conveniently from Toynbee's list of civilizations. For the theory to be persuasive—to be more than a working hypothesis—it must be seen to be valid not only for remote civilizations viewed in their *finished state* through powerful historical telescopes; it must also pass the better or added test when applied to a much more contemporary and important historical phenomenon. That phenomenon—and the term is far from being an exaggeration—is the struggle for control of *North America*.

A deserted eighteenth-century New England village, practically repossessed now by nature after its abandonment by hardy settlers, impresses Toynbee. Where had the settlers gone? And were not the speed and determination of reassertive nature testimony to the heroic scale of the settlers' original efforts in carving a home out of the wilderness? This episode set Toynbee to speculate on how the probable outcome of European rivalry in North America might have appeared to an observer in 1650. He would probably have ruled out the Spaniards who, despite their springboard in Mexico, had fared poorly in the recently concluded Thirty Years' War. France seems likely to achieve military primacy in Europe, but to concede naval primacy to Holland and England. Holland seemed perhaps the stronger of the two, and possessed moreover the incomparable advantage of New Amsterdam and entry to the interior through the Hudson Valley. However, France sits astride an even finer water-gate—the St Lawrence—and could also project overwhelming military pressure back in Europe and onto Holland itself. He would have concluded that the English in Virginia and the Carolinas might 'survive as an enclave' but that—for certain—the hard-pressed, straggling settlers of New England were going nowhere.

By 1701 Toynbee's long-lived observer notes that he was off-target with the Dutch—New Amsterdam having been renamed New York by the victorious English—but that his bet on the French was surely paying off as he espies them penetrating to the Great Lakes and the Mississippi and establishing a bridgehead in Louisiana. A century later, however, and his wager is lost: the tricolor flies only over St Pierre and Miquelon, and the Southern States of the new Union are fair set to win the West, although not without an assist from the Yankees of New England whose inventiveness would furnish them with the Mississippi steamboat and the cotton-gin. But a mere sixty years later Toynbee's weary observer would note that 'The New Englanders are now masters of the Pacific coast all the way from Seattle to Los Angeles'[21]; the Yankee railroad is knitting the country together in tribute to the North-East; and the Civil War has confirmed the supremacy of the North. 'It is impossible to deny that the original colonial home of the New Englanders was the hardest country of all. Thus North American history tells in favour of the proposition: the greater the difficulty, the greater the stimulus.'[22] This is a sweeping characterization of North American colonial settlement, but it is a persuasive endorsement of challenge-and-response in theory and practice.

What happens next in Toynbee's cycle-within-a-cycle, now that the historical process has been energized? The challenge-and-response mechanism operates, as we have observed earlier, somewhat as Hegel's dialectic: it generates its own dynamic and the society will continue to grow unless and until the creative response fails. At such a point, the creative minority loses the obedience and compliance of the majority which then becomes a passive or surly or even hostile 'internal prole-tariat', in Toynbee's words. This *breakdown* may not be irreversible, there may be a recovery of the creativity by the old leadership; but if it does not respond, then *disintegration* sets in and the society splits in two, leaving a dominant but no longer creative junta, the hostile internal proletariat and, since the society cannot any longer project or 'radiate' power, an external proletariat as well—that is, the barbarian at the gate. This period ushers in Toynbee's 'time of troubles'—akin, once again, to Spengler's 'Contending States'. The time of troubles is a 'rout' and there follows a 'rally': indeed, in one of Toynbee's less convincing passages, he even claims to have been able to detect—with almost military preci-sion—the amplitude of the rout-and-rally rhythm in a number of disin-tegrating societies as being 'three-and-a-half beats'![23] Whatever the number of beats—rout-rally-rout-rally-rout-rally-rout—there follows the establishment of the *universal state* to dominate the entire area which had been involved in the process. Our best example is the Roman Empire which both absorbed and destroyed Greece and extended its hegemony over the entire reachable world.

Judged by Toynbee's own analysis, every Universal State *seems* fated to fail: in each, the majority becomes estranged from the parasitic dominant minority who are confronted also by the external foe, and militarism and nationalism are inevitable products. The State, the civilization, dies but, through the death-throes, there survives a seed which may offer the chance of rebirth, of a new cycle of the familiar challenge-and-response mechanism which has offered a cogent explanation of the way in which all earlier societies had become dynamic. All very redolent of redemption and everlasting life after death. But what of Toynbee's overall system and the cycle from genesis to disintegration? And how does it now rate—40 years after completion?

There are some clues in Part XII—the last, which came out in 1955—to Toynbee's *own* opinion of the validity and durability of a thesis which he had, after all, first formulated at least thirty years earlier, and in a very different world. Let us go back first to his analysis of the *breakdown* process, where he finds that of his original roster of twenty-eight civilizations, no fewer than eighteen are now dead and buried; and that nine of the remainder are either 'in their last agonies [or] under threat of either annihilation or assimilation by the eighth, namely our own civilization of the West',[24] as a result, we have been taught to conclude, of their failure to respond to a challenge. Later, however, Toynbee seems to indulge in some judicious trimming of the *universality* of his system: 'Though all the other civilizations… may be dead or dying, a civilization is not like an animal organism, condemned by an inexorable destiny to die.'[25] Well, we know that Toynbee does not hit it off with Spengler in this *biological view* of history, despite the similarity of the *cyclical* approach common to both historians. But he then goes on to imply that the West might qualify for what we would now call a 'get-out clause', exempting it from the fate which will eventually have befallen the other twenty-seven. 'There is no law of historical determinism that compels us to leap out of the intolerable frying-pan of our time of troubles into the slow and steady fire of a universal state where we shall in due course be reduced to dust and ashes.'[26] There may, indeed, be no such law, but one could not help detecting in these lines a sense that Toynbee was close to making a special case for the West. He is at least certain that 'Western Civilization… has manifestly not reached the stage of a universal state.'[27] So let us now turn to Part XII.

Has the Western Civilization so differentiated itself that, even in the very process of submitting to Toynbee's tests, it either should not have been included in the List of Twenty-eight in the first place? Or, if it is not yet a universal state (or wasn't, at least, in 1955), is it now set to be the agent by which the entire world becomes not only a universal state but a *unitary* one as well? Toynbee sets about writing Part XII—'The Prospects of the Western Civilization'—with consciously expressed 'distaste': one of the cardinal principles in the Study was to regard the West as just one of a number of civilizations—to revolt against the notion that West = History. Indeed, by Part VII he had already found cause to demote the West in favour of the superior *spiritual* attainments of no fewer than four earlier civilizations. What, then, obliged him to change his mind?

The answer lies in the Prologue, and in the unashamedly 'West-European-American' orientation of Hegel and Spengler. Toynbee explains that, in departing from the cardinal principle, 'he was bowing to the logic of three facts which had lost none of their cogency' since 1927. First, 'the Western civilization was the only extant representative of its species that did not show indisputable signs of being in disintegration.' Second, 'the expansion of the Western society and the radiation of the Western culture had brought all other extant civilizations... within a world-encompassing Westernizing ambit.' And finally, 'for the first time in the history of the Human Race, all Mankind's eggs had been gathered into one precious and precarious basket', and 'the fate of all Mankind lay on the finger-tip of one man in Moscow and one man in Washington.'[28]

These two phenomena—unprecedented and utter economic domination of the entire globe by one surviving and overweening civilization, and the prospect of instant, clinical Armageddon without years of tedious trench warfare—led Toynbee '*reluctantly* to endorse in 1950 AD the conclusion... that an inquiry into the prospects of the Western civilization was a necessary part of a twentieth-century study of History.'[29] [my italics] But before we leave Toynbee, there are three other clues which we should at least flag so as to understand better his own evolution as he approached the end of his life; for they are evidence that his work—like history itself—remained unfinished; and it is intriguing to speculate on how and whether Toynbee might have concluded his 'Study' had it been 1975 and not 1955.

First is the matter of the physical environment. There is little attention paid to, and certainly no *systematic* treatment of, the issue of natural-resource depletion; but there is, buried in a section on Technology, Class-conflict and Employment, an awareness that the ghost of Malthus had returned to press his hitherto discredited case. 'In thus forecasting a posthumous fulfilment of Malthus's expectations, we should also have to forecast that, by the time of "the great famine", some *oecumenical authority* [my emphasis] would have made itself responsible for looking after the elementary material needs of the whole population of the planet.'[30] And 'Would Western civilization itself be able to survive the death of a mechanized industry, to which it had given hostages by allowing its population to increase in the Machine Age far beyond the numbers that any non-industrial economy could support?'[31]

Second, in a reflection on the unwelcome nature of these intrusions on his thesis at the very moment of its completion, Toynbee fore-shadows a form of World Government—at least to ensure the abolition of war through 'the control of atomic energy... concentrated in the hands of some single political authority.'[32] The United Nations being unsuited to this role, Toynbee has no hesitation in nominating either the United States or the Soviet Union as the 'demi-mundane' nucleus of such a development.

The third and final clue lies in Toynbee's view of religion and of God's involvement in history. He states quite uncompromisingly that 'in AD 1955 the crucial questions confronting Western Man were all religious'[33], and he wonders 'How long would Western souls find it bearable to go on living without religion?'[34] I said earlier that I did not intend to comment further on the responsibility which Toynbee pins on God for the direction of history; and I haven't. But there is no doubt that poor Toynbee was having to come to terms with the growing contradiction inherent in the concept of history as the living expression of God's will in a surviving Western world-civilization where God had lost street credibility in the late twentieth century. Might Toynbee have gone on to postulate a diminished role for God in history? Some syncretic faith? Perhaps we should finish with Toynbee's discovery of a role for the descendants of Negro slaves in America in whose 'hearts the divine fire glows again [whereby] Christianity may conceivably become the living faith of a dying civilization for the second time. If this miracle were indeed to be performed by an American Negro Church, that would be the most dynamic response to the challenge of social penalization that had yet been made by man.'[35] Perhaps the 'oecumenical authority' would turn out to be divine.

Salvage

Can anything be salvaged from these theories? Or has history—the very phenomenon which they were designed to arbitrate—overtaken them? It is neither possible nor desirable to try to syncretize the views of the three world-historians whose thoughts we have been traversing. Each will attract adherents and repel opponents; all three will, I hope, encourage extreme apostasy. The very idea of *reconciliation* is perhaps a reflection in the late twentieth century not only of a desire to consign prejudice and irrationality to Hegel's lumber-room of history; but also—regrettably—of the relativist's wish to avoid making clear moral and intellectual judgements, and of the desire of the reductionist so to particularize and atomize that the result is not worth a candle of any useful length.

But although we cannot square the triangle, we can take from each of the theories certain elements which seem to have relevance to our contemplation of the third millennium. We detected parallels between Hegel's *dialectic* and Toynbee's *challenge-and-response* as vital moving parts in an historical orrery; and we noted, but dismissed as irrelevant clutter, the view of both men that history was God's purpose being acted out in real-time. There was similarity between Toynbee and Spengler in their notion of an historical *cycle* of birth, growth, maturity and decline; and we concluded that Spengler's analogy of history to an *organism* did not seriously diminish the parallel. We noted that Spengler's concept of a cycle *did* seem to harmonize with a survey of all of *recorded* human experience; and that there were no rational grounds for conviction that the future would deviate in this respect from the past. The charge of *pessimism*—whatever one's interpretation of Spengler—was, and remains, quite pointless, and it may be that the incompatibility of pessimism with a belief in God's role in history is the true problem that Toynbee has with Spengler. Finally, all three historians unite in the need history has for *great men* and *creative minorities* to power it forward; and we are now able—if not to square the triangle—at least to triangulate our position in 1995 from the bearings of each historian.

From Hegel, remarketed through Kojève by Fukuyama, we have a form of political organization which is practised by the dominant civilization in the late twentieth century—the West—and which is being adopted by a growing number of peoples who had not been part of, or contributors to, the process of Western enlightenment. Spengler bequeaths us an historical perspective which has the virtue of being instantly recognisable; and he has painted a picture of a world and a set of prophecies which are uncomfortably difficult to dismiss. As for the last of our universal historians, if we substitute for Spengler's *prophesies* the notion of Toynbee's *challenges*, then it is clear that we shall require in the third millennium *responses* of heroic vision from men and women with a creativity and imagination the like of which has not been seen in history.

Chapter Two

Bringing us Up to Date

'One may indeed conclude that the more advanced the material culture the greater the investment required to sustain, let alone improve it. The more insistent the needs and expectations the more pressing the necessity of anticipating the future.

Conversely, the greater the requirements of the technology the greater the pressure on natural resources. It is no wonder that the vast increase in population and the greater impact made by modern technology should have led people to think more intently about the future of the environment itself, including even climatic and geological change.' Grahame Clark: *Space, Time and Man*

MY HISTORY BEGAN in 1937—not an otherwise very special date but a conveniently half-way point between 1875 and 2001. Nor, perhaps, is there anything very special about 1875: however, not only is it a nice round date but those 125 years have a great deal to answer for. For Hegel, the world of 1830 must have seemed like just another waypoint on the smooth course being charted through history by an unerring God, from man's promordial battle to the eventual triumph of liberty and democracy. He could have seen nothing likely to derail this political, social and economic momentum. Prussia was on the move and bore the Christian standard aloft on behalf of all peoples.

Hegel would have been horrified by these 125 years, and what they have inflicted on his divinely-guided history, and as we continue our exploration of history we may have good cause to fear that they have made a mockery of any theory of history other than that it is a random walk with a Greek tragicomic undertow.

Taking 1875 as the base-year, Table I presents some comparative statistics of human activity reaching forward to 1937 and 1990, and concluding with illustrative extrapolations to midnight on 31 December 2000—the eve of the third millennium. (These statistics form the curve which is reproduced as Graph I after Table I.) *Population* is the only element for which there are values in 1000 and 1800: this means that none of the others were observable until late in the nineteenth century. (The extrapolations are simply for aesthetic purposes: accurate or not, midnight 2000 is very close to 1995, and getting closer, and the projections serve simply to focus our attention on the twenty-first century.)

Table I
Some Comparative Statistics of Human Activity
Sources: UN, IEA, Mitchell, Mulhall, Kolb & others

	1000	1800	1875	1900	1937	1990	2000
World Population (M)	450	978	1500	1650	2295	5292	6100
Coal Production (Mmt)	0	0	268	707	1393	3517	4500
Crude Oil Production (Mmt)	0	0	3	29	256	3005	3000
Independent Countries	0	0	50	75	100	185	200
Sulphuric Acid Production (Mmt)	0	0	0.9	4	15	133	150
Private Car Population (M)	0	0	0	11	38	469	550
Livestock (M)	n/a	n/a	367	493	634	3447	4000
Steel Production (Mmt)	0	0	1.7	26	121	899	1000
Number of Phones (M)	0	0	0.3	2	32	450	550
Refrigerator Production (M)	0	0	0	1	5	53	70

This is not the place to analyse these statistics; it is enough for the moment to register the enormity and the precipitate speed of their impact on humanity since 1875; and the relentless upward flexing of the curve as it appears in Graph I on page 60.

Common sense allows me no time for the Biblical Apocalypse, or Marxist certainties. But there is something in the notion of inevitability—though without the Marxist imprint—which troubles me. And attracts me. I want a theory of history; but I am not looking for a complex one laden with eternal verities because I now have reason to doubt that the search would bear fruit. My cross-examination of Spengler, Hegel and Toynbee already inclines me to the persuasion that there is no 'sense' in history, and that it is only with this deep realisation that we can handle further instalments of it without the mistaken comfort that some intrepid force is all along directing it towards the right destination.

No. Isn't there an American Indian proverb which says that 'Today is the first day of the rest of your life'? Well, perhaps that is the way to view history: it starts today, as the next piece of the future is transformed into the past; but such are the scale and speed and force of the demons pointing their muzzles at us out of the future that none of the old nostrums and theories and certainties—none at all—are going to avail us. We shall have to seek new ones.

Challenged by the search for a theory of history, a key to the anthropocentric clock-work, I used to believe, or at least to hope, that somehow and somewhere it was absolute and eternal and might one day be found, however elusive the quarry might be. That's where I now see that I have been wrong, along with all the professional optimists, pessimists and religionists. Since I had always regarded *individual human life* itself—tiny subsets of history—as a random walk, with only oblivion at each end; had always treated life as something you did when you couldn't sleep, how on earth could I have sustained a different order of belief about history? About the stage on which these lives would be acted out?

Well, the Indian proverb makes sense: history starts today; and so, therefore, must a new and much more valid theory of history.

The Soviet implosion has swept away, in an historical nano-second, a huge part of the philosophical and attitudinal baggage which has burdened the First World—and the Soviet empire—in its view of recent and contemporary history, and in the way it has been accustomed to handle the future. It is a paradox that the fears and uncertainties of the Cold War were themselves a source of comfort—*Dr Strangelove or How I Learned to Love the Bomb* and all that—because they were a very large and constant part of the existential landscape, albeit indistinct for most people but no less real for that; and, in that way, they acted as a proxy and a cover for other and, as we shall see, for far more intractable concerns.

Current images of the end of the Cold War are all to do with voids and vacuums—empty barracks in eastern Europe, the Black Sea Fleet tied up for lack of diesel or agreement on who owns it, retrenchment of the military-industrial complex, demands for peace dividends, early retirements, unemployed arms dealers, tribal wars between ex-Superpower client states, inane pronouncements by politicians and statesmen, redundant institutions looking for something useful to do.

These voids and vacuums are going to be filled up very rapidly and unpalatably, stuffed in fact to overflowing, with a number of infinitely more dangerous and desperately sinister demons which had hitherto occupied a position of only secondary importance in the affairs of governments primarily concerned, as they had been for half a century, with freakish doctrines such as Mutual Assured Destruction, and with the constantly changing calculus required to preserve the doctrine.

Chapter Three

Sowing the Seeds

'In all parts of the world men fled from one place to other places, and there was a confusion of tongues. Much wrath was kindled against the princes and the servants of the princes and against the magi who had devised the weapons. Years passed, and yet the Earth was not cleansed.' Walter M. Miller Jr: *A Canticle for Leibowitz*

I REMARKED EARLIER that there is nothing especially significant about 1875 but it is convenient and easy to remember. But, most importantly, it is necessary, for the thesis of this book, to identify a *period without precedent*, which can be singled out as containing events unique in human history and uniquely critical to our future, and we must therefore assign it a beginning. The period identified must differ from all predecessors in at least one key and defining respect:

Graph I below uses the statistics from Table I but brings out their impact in a dramatic curve whose impact is instantly observable. Along the x-axis of the graph are the dates—milestones stretching back to 1875, distant yet sufficiently close to 1995 for most of its events and features to be recognisable to the reader, and forward to 2000; and I've added a couple of earlier observation platforms—1000 and 1800.

The y-axis is trickier. I've talked earlier of a nexus of intertwining events and factors which operate on each other and, through a form similar to the accelerator and multiplier effects familiar to economists, moderate their own direction and momentum. These 'factors' could comprise a whole host of scientific discoveries, industrial inventions, modes of thought and many other key aspects of human activity, as well as 'developments' which might seem to be random and not human-driven.

Our y-axis sets out to capture and portray, in the form of the composite curve, a small but vital and *representative* number of these factors which first appeared on the horizon late in the nineteenth century. They reflect and characterize industrialisation, and from statistically insignificant values a hundred and more years ago, they now symbolise the economic and cultural dominance of an industrial and economic monster which now seems set to deliver a rain of deadly blows to both the End-of-History notion, and to this book's own original and

intended purpose of discovering a Universal History. 1875 is a somewhat arbitrary date and therefore I emphasise that the factors contained
in the curve have not been, so to speak, parthogenetically conceived in
the hundred-odd years since then, that is to say without lines of causation stretching back and disappearing off into time.

What is quite *novel* about the factors in the curve is that their rates of
growth—the steepness of the curve—starting from around our arbitrary
date and then accelerating, are such that what we are seeing is, in fact, a
statistical discontinuity: in terms of calculus, a quite new order of deriv-
ative—a break which is quantitatively so great that it becomes qualitative—a break which sets the period apart from all others. The same is
true of population, which forms the spine of the curve.

James Lovelock puts it like this: 'Small groups hunting and gathering...once lived in symbiosis with our planet...We had the potential
to sustain our own environment at the expense of the Earth; to break
our contract with Gaia...But right up until the beginning of *this century*
[my emphasis] none of this, nor the industrial civilizations that had
evolved, were significant in themselves to the Earth...The danger lay in
the potential for further growth and development. Now the consequences of that growth in our numbers and development of our

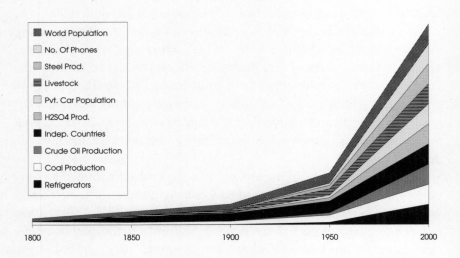

Graph I
Sources: Various, as in Table I

capacity to displace the rest of planetary life, threaten both us and our planet.'[1]

In this respect, this 125-year period most certainly *does* differ uniquely from all predecessors and so meets the criteria set out earlier. It is unique in a sense that no other century has ever been.

The y-axis plaits together the following handful of observable factors: global population, coal production, crude oil output, independent countries, sulphuric acid produced, motor vehicles on the road, horse, cattle, pig and sheep numbers, crude steel poured, number of telephones in use and production of refrigerators.

Are these particular factors being demonised? Why have they been singled out to form the composite curve whose components 'will deliver the [promised] rain of deadly blows' to hitherto accepted theories of Universal History? Do they have no redeeming features, and have no compensating factors arisen during the same period to redress the balance?

Of course, there *have* been many enormously important and beneficial gains during the period: in most of the West, at least, lower infant mortality, longer life-expectancy, better health and sanitation, better housing, anaesthetics, universal suffrage, wide literacy, better diet, greater protection of personal liberties, human rights, access to justice, social security—the list of benefits to a large part of humankind is endless, and many of the more purely *material* gains would have been impossible without the industrial innovations and processes exemplified by the production figures set out above, or the beneficial social purposes to which they have been applied.

Indeed, economists would argue that the wealth created by this industrial development was indispensable in bringing about *social* betterment; and I certainly do not grieve for the passing of a world where I myself might not have enjoyed these blessings as a matter of right.

There are, then, redeeming features.

Nor are the industrial factors which appear in the curve—or the thousands of other industrial artifacts which could have gone into it— *in themselves* the cause of the malaise which is associated with the emergence of the industrial state: it is their scale and speed and direction, and the failure of twentieth-century humankind to accommodate their impact—to absorb fully their costs—while continuing to enjoy their benefits.

Unfortunately, we are *not* dealing with a balance sheet where, by definition, assets = liabilities. What we *are* dealing with is an equation of inconceivable complexity where changes in the terms and inputs on one side must produce a like shift *overall* on the other, but where there is no assurance that the result is *qualitatively* neutral. In fact, the probability of a qualitatively neutral impact is, at even a simple intuitive level, so low as to be dismissible. This is a sufficiently useful working hypothesis that it is unnecessary to address the infinitely complicating effects which come into the equation when time-lags and loops, compounding by-processes and feedbacks are considered and the whole interaction reiterated infinitely.

Let us now go just a step or two further and see where the logic may lead us: we acknowledge that human impact on the environment has become *truly* visible and tangible at the level of everyman in the space of only two lifetimes, i.e. our 125 years; that Nature *may* be able to return the impacted part to its previous state of equilibrium but only at a speed infinitely slower than that at which humanity created the change in the first place (and if left alone to do it); and that it is almost hubristic to think that human activity might, during that time, actually have *improved* the environment—except in the narrowly utilitarian sense of draining the odd malaria-infested swamp, building a golf-course or covering a mountain with ski-lifts. With an acknowledgement of the simple strength of these propositions in the context of the earlier equation, then the conclusion can only be that there has indeed taken place *net tangible damage* to the environment, and to our prospects of continuing to play a part in helping the God we have created to carry out His great plan.

This is the simple truth: there does not exist some benign calculus which works unbidden and unseen to correct the imbalance and undo the damage except through the operation of James Lovelock's Gaia mechanism, even though some may not accept the precise organic analogy of the Gaia mechanism any more than they had accepted Spengler's. And unfortunately for the apologists, religionists, professional optimists and all the other charlatans whose prejudices, piousness or stupidity operate to impede proper and full public understanding of our dilemma, Gaia has not made a special dispensation for man. Gaia can flick humanity off any time she wants, and get back to the business of self-healing.

Once these charlatans are exposed, then the question of damage will resolve itself into: How much? Is it tolerable, weighed against the material benefits brought about by industrialisation? How irreversible? And knowing, as we shall see, that the process of the economic imperative is unsustainable; and assuming, as we might, that all governments throughout the world—and it would have to be global—were to receive miraculous visitations of responsibility, altruism and effectiveness and mount a concerted public relations crusade followed by a gigantic long-term programme to reverse the damage, could the necessary political, social and economic revolution—for that is what it would be— actually be contemplated?

This is the paradox, the dilemma: the required revolution may be almost too monstrous for a complacent and materialistic world, still— even increasingly—tribal and led by Throttlebottom governments, to contemplate as being more than a tedious chore of history which will demand grudging attention *at some time in the receding future*, and certainly not as something to countenance as a central plank in today's election platform; particularly disagreeable, too, to all the nations now signing up to join Fukuyama's neo-Hegelian club. The equally intractable alternative, by contrast, is 'business as usual'.

There must be substantial doubt that a sufficient number of the world's most important nations and, *a fortiori*, the less important, have either the will or literally the means to stem the drift or to create the revolution required to prevent or solve this dilemma. Far more radical and unconventional means will be required than have ever been previously assembled. The most distant political horizon is never further than the next election, the time is too short and there is too much already in the pipeline and on its way to the outfall for third millennium humanity to expect itself likely to avoid convulsions of inconceivable magnitude within a lifetime.

Bill McKibben, in *The End of Nature*, barely touches the *political* terms in the equation. He introduces his last chapter—his proffered solution to the *political and cultural* crisis amply and convincingly described in the rest of his book—whistling these words from the graveyard: 'Or, just possibly, we could change our habits.'[2]

He pleads for an approach of *humility* to nature in place of the *defiance* traditionally wielded by man—the 'Power Drive' propounded as a central thesis of this book in Chapter Six below. In practice, McKibben fears the jig is up: he admits that he has no great desire to trade down his car or his large house. For him, 'The inertia of affluence, the push of poverty, the soaring population'[3] make him pessimistic that we will be able dramatically to alter our ways of thinking and living. And his tangible suggestions are but ritual exhortations which attract, in equal measure, my sympathy and my despair:

—more efficient washing machines
—'cut back on fossil fuel use'
—human population must get smaller

The Power Drive succeeded, and reached its peak of sustainable domination over nature at some point during the last 125 years, when the material benefits of industrialisation were not challenged by more than locally containable and short-term damage—'externalities' in the felicitous language of economists and industrial apologists. Certainly: nothing wrong with a bit of pollution.

This was a kind of Pareto efficiency—an idealistic condition where no man's lot might be improved without a corresponding debit to that of his neighbour.

Now the Power Drive has failed and history is out of control.

Before I move back to the future, we should pause to savour an odd and intriguing consonance here between the view of the cosmos taken by the creationists, the Gaia theory expounded by James Lovelock, and the thesis of this book.

Lovelock has no doubt of the dire condition in which late twentieth century humanity finds itself and its world. He suspects that our crisis is quite irredeemable and that our role on earth will ultimately be seen—highly retrospectively—as both pointless and terminal, and the matter of a second of geological time.

Neither meliorist nor hand-wringer, Lovelock's central theme is that Gaia herself is a self-regulating organism and that she will—by definition—'survive'. However, he has been popularly misunderstood so that the issue of *human* survival as part of Gaia is seen as being somehow related to the survival of Gaia herself.

In fact, Lovelock says 'For Gaia, ozone depletion and the ozone hole over the Antarctic are not a serious threat.' The threats, to human beings not to Gaia, are ultraviolet radiation, chlorofluorocarbon gases, carbon dioxide and 'much more seriously… methane gas from rice paddies and from cattle' which it 'is all but impossible' to stop.[4]

The creationists' view is, as Bill McKibben points out, mistaken and muddled scientifically. However, looking back at *their* Big Bang on October 1st 4004 BC, courtesy of Bishop Ussher, we must, for all the wrong reasons, concede that they 'may intuitively understand more about the *progress* of time than [third millennium man].'[5] After all, an historical horizon of six or seven thousand years is comprehensible, and there is no earlier human history which needs to be understood in order for us better to understand what has happened since. Their view of the cosmos and their time-scales have much to do with the thesis of this book—with the profundity, the newness, the historical suddenness of human impact, when set against the almost geological pace at which that impact might be neutralised.

I don't happen to know any creationists; but my guess is that their time-scale, their 6000-year proxy for geological time and their view of historical processes, would fit in very well with James Lovelock's conclusion that Gaia is ultimately self-regulating and, therefore, self-regenerating—once, that is, that the pathogen has gone and then only over expanses of time which are incomprehensible and beyond political tinkering.

Even the most responsible of the independent environmental movements have occasionally done and said some pretty silly things amidst the bulk of their good works, but I shall conclude this chapter with an elegiac passage from Greenpeace:

'Planet Earth is 4,600 million years old. If we condense this inconceivable time-span into an understandable concept, we can liken the Earth to a person of 46 years of age.

'Nothing is known about the first 7 years of this person's life, and whilst only scattered information exists about the middle span, we know that only at the age of 42 did the Earth begin to flower.

'Dinosaurs and the great reptiles did not appear until one year ago, when the planet was 45. Mammals arrived only 8 months ago; in the middle of last week, human-like apes evolved into ape-like humans, and at the weekend the last ice-age enveloped the Earth.

'Modern humans have been around for four hours. During the last hour, we discovered agriculture. The industrial revolution began a minute ago.

'During those sixty seconds of biological time, humans have made a rubbish tip of Paradise.

'We have caused the extinction of many hundreds of animal species, ransacked the planet for fuel and now stand like brutish infants, gloating over this meteoric rise to ascendancy, on the brink of the final mass extinction and of effectively destroying the oasis of life in the solar system.'[6]

Chapter Four

No Pollution but People

'Come and see the exciting story of America's population explosion.' —banner at the pavilion of the Equitable Life Insurance Company of the United States at the New York World's Fair in 1965.

'If you continue to multiply without constraint or consideration for the rest of the world, you will swiftly exhaust irreplaceable resources, animal, vegetable and mineral, which will surely lead to the destruction of your DNA and the desolation of the planet...I hope you become *Homo SAPIENS*, the alternative is *Homo EXTINCTUS.*' Sir Roy Calne: 'The Creator's Testament to Modern Man' in *Too Many People*, 1994.

IN THE COURSE OF planning and researching this chapter, I decided that it would be instructive first to delve back into my half-shelf of books on the environment and assess how some of its dustier occupants had fared over the 30-odd years which separate the solecism which slithered off the pen of some oafish public relations executive in 1965 from the wiser words of Sir Roy Calne in 1994.

I was pondering the possibility that the Boy-who-cried-Wolf syndrome might have been operating all along to weaken the case of the so-called 'environmentalists' and to give comfort to their opponents. (It is tragic that the whole ecological issue should have become, as it has, polarised and frequently trivialised; that a matter of such elemental importance to all mankind should have given rise to embattled salons of prejudice and self-interest. But more of this later.)

My delve proved to be a fruitful exercise.

I looked first at Rachel Carson's *Silent Spring* of 1962, without doubt a touchstone for all subsequent writing on the environment. It comes through with flying colours: as a symbol of her work, DDT was banned in the United States in 1971—matched by the self-contradictory 'voluntary ban' in Great Britain which persisted until 1984 when it became mandatory—and the American Bald Eagle owes its survival and increase in numbers to this saint of environmental awareness. Little would need revision in a new edition although, were Carson writing today, she would find that her crusade remains unfinished and that there are muscular successors to DDT in the form of CFCs, PCBs and TCDD.

Then I turned to Barry Commoner's *The Closing Circle* published in 1971. It was and remains a remarkable book—elegant, restrained, sad and in its last chapter—which bears the name of the book itself—almost wistfully optimistic. Barry Commoner would have little cause, twenty-four years on, for either revising his views or rejoicing that they had wrought the changes he advocated.

Finally I picked up *The Limits to Growth* produced by Potomac Associates in 1972 for the Club of Rome's 'Project on the Predicament of Mankind'. It is worth reproducing in full the Introduction by the then Secretary-General of the United Nations, U Thant, in 1969:

'I do not wish to seem overdramatic, but I can only conclude from the information that is available to me as Secretary-General, that the Members of the United Nations have perhaps ten years left in which to subordinate their ancient quarrels and launch a global partnership to curb the arms race, to improve the human environmment, to defuse the population explosion, and to supply the required momentum to development [sic] efforts. If such a global partnership is not forged within the next decade, then I very much fear that the problems I have mentioned will have reached such staggering proportions that they will be beyond our capacity to control.'[1]

Well, I thought, which of the two salons should take comfort: the 'environmentalists' or their detractors—the business-as-usualists? After all, U Thant's ten years have come and gone more than twice over, *and we're still here*, aren't we? The Bald Eagle is back—I saw one in New York State only last November; and Barry Commoner might search in vain for a publisher today: the Contents page of his book seems almost trite until one remembers that he was writing almost a quarter of a century ago.

The unequivocal answer to the question lies in the last three words of the sentence: 'U Thant's ten years have come and gone more than twice over, and we're still here.'

When Barry Commoner found his publisher, 'we' were about 3,700 million; some twenty years later we had managed to add—to these already obscenely unsustainable numbers—one more person in 1993 for every two in 1972, 1,850 million—more than the Earth's entire population in 1900—to bring today's total of 5,500 million, and counting. Popollution, indeed.

I shall demonstrate in this chapter that unbridled population growth in the last century or so is the only stand-alone source of pollution; that all of the other types of pollution, which are discussed in some detail in the following chapter, are simply derivatives—literally by-products—of humanity's now pestilential numbers.

The second thesis of this book is that, from origins somewhere in the late nineteenth century, there has erupted an interrelated set of industrial and technological threats to humankind's survival—at least, survival in a way we would wish—fuelled by the breeding binge of this century.

It is not my purpose to strengthen the beliefs of the 'environmentalists', or to enlist the support of the agnostics or to challenge the complacency of the professional optimists—to populate one salon at the expense of the other. My principal concern is to show that we are not dealing with simple matters of degree in the condition of the environment at the end of the twentieth century, with *marginally* too much pollution here or *undesirably* high levels of deforestation there—just a few steps further than we should prudently have stepped, but easily retraceable, down some dysecological continuum. I shall show in the rest of this chapter that we have gone well beyond the point of no return: we are already at McKibben's End of Nature and must now decide what we're going to put in its place now that we have so certainly overshot the runway of Fukuyama's End of History.

We start with human numbers and with a defiant piece of maximalism: there are *no* redeeming features in population growth—unless yet further economies of scale in industrial production and the satisfaction of ever-greater consumer demand are *ipso facto* desirable. Consequently, increased industrial production attributable to population growth is, by definition, pointless and harmful. The numbers have risen and broadened into an unstemmable torrent, as in Graph II on the next page.

It is impossible to misunderstand or overestimate the impact of these bland figures. *Population* is the rogue independent variable in the great ecological equation; none of the other ecological villains discussed below operates independently from humanity's numbers. All are products and functions of human activity. Some, like 'old' DDT in the food chain or yesterday's mercury batteries dumped in the oceans, will continue to present lethal and unpredictable i.o.u.'s in the future long after they had served their original intended purpose, but all arose through human agency at a certain point in the operation of the equation.

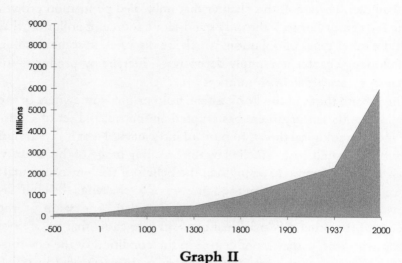

Graph II
Population Growth (X axis not to scale)
Source: Various, incl. Marsh, Earth Report 2, Global 2000 &c.

The Global Equation is: Ed = P(Cnr) where Ed =ecological demand, P= population and Cnr = consumption of non-renewable resources.

Non-renewable resources are precisely that: non-renewable and increasable, i.e. extractable 'economically', only by ever-greater inputs of energy, capital and technology: ever-larger mackerels to catch ever-smaller sprats.

Population at current and forecast levels—and it really doesn't matter if the forecasts are too high by the odd billion or so—is unarguably an infinitely more malevolent pollutant than cadmium in our rivers, human sewage and hospital detritus lapping round children's sand-castles on the beaches, DDT in our fatty tissues and CFCs discharging from half-a-billion refrigerators. It is, in fact, the worst pollutant because it is the exponential generator of all the others through the operation of the economic imperative, which we shall look at later. Moreover, the statistics, as presented, do not reveal that it is in the Third World that the greatest growth has been taking place and will continue to do so—precisely those parts of the world which are incapable of sustaining even existing populations and of absorbing—or exporting—the ecological stress.

Pollution is not an absolute: it has to do with the ability of the (micro) environment to digest the pollutant completely or, at least, to an extent that the environment is not compromised. I live in the countryside.

Most days I can see a herd of red deer which I have sometimes counted as numbering anything up to a hundred or more. They must make a terrific demand on their environment, but it works: they live off the land and their bones and blood, their urine and faeces, their hides and hooves return to the land unseen. In ill contrast is the cattle feedlot down the road which leaches a rich bovine cocktail into our river where it mixes with dioxins from a local industrial tip.

Anyway, How Many People is Enough?

'There is no infallible head for a church on earth. The dream of believing man has been tried, and we see... what has come of it.'
Anthony Trollope: *Barchester Towers*

Population growth seems to have been regarded with a degree of official equanimity by the Council of Trent 450 years ago, but then the numbers were not threatening. Indeed, folk memories of the Black Death and the needs of the Argument of Kings might rather have favoured such growth. Our growing numbers managed without Papal infallibility until Pius I (died 1878) felt that he, at least, certainly couldn't; and were given an unnecessary boost for the future in 1968 with the publication of Paul VI's encyclical *Humanae Vitae*. Islamic Fundamentalism has added its support[2], and both religions find a bizarre bed-fellow in the transnational corporation, many of which anticipate with eager relish ever-growing global consumer markets.

The arguments of some businesses in favour of larger populations are rarely articulated—the deliberations take place in boardrooms and long-range budgeting departments. But we know that great account is paid by manufacturers of consumer products to forecasts of demographic changes when decisions are made concerning capital investment, product development and planning for their obsolescence or market 'repositioning'. It is no accident that Western manufacturers of baby food and cigarettes, wheat flour and perfumes must look outside their traditional markets for the growth required by their shareholders: once again, these are precisely the less naturally well-favoured parts of the world—the so-called 'developing' countries—which need like a national hole-in-the-head to squander their scanty reserves of hard currency on frivolous imports.

The position of the Church is rather more inscrutable and, unless some nuance escapes me, less obviously self-interested. I know what Genesis 1.26 and 1.28 *says* but I can't believe that God's injunction to 'replenish the earth' meant standing-room-only humanity, or that to 'have dominion' over fish and fowl, cattle and every creeping thing was intended to require the genocide of so many of the very species which He'd spent verses 1.24 and 1.25 creating. It is also unclear why Onan and, for that matter his brother Er, should have been singled out by God for such extreme and irreversible treatment especially when they were only following the orders of their father Judah, who went in unto their mother Shuah without the sanction of marriage.

But no matter. Since both the Catholic church and some Big Business share this equanimity, let them share also the same dock and answer to what is, in effect, the same indictment: even if either God or the transnational corporation *could* provide food, clothing, shelter, heat and light and meaningful employment for all these numbers—a feat which neither putative benefactor has proved capable of achieving at any identifiable point up to 1995—would either God or the terrestrial company president gaze with pleasure upon the condition to which the Earth had been reduced under its burden of 14-billion souls, five for every two of us today? And would those extra 8½-billion feel any worse off for not having been born? Only the Church—secure in the knowledge that God's long-term will is being carried out with an invaluable assist from Papal infallibility—could answer in the affirmative.

The answers are clearly no, there are no benefits in present levels of population, let alone its further growth; humanity's lot is impoverished and neither spermatozoa nor unborn foetuses have a vote in the matter.

None of the environmental villains we discuss in the next chapter— the shaving of the rain-forests, desertification, pollution of our oceans and skies, acid rain, greenhouse gases and rising expectations—would have reached crisis proportions without the growth of the Earth's population to the point where it became exponential. Most of the West (although the United States *seems* not to be a good example largely because of its policy—cynics would say lack of one—of untrammelled immigration) has accomplished what is called the *demographic transition*, where the birth-rate, infant mortality and live-expectancy curves intersect and combine with a high level of industrialisation to produce effective population stability. However, the West is itself grossly overpopulated and can therefore serve as no example of a way out of overpopulation: it is a partner with the Third World with its own assigned role in the despoliation of the Earth, both in its own backyard, and through its prodigious gluttony in consuming ecologically under-priced Third World raw materials; whilst the Third World complements its Northern partner partly by enforced complicity in the process of maximising exports of raw materials to finance an import bill containing a high percentage of socially worthless manufactured goods, and partly by ravaging its own environment in a zero-sum game to feed its purposelessly exploding populations. Finally, as we shall explore in a later chapter, a world already saturated with consumer goods produced by the labour of a few score *millions* in the West and in East Asia can scarcely contemplate an ecologically tolerable level of industrialisation to provide employment for *billions* in the Third World.

Thus Third World countries, whose combined population will have risen from 1,700 million in 1950 to 7,200 million by 2025—an average growth of 201,000 per day—are leagues away from that transition and there are insidious obstacles to their ever reaching it. We will examine later the myths propagated by the United Nations and its agencies, and other international aid organizations, that just one more upward push in many of the world's *naturally* blighted areas will lever them up on to the plains of abundance and balance-of-payments surpluses to enable them to discharge their present insupportable levels of hard-currency debt, and to join in the spiral of suicidal extraction, production and consumption.

Particularly since World War II, cheap and phenomenally powerful inputs such as DDT (which were environmentally digestible as long as their use was largely restricted to Allied armies operating in the jungles of Asia and the Pacific), and widespread vaccination against smallpox and other traditional killers, have dramatically reduced infant and maternal mortality in the Third World. Then, even as this phenomenon combines with rising birth-rates to increase life supply at one end, what we might call 'death demand' at the other end has in effect been reduced through longer life-expectancy. These complex processes, rather than just absolutely higher birth-rates, have had a massive and, in historical terms, almost instant impact on human numbers.

However, these inputs are part of the Global Equation set out above. While they are cheap, indiscriminately effective and their handiwork virtually instant, there is no *benign* compensating term in the Equation. The West's death rates fell far more slowly to bring about its demographic transition but the Third World had engineered neither the required agricultural or industrial revolutions when these inputs began their work, nor are there colonial safety-valves to take the strain. Nor, as

I have touched on earlier and shall discuss later, does most of the world exhibit uniform and naturally favourable conditions for its inhabitants.

But there has to be, of course, *some* compensating term in the Global Equation. It lies in Newton's Third Law of Motion, that 'to every action there is an equal and opposite reaction' but it is *malignant*: it is environmental degradation and, in a piece of supreme irony, it is propelled by *development*—the process perversely advocated, abetted and advanced by the United Nations and its agencies and in the overseas aid programmes of individual nations, and given new vigour, and indeed respectability, in the madness of the renewal in December 1993 of the GATT treaty.

Since we are, then, no longer in control of our numbers, whereby in the third millennium humanity will have not only to contend with the End of Nature but also contrive a sequel to the End of History, it is appropriate to ask a question: What *was* the 'global optimum' level of population? Or even, was there ever such a thing? My guess is that since population growth seems to have been an historical inevitability, so that no permanent state of Rousseauesque simplicity was ever in the cards, then almost any pre-twentieth century level could have been considered 'optimum', particularly when the world was an atomised and highly parochial place, there were only minimum global trading and cultural contacts, and little industry powered other than by water, wind and human or animal muscle. The question should therefore be rephrased and 'global maximum' substituted for 'optimum', since the answer cannot simply comprise the sum of clusters of population from all over the world.

Consequently, we shall define 'maximum' as being that *stabilised* number of people beyond which ecological demand, that is the 'summation of all man's demands on the environment, such as the extraction of [non-renewable] resources and the return of wastes'[3], had clearly begun to cause *irreversible* or *unsustainable net environmental damage*. However, definition of that damage and an attempt to date its appearance will not be limited to the more currently fashionable areas of environmental concern such as the destruction of the rain forests and the puncturing of the ozone layer.

The definition must be broadened to capture a number of far less sensationalist factors which are a part of the late nineteenth- and twentieth-century experience and which have become inseparable elements in our political economy. In turn, these factors must be defined as having constituted, from their inception, ultimately insupportable demands on the planet, either because the resources demanded are finite in supply, such as petroleum and groundwater and even—as we shall see—air, or because the factors are directly destructive, such as toxic waste and global warming. And this will enable us to seek to date the reaching of that maximum population level. We need not go back centuries to some imagined pristine age when the earth had to contend with no more than a few million happy savages: it's much less remote than that. This is not a work on demography; but mathematicians and economists, enlisted by demographers to propose and date an 'optimum maximum', might employ the techniques of mathematical induction or regression analysis to suggest that the 'date' was around 1850-1875 and that the 'number' would not have exceeded some 1.25 billion but, as I have emphasized, necessarily undifferentiated by region or per capita GNP.

Although this is a highly conjectural, even a tendentious, piece of calculation, we need only cite, with the benefit of accurate retrospection, the catastrophes visited upon the earth in the century or so which has followed, and attributable to the blight of numbers.

Let Thomas Malthus, a much misunderstood writer, provide some thoughts before we conclude. His *Essay on the Principle of Population* first appeared in 1798. Malthus' object in writing his Essay was to enquire into the effects of a 'great cause' which is 'the constant tendency in all animated life to increase beyond the nourishment prepared for it.'[4] He says that plants and irrational [sic] animals are impelled to increase their species having 'no doubts about providing for their offspring... Only want of room and nourishment' represses this effect.[5]

'The effects of this check on man are more complicated. Impelled to the increase of his species...he asks whether he may not bring beings into the world for whom he cannot provide the means of support. If he attends to this natural suggestion, the restriction too frequently produces vice',[6] i.e. abortion and infanticide. 'If he hear it not, the human race will be constantly endeavouring to increase beyond the means of subsistence... But... population can never actually increase beyond the lowest nourishment capable of supporting it... [so there is] a strong check on population.'[7]

For Malthus, then, there were three checks on population growth and the slide into Misery: *positive* checks in the form of famine, pestilence and war; and *preventive* checks in the form of either Vice, as exemplified above, or Moral and Prudential Restraint. His opposition to the Poor Laws of the day must not be viewed as the callous indifference of a conservative moralist to the lot of the poor. The Speenhamland System of welfare accorded help to the poor in accordance to the size of the family. Malthus felt that this open-ended mechanism would only further distort the intersection of the population and food curves to the extent that it actually encouraged larger families. Research suggests that Malthus was probably wrong in this belief; but given the *apparent* evidence available to him, he cannot be faulted for his sincerity in advocating 'moral restraint' as superior to money hand-outs in producing a long-term solution to the problem of the poor, and in proposing amendments to the Poor Laws which, while causing considerable suffering in the short term, could only improve the lot of most poor people in the longer term.

Malthus' views in this respect are eerily similar to the positions taken up by some people in arguments raging currently in the West over the provision of welfare to today's underclasses. But much more important is their relevance to the debate which takes place later in this book over the merits or otherwise of 'development' and foreign aid when related to population growth and environmental degradation in the Third World of the 'developing' countries.

Malthus died in 1834. His influence then waned until well over one hundred years later although the force and novelty of his argumentation, as a pioneer demographer, historian and sociologist, seem never to have been in danger despite the complete contempt of later generations. His writing and research and methodology were unusual for his times, and this is borne out by the illustriousness of both his supporters— David Ricardo and William Pitt, Thomas Macaulay, John Stuart Mill and Charles Darwin—and of his adversaries—Karl Marx, William Cobbett, Tom Paine and Robert Owen.

Malthus' weaknesses, as perceived a few decades ago, lay not in astigmatic views of the world which he did so much to analyse with such data as he could marshal at the time; but—excusably—in his being unaware of the changes in agriculture, trade and medical and sanitary conditions which would begin to assert themselves by the second half of the nineteenth century and increasingly in the twentieth. New lands were being opened up outside Europe, agricultural science was improving, the clipper ship had arrived to bring rapid and cheap transport of foodstuffs from the New World to an Old World, where industry would create the wealth and employment to support the growing numbers (and, of course, the beginnings of mass consumer demand upon which industrial society would come to depend for its efficiencies of scale); and birth-control would begin to interact with lower infant mortality to complicate the demographic equation still further. Malthusianism had been seen off by technology.

Until, that is, technology itself began to recreate the conditions of Malthus' nightmare: certainly, Malthus would have extended his reference to 'plants and irrational animals' to include his own species.

Chapter Five

Demons of the Third Millennium

'It would be prudent...to regard every man-made organic chemical not found in nature which has a strong action on any one organism as potentially dangerous to other forms of life...The fact that DDT is nowhere found in nature..[suggests] that somewhere, at some time in the past, some unfortunate cell synthesized this molecule (DDT) and died'. Barry Commoner: *The Closing Circle*

Introduction

I FOUND THIS TO BE one of the most difficult chapters to write, notwithstanding the essentially factual and straightforward nature of its subject. So, having finished writing it, I decided to write this Introduction. The problem is that environmental issues and the environmental 'movement', as it is sometimes arcanely called, are for most people a cause of either great unease or even greater boredom. The business-as-usualists are certainly bored: they 'know all about it' and, if challenged, will react quite predictably by saying that 'it'—the environmentalists' apocalypse—hasn't happened. Witness U Thant's warning quoted earlier: twenty-five years have filed past and we're still here.

The fact that no accredited 'environmentalist' has, to my knowledge, ever forecast the precise nature and date of the apocalypse—or has even said that some such discrete event would happen—gets forgotten amidst the complacency generated by the rhythmic passage of the years and the substitution of comfortable consumer short-termism for strategic thinking and planning for the future: a great global dose of valium. As for criticism of U Thant's warning, the ripostes could be many but it need only be said that while his entreaty for a 'global partnership', has quite simply gone unheeded, yet in the years since 1969, the viruses of which he spoke have continued insidiously to multiply and infect the system. And U Thant had never heard of global warming and destruction of the ozone layer, knew little of Somalia or Rwanda and nothing at all of Chernobyl.

Then there are those whose awareness is piqued, their complacency is shattered, but they are uneasy—indeed, they are aghast—at contemplating either the practical consequences of responding to the pleas of the planet or the moral quandary posed by ignoring them: it is not part of their future history.

Both groups exhibit degrees of what psychologists call 'cognitive dissonance'—hostility to distasteful ideas and a reluctance to acknowledge the divergence of today's world from a sustainable path. For both groups it is as if 'the environment' was something which one had the choice to support or oppose; as if the 'environmental movement' was rather like the Conservative Party or Alcoholics Anonymous: something you join if you want to, or slope off to on Monday evenings. Partisans of the business-as-usual salon need not instantly make the crossover: they need only to look at the evidence which follows, and to conclude that the 'issue' will neither go away nor heal itself.

★ ★ ★ ★

I have earlier insisted that this is not a book about the environmental degradation and related abnormalities which are so much a product of the twentieth century and which are poised to come centre-stage as demons of the third millennium. There are sources far better than this book for those readers who need an exhaustive analysis of the environmental state-of-play. What this chapter seeks to portray is the environmental crisis as a set of interrelated phenomena with one cause and ultimately one outcome; it will enable the reader to follow the book's central thesis and to understand why it is that the consequences of this century's ravishing of the planet cannot be measured only in simple materialistic terms. Our treatment of the environment must be viewed on the wide screen—for its linked and imminent social, economic, cultural and political impact.

Of course, environmental damage is not a feature unique to the twentieth century. Geographers say that the voraciousness of Roman goats grazing in the early first millennium contributed significantly to the desertification of the Mediterranean littoral with effects which persist to this day. Johann Mathesius, writing in Nürnberg in 1562, tells us that 'quicksilver and rotgültigen ore...cobalt and wismuth fumes are the most poisonous of the metals... and kill flies, mice, cattle, birds and men. Fresh cobalt and kisswasser (vitriol?) devour the hands and feet of miners and workpeople who do much work among the fumes of the smelters.'[1] Not for nothing was Edinburgh known as 'Auld Reekie' for the smell that arose from untreated sewage lying in the congested streets;

and the cobble streets of London no more than a hundred years ago offered round-the-clock sanitary facilities to no fewer than 145,000 working horses, most of them very large.

However, we have witnessed since the second half of the nineteenth century the growth, at an ever-accelerating pace, of environmental degradation and destruction on a scale which is without precedent and is certainly not a simple extrapolation from the folkloric examples cited above. Furthermore, the causes and nature of this phenomenon are inseparable from the very tissue of our consumer economy and the political and social systems which depend upon it. They are therefore not amenable to nine-to-five political pieties and bottle-bank cures.

It is for these reasons that the environmental dilemma is by far and away the dominant issue of the third millennium because it alone can—and most certainly will—challenge the supremacy of the liberal democracy state of equilibrium postulated in End-of-History theory. It should transcend party politics; and it is not a question of saving the Minke whale, the Ring-tailed lemur or the California condor: it is to do with preserving and, in an ironic sense, justifying the very liberal democratic society which has, quite literally, delivered the goods we want and the problems we can do without. Or would like to.

The Demons are environmental destruction and the depletion of air, water and oil, but they are abetted by a number of supporting gremlins which are products, in the main, of the twentieth century: technological tyranny, rates of change, the Global Village, free trade and mass consumption, rising and unreasonable expectations and, finally, political hypocrisy and short-termism.

None of these, the reader will note, is news. There has been popular awareness of environmental destruction at least since 1962 when Rachel Carson published *Silent Spring* and resource depletion has become almost a dangerous complacency, even though its eventual corollary—brutal and brutish competition for the resources being depleted—has barely begun to appear in the coffee-table glossies; and there has been a consciousness of technological tyranny at least since William Blake wrote about Dark Satanic Mills in the early 1800s.

Rates of change are an altogether more subtle and insidious gremlin: a phenomenon invisible in itself, it operates silently and with exponential destructiveness upon the other Demons. The virus was first isolated by Alvin Toffler in *Future Shock* in 1970, but it is not as evocative and merchantable as these others and its true malignancy has therefore been undervalued.

The last three gremlins are also less tangible, and present quite different threats and dangers. They are instrumental not so much in creating the perils themselves but in fostering an environment favourable to their spread and erecting formidable obstacles to their recognition and solution.

The Global Village is a cosy, sugary, mindless, vapid construct born with missionary zeal in the West—on Madison Avenue, in company boardrooms, amongst misguided charities and disingenuous do-gooders, and in pseudo-liberal gatherings. It reflects the penetration by the West and all its works to every corner of the earth and it postulates an electronic geo-suburban planet of instant and overwhelming communication. It sells product, it salves consciences and it spreads a comforting anodyne of smugness and complacency over the missionaries, if not the Villagers themselves. It is the culmination of the human campaign to achieve our total alienation from nature by elevating frenetic economic activity to the central role in our occupation of the earth.

Rising and unreasonable expectations reflect the frivolity of consumerism and the illusion of the attainability of universal material equality and limitless economic growth as not only feasible but posi-tively desirable global goals—the one-sided equation. It is a phenom-enon aggravated by the inability and unwillingness of governments collectively to confess to the world's people these undeniable lies.

This leads us finally to government itself and to the issues of political hypocrisy and short-termism. We shall be considering these matters in later chapters and in the Epilogue, but meanwhile we shall proceed to a more detailed dissection of the two Demons which governments of all colours will surely confront in the third millennium—even if popula-tion growth blessedly ceased and went into reverse on 31 December 2000.

These are the principal betrayals by humanity of our bond with nature and of the ecosystem of which we have long ceased to be a welcome part.

I. Environmental Destruction

In an earlier chapter I said that we would look back from 1937—as a midpoint—to 1875 and then forward another 60-odd years to the year 2001 to see whether and how the two periods might seem to have differed from each other when viewed from today's vantage point on

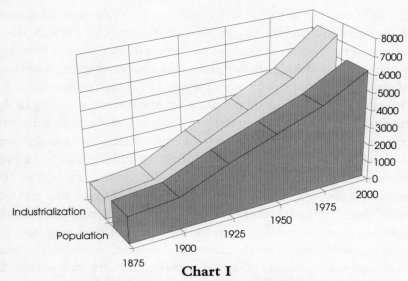

Chart I
Industrialization and Growth of Population
Sources: UN, FAO, Mitchell & others

the eve of the Third Millennium. The means of measurement start with Chart I, which plots growth in the production of the same key industrial raw materials and finished products which appeared in Table I, but focussed close-up over this far shorter 125-year period. Population growth appears alongside—always as an undertow to the other dependent phenomena. Is there anything more than a difference of quantity between the two series 1875–1937 and 1937–2000?

Precision—to a year or even a decade—is both unnecessary and impossible; but some elementary eyeball calculus suggests that, taken as a whole, the curves begin to break out towards the end of the first series, that is to say that the differences clearly begin to become qualitative: industrial processes, the now indispensable reliance on petroleum, and the accelerating pace of population growth have now clearly combined to create a quite new form of political economy and a quite new order of demand upon the earth's resources. The spreading use of cheap oil had endowed the West and its imitators with unprecedented freedom and flexibility in projecting limitless power to literally every corner of the earth and to endeavours previously beyond imagination, and through a single supreme invention: the internal combustion engine.

In the second series, the process has initially been checked in the Great Depression and then given a meteoric boost by the exigencies of World War II. Urbanization now becomes a phenomenon in its own right: over one half of the world's population will clot—one hesitates to use the word 'live' in—the city by 2001 and the process by which people and nature have become disconnected one from the other is essentially complete as economic growth and the bland but grim statistics of material development displace all other measures of human performance. For urban dweller and alienated peasant alike, the operation of the Global Equation becomes ever more irrelevant and yet, at the same time, ever more domineering. Gigantism is now a commonplace in virtually every sphere of human activity: office and apartment buildings, ships, coal and copper and iron mines, factories, media and communications, transport systems, armies, man-made disasters, crime and poverty and environmental degradation. But these phenomena are endowed ironically with their own form of invisibility precisely because of their hugeness, the insidiousness of their development, the dislocation of people from nature and—most sinister of all—a universal aversion to confront the unsustainability of the system we have created. Some other, some quite new consequences of our treatment of the planet must be identified so as to correct our failing vision.

Chart II, covering the entire period, begins to measure as it enters the second series just such a consequence. These are phenomena which were either, to all intents and purposes, unknown in the first half or which, if known, had little impact on the environment. They are emissions of sulphur dioxide and carbon dioxide; and the production of

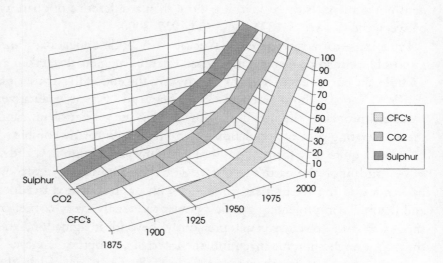

Chart II
Carbon Dioxide, Sulphur Emissions and CFC Production
Sources: Goudie, UN

chlorofluorocarbons.

And how about petroleum? In his will, George Washington says that he had bought a piece of land on the Pennsylvania frontier because of a 'bituminous spring which it contains, of so inflammable a nature as to burn as freely as spirits, and is as nearly difficult to extinguish'. The first oil well—Drake's Well—was drilled in 1859 on Oil Creek near Titusville, Pennsylvania, by two men looking for salt. American aborigines had used oil as a medicine—from surface deposits—from times beyond memory. We don't know whether this was Washington's land but, in any event, Drake struck oil on 17 August and the oil age was born.

Production grew rapidly in the later nineteenth century—of course from a zero base—but, as Graph III below shows, by 1900 petroleum still represented little more than 1% by weight of total fossil fuel consumption: coal and its derivatives, which are also shown, powered essentially all industrial processes in the West and provided most domestic heating. Merchant and naval ships, locomotives and traction-engines were coal-fired and the world's total stock of commercial internal combustion engines would not have filled a barn.

Towards the end of our first 60-year period—the outbreak of World War II—there were 38 million cars, buses, and trucks operating on freshly paved-over parts of the world—3454 times the number in 1900—and several million petrol- and diesel-powered engines in use in industry and agriculture. Applied chemistry had emerged from the First

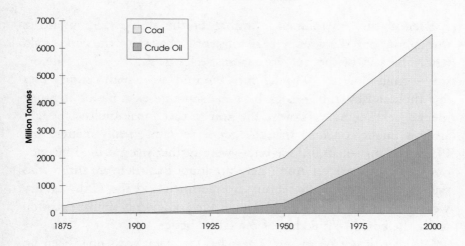

Graph III
Production of Crude Oil & Coal
Sources: Mulhall, Kolb, IEA/ OECD, UN, various

World War and began to generate an ever-widening flood of indi-
gestible chemical products and techniques for industry and agriculture,
and for personal consumption: DDT and the first non-biodegradable
plastics are blessings of these years.

Let us turn now to Chart III where we plot over the entire period
the fortunes of three organic phenomena—the American buffalo, the
world's forests seen through roundwood production and the great
global farmyard with its sheep and cattle, pigs and goats; and we add a
new marker of geosuburbanization: the appearance of the refrigerator.

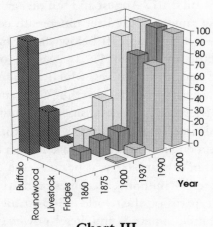

Chart III
Forests, Farmyards and Fridges—and the odd Buffalo
Source: Mulhall, UN, various

Even if the environmental impact of the smokestack industries
throughout our 125 years were not instantly observable, the same could
hardly be said of the buffalo curve: species genocide on this heroic
scale—from close to 100 million in the mid-nineteenth century to a
few thousand by 1900—is perhaps the supreme example of environmental jackbooting. Of course, the irony is that a macabre cost-benefit
analysis might conclude that the genocide 'didn't really matter': the
Plains Indians—marginal anyway—were further marginalised but no-
one else was worse off. And I have no doubt that there are those who
will say that nineteenth-century frontiersmen and the Fifth Cavalry
were ecologically illiterate and that, in a hypothetically similar situation
today, the buffalo would have fared rather better.

Well, let us not be so sure. There has for many years now been no
justification for ecological illiteracy and yet there is now a long queue
of latterday buffaloes lining up for either extinction or a new Ark: the

white rhino, Indian tiger, mountain gorilla and now even the African elephant are just the lucky ones which make it to the Sunday colour supplements. But less photogenic examples, like the Spotted Owl of the Pacific Northwest in its conflict with clearcut logging, are every bit as effective in forcing us back to the inescapable discipline of the algebra in the Global Equation set out earlier. Or should be. Unfortunately, the ordeals of these animals and, for that matter, of the wild flowers which used to adorn our hay meadows and hedgerows, the butterflies which helped them pollinate, and the grayling which once darted about in our drying up riverbeds—these ordeals have become subliminal because they don't impede us in our pursuit of ever greater accumulation of consumer goods and in creating ever greater numbers to perpetuate ultimately insatiable demand in an ultimately uninhabitable world. Or, at least, in the End-of-Nature world which may be on the way.

No animal, no butterfly, no fish, no flower, is indispensable to the earth or human tenancy of it. Indeed, a variation on the Gaia theory might have it that the one creature whose dispensability would materially assist both Gaia and the rest of creation to revive and prosper would be the human being. But that is an untimely blasphemy.

How, then, are we to make the experience of these species relevant to our perception of our own relationship to the world in 2001, granted that even the most proselytic ecologist would concede that any number of animal and plant species might perish without causing us to do more than express regret and to note that it is no doubt all part of some perfectly normal evolutionary process? The great industrial processes upon which our political economy depends, and the environmental trauma they inflict, are now too much part of our internalized social landscape for society as a whole to be able to view them dispassionately and to comprehend with any adequacy what will have to be done if we are to live with them—since we are no longer able to live without them. They are at once too remote and yet too familiar: we don't see the cadmium and the mercury in the rivers or the lead in the air we breathe or the DDT in our bodies. And the animals don't help: they and their plight and our reaction to it all too readily become part of a sort of cosy 'Bambi Syndrome' approach to species survival. Better to turn to Chart II (sulphur, carbon and CFC emissions) and Chart III (the buffalo and the forest, the farmyard and the fridge) to give urgency and meaning to the ecological calculus in the third millennium.

These phenomena of ecological predation are of a quite different order from those which it was fashionable to debate in the 1960s and

1970s and they are infinitely less tractable.

First, a highly abbreviated overview of the scale and nature of these truly apocalyptic challenges, and why they are so different in kind from the traditional smokestack forms of pollution with which people had almost learned to be comfortable.

By 2020 the world's forests will have been hacked down, killed by acid rain, flooded, burned and converted for ephemeral agricultural use so as to cover only about 14% of total land area compared with 25% in 1978. The percentage in 1950 was about 40% and in 1900 about 50%. This ravage is ultimately driven by disrespect and disregard for the operation of the Global Equation—for the principle that changes in ecological demand must be reflected in changes in supply. There must be a point of sustainable equilibrium—although it is probably indeterminable—at which the stock of forest is adequate to support, through regeneration, the demands placed on it by the manufacture of acid rain and carbon dioxide, on the one hand, and by logging and agriculture on the other. However, we unfortunately do not have the luxury of being able to calculate and agonise over where that point is: it is sufficient to be able to state, and no amount of economic and political sophistry can contradict it, that this point will have been reached and passed when the forest can be seen to be shrinking irreversibly, and the demands upon it—as recited above—increasing and showing every sign of continuing to do so indefinitely and exponentially. That point has incontrovertibly already been reached and passed.

There is, of course, disagreement over the rate at which the tropical forests are retreating before the onslaught of chain-saw and flame-thrower. In his fine and thoughtful book *The Human Impact on the Environment* the geographer Andrew Goudie cites estimates that the loss amounted to '2% of total forest expanse' in 1991 alone; that deforestation in the 1980s may have increased by as much as 89%; and that the FAO puts the total loss in 1990 amongst countries with 78% of the world's total tropical forests at 16.8 million hectares. He adds that exploitation is so rapid that 'minimal areas will be left by the year 2000 in the Philippines, peninsular Malaya, Thailand, Australia, Indonesia, Vietnam, Bangladesh, Sri Lanka, Central America, Madagascar, West Africa and eastern Amazonia.'[2]

There can be no disagreement over the *fact* of deforestation: even if the 1990 loss were only half the FAO estimate, we would still be contemplating a charred and mutilated graveyard the size of Scotland in one year alone.

Pleas for the forest to be saved because of its role in providing refuge for endangered species, or as a potential storehouse of natural medicines, are touching but of tertiary importance to its operation, along with the oceans and the atmosphere, as one of the great global ecological regulators. At precisely a moment in history when population is growing at an unprecedentedly prodigious rate, and when we need every last tree to absorb its quota of the carbon dioxide being generated with comparable irresponsibility, the earth's protective forests are disappearing. The case rests—it is unanswerable.

But what of another phenomenon on Chart III—the global farmyard? A by-product of the profusion of human numbers is the only slightly less exponential growth in the population of the cows and pigs, sheep and goats required to fulfil our hunger for meat and dairy products, an explosion by no means offset by the near-extinction of the buffalo and other species. Not only do these worthy beasts consume prodigious quantities of fodder—an exceedingly inefficient use of plant protein—but they fart. So do people. And farts are methane, and contribute about 20% of the so-called greenhouse gases.

It is tragic that issues of such incomparable importance to humanity's survival as the greenhouse effect should have become the object of polarization between rival camps of vested interests, even supported by panels of rival scientific advisors, seeking either to downgrade or even to dismiss the existence of the effect; or, on the other hand, jeopardising a common appreciation and handling of the issue by naive calls for impossibly large and immediate curbs in the generation of greenhouse gases.

Even if there were no incontrovertible proof of both the existence of the greenhouse effect and of its probable consequences, simple prudent observation alone would suggest that something in the climate is amiss, and that the detractors of the effect will eventually go the way of those who once rejected, and even continue to do so at this late stage, evidence that cigarette smoking promotes lung- and heart-disease along with the vaunted social and sexual success.

This is not the place to analyze in depth, or to attempt to date in the early third millennium, the nature and timing of the greenhouse effect catastrophes portended by the continued release into the atmosphere of carbon dioxide—50%, methane 20%, nitrous oxide 6%, low-level ozone 12%, and increasingly chlorofluorocarbons (CFCs) for most of the balance; nor the carcinogenic consequences of ozone depletion caused mainly by the same CFCs. It is sufficient to say that extreme climatic changes are already unavoidably programmed into the future as the result of past emissions, let alone those being, and waiting to be, generated; and that the economic, political, social and military consequences of this stratospheric pollution will make us nostalgic for its smokestack forerunners.

This has been but a brief and quite incomplete survey of the scale and nature of current and prospective environmental depredation. It is not intended as a Green polemic, and it will have served its purpose if it succeeds simply in convincing the broad readership—committed to neither of the extreme wings of the 'environmental debate'—not only that extraordinary damage had been done to the environment by decades of conventional industrial and agricultural activity; but that there is now at work an entirely novel set of imminently catastrophic forces.

II. Resource Depletion

I was first employed in the mining industry as a commodity economist. The time was the early 1960s and, following the recession of the late Eisenhower years, the economy was beginning to respond to the neo-Keynesian banners fluttering over the White House.

The mining industry was an exciting place to be. Production and consumption of an ever-lengthening menu of minerals were expanding; people were drilling holes where none had been drilled before and to unheard-of depths; mines of unprecedented scale followed the drilling-teams; railways were driven through the wilderness to bring out the extracted ores, and deep-sea loading terminals were built to accommodate bulk-carriers of gargantuan size to carry the stuff halfway round the world. In the United States there persisted a fear, born out of the Korean War ten years earlier, of being starved by hostile forces of those metals and minerals in which the country was not self-sufficient—meaning, to all intents and purposes, almost all of them, given the prodigious levels of American consumption.

To help allay the fear, Festung Amerika was underpinned by the construction of the Strategic Stockpile, which consisted of huge dumps of minerals and metals which could be, as it were, re-mined courtesy of the Federal Government in the event of either interdiction by enemy action of seaborne supplies, or market-cornering by foreign monopolies. The United States itself showed how certain metals might become chips in the Cold War game by banning sales to the Soviet Union of key military-use metals such as vanadium, molybdenum and titanium.

I used to spend fascinating days on end at the US Bureau of Mines in Washington, DC, talking to Government analysts and reading reports on the supply-demand prospects for nickel and chromium, copper and manganese, platinum and rare earths and half the rest of the Periodic Table. From all this would come—and I do not use the term with more than an allowable degree of facetiousness—'flavour-of-the-year' fads for this or that metal or mineral. And exploration budgets followed.

Not many years later, but unfortunately just *before* the first oil shock of 1973, the Club of Rome published *Limits to Growth*. One obvious limit was the earth's theoretical stock of the raw materials required to feed that growth; but, of course, a definition of 'stock' of any particular raw material, at any particular moment, entails a complex set of inter-active calculations which include amortization of the cost of exploration and discovery, mining and processing technology, transport, cost of capital, depreciation, taxes, return on investment, price of alternative materials and—not least—the cost of fuel. *Limits to Growth* reproduces US Bureau of Mines statistics of global reserves, a range of three rates of annual percentage growth in consumption, and complex forecasts of the number of years remaining until exhaustion of the reserves for sixteen metals and for coal, natural gas and petroleum.

(For the record, these estimated reserves vary according to whether a static or exponentially growing rate of consumption is used, and clearly the actual or probable rate for most metals will tend to lie above the static but below the exponential. The *static* rate projects a range for the metals from 11 years for gold to close to 240 years for a major metal like iron, the *exponential* rates being 9 and 93 years respectively. For coal, gas and petroleum the *static* rates are 2300, 38 and 31 years respectively, and the *exponential* rates 111, 22 and 20 years.)

These were stern warnings. But it is instructive to note that the concerns of *Limits to Growth* with respect to resource depletion were restricted to the so-called non-renewable resources and paid no *special* attention to the fossil fuels, and no treatment at all of two other raw materials of literally consuming interest, namely air and water.

Of course, air and water have long been regarded as 'free goods' and, as we shall shortly see all too plainly, wrongly so. Perhaps this is why they have not normally featured in the forecasts of supply and demand. And oil, while not being regarded also as a free good, has nevertheless gener-ally been classified in the supply-demand statistics as if it were just

another of the non-renewable raw materials. In practice, air and water
are no longer free, and oil ceased to be just another raw material many
decades ago—when man broke off his affair with the steam engine and
plighted his troth with the automobile. Faust and Mephistopheles.

Where, then, have the stern warnings now left us? Forecasts of imminent shortages of metal 'X', or of the certain exhaustion of exploitable
reserves of metal 'Y' within so many years at current rates of consumption, should be matters of urgent *microeconomic* concern principally to
the companies which extract, refine and supply that particular metal, or
to others which use them in a manufacturing process or in end-prod-
ucts, for example copper mining companies at one end, and copper wire
drawers at the other. They are not of great *macroeconomic* concern even
though reserves of many of the most industrially important metal ores
seem likely to become scarce during the twenty-first century, even after
allowances are made for improvements in technology and higher prices.
Few of the metals and minerals which may become 'scarce' in the early
third millennium are so unique in their properties as to be without
substitute, albeit imperfect; advanced metallurgical techniques will tend
to make a pound of metal do the work of two pounds ten years earlier;
and one promising result, at least, of environmental preaching has been
the huge growth in recycling; and landfill sites are potentially
exploitable mines.

However, the supply and demand forecasts hinted at earlier seem
sufficiently menacing in the more immediate *commercial* sense that the
mining companies will probably have retained their analysts and economists and long-range planners, and government agencies around the
world will continue to construct graphs and equations to produce what
are—in historical terms—rather short-run forecasts of supply and
demand for the everyday metals and minerals considered to be so indispensable to our industrial consumer economies. But, for the reasons
cited above, none of these commodities merits inclusion on a rather
special type of critical path which we might construct to stretch out of
the late twentieth century and as far into third millennium horizons as
these rather more mundane forecasts normally extend, say to 2030 or
2075 or 2099.

The only commodities which would appear on *this* critical path are
air, water and oil (defined as including natural gas) because they alone
are, or have become, indispensable to life as we live it, and—against all
ingrained assumptions—air and water are now about to join oil as
depletable, and already substantially depleted resources. We shall,

however, allow the commodity economists to continue their work, hoping only that those who employ them realise that their forecasts and calculations are quite meaningless unless there are available enough energy to power the mines and industrial processes downstream and, above all, adequate supplies of the basic elements required by society—air and water—in order to power to the checkout counter the consumers of the products of those industries.

Air

'Air quality today will be a carbon copy of yesterday.' Weather forecaster on KLAX, February 10, 1987.

I picked up these ironically prophetic words on the car radio one fine morning while driving across the Mojave Desert from Las Vegas to Los Angeles. Their prophetic quality assumed more immediacy as I reached the last crest and looked down into the atmospheric soup clothing the city to the horizon. Detailed elaboration on the matter of air pollution is unnecessary: for most people, deterioration of air quality caused by emissions from automobiles, power stations, petrochemical plants, industry in general and the destruction—often by burning—of the very forests which consume carbon dioxide and swap it for oxygen, is the most easily perceived and personally experienced type of environmental pollution. Less apparent but no less cumulatively lethal are the innumerable types of chemicals and particulate matter which now inhabit the atmosphere. The presence of these foreign matters, often carcinogenic, in the atmosphere is irreversible and can only increase as a consequence of growth in the mass of industrial activity responsible for their release as pollutants even if, as may well happen, there is a decline in the *relative* output of pollutants per unit of production or mile driven or, as will certainly *not* happen, an immediate and total halt to deforestation.

This is the air we breathe—the same air which must also, even as it will surely become more and more unbreathable, be shared out to fill almost three times as many pairs of lungs in the year 2100 as it does today; and it is the same air which will be required at the same time to tolerate, i.e. to absorb, the toxic output of an ever-growing number of cars, trucks, buses, power stations, petrochemical plants, factories and households. Here, the candle is being burned at both ends: the demands which remorseless population growth and the accompanying industrialisation will make on our air supplies will be compounded by the equally remorseless assault being waged on the earth's forests whose role is so vital in regulating the weather and generating oxygen.

But that is only the air we breathe: more insidious, as we have noted earlier, and ultimately more unarguably lethal is the ecological dislocation *already programmed* into the third millennium by global warming and ozone depletion; and the destruction in this century of the Northern Hemisphere's forests and lakes by acid rain, and its relentless gnawing of masonry and statuary. Although this trio of menaces does not directly affect the chemical composition of the stuff we're going to be breathing in the twenty-first century, it is through the medium of air—the atmosphere—that their effects will be manifest.

I am aware that the very existence of the phenomenon of global warming is contested by some scientists, although no-one seems to disagree that there has taken place an increase in global temperature of about one-half of one degree centigrade over the last 100 years and that a continued increase—whether man-made or the product of long-term climatic changes—would have cataclysmic consequences. Uncertain as these may be in their timing, they would include massive disruption to cereal production in the Northern Hemisphere and a rise in sea levels, as the polar icecaps melt, sufficient to overwhelm towns, cities and rural coastal areas which are home to a billion or more people; and melting permafrost in Arctic regions would release more methane into the atmosphere and so add to the cycle.

Those inclined to scoff at the evidence and those already persuaded by it, will have reacted with alarm and relief, respectively, when no less an environmental illiterate than Mrs Margaret Thatcher, Prime Minister, endorsed the views of the latter in a speech in 1989. However, as long ago as 1971 Barry Commoner had first used the analogy of the greenhouse to describe the similarity between glass windowpanes and increased carbon dioxide levels in the atmosphere in trapping infrared energy—the longer wavelengths of light—and preventing it from escaping. Since heat is really light, there is the greenhouse effect—the global warming.

Carbon dioxide, methane, nitrous oxides and chlorofluoro-carbons are the culprit gases and there is already enough of them up there, let alone what will ineluctably be released before there could conceivably be a reduction or complete cessation, to mean the certainty of major global warming. There is a delayed-action effect but, as James Lovelock says of carbon dioxide, methane and CFCs, 'We have changed the atmosphere more already than took place between the last [ice-age] and now. The consequences, a rise of temperature comparable to that between the glaciation and now, are inevitable.'[3]

Ozone depletion does not need prime-ministerial acknowledgement of its existence: but Greenpeace is said to have sponsored development of a refrigerator which does not use CFCs in response to her appeal following her Damascene experiences of 1989. Stratospheric ozone is a thin layer of O_3 (a molecule comprising three oxygen atoms) which sits at altitudes ranging from 16 to 25 kms above the earth. In the stratosphere, ozone acts to shield the earth from the full dose of ultraviolet solar radiation. Chlorine contained in CFCs, which are used in aerosol cans, foam food-containers and refrigerators, seem to be the main agents of ozone depletion. As the gases reach the stratosphere, they are broken down by ultraviolet solar radiation and chlorine is set loose. One chlorine atom binds with the ozone molecule to produce O_2 and Cl_0. The Cl_0 then attacks another blob of O_3 to produce two molecules of O_2 and a pure Cl atom which then reiterates the deadly cycle.

The Chinese have 30 million refrigerators today. By the year 2030 they plan to have over 350 million; and 'Greenpeace' is not translatable into Chinese.

Ozone depletion has been detected particularly in the Antarctic, where low temperatures and long sunlight favour chlorine release, but is now being detected in the Northern Hemisphere. Increased ultraviolet radiation reaching the earth is feared likely to produce greater incidence of cancer and blindness; and to have adverse effects on photosynthesis in crops and the plankton which is the root of the marine food cycle. CFCs have an unfortunately tenacious drive for survival: those already up there can last and continue their search-and-destroy missions for a century and their numbers will continue to be reinforced for many years to come even after the last one is pensioned off on earth.

Acid rain is formed through the reaction of sulphur and nitrogen dioxides and hydrocarbons with rain and sunlight—the main sources being emissions from power stations, motor vehicle exhausts and industrial processes. Metals such as lead, zinc, mercury and aluminium are also reaching fresh water supplies. The main consequences are already visible in dying or dead forests throughout wide tracts of the United States and Canada, and from the British Isles to Russia and from Sweden to Greece; in mutilated statuary from Exeter Cathedral to the Parthenon and the Taj Mahal; and in lakes which no longer support fish.

The issue has in recent years become highly political as the evidence becomes irrefutable that the building of ever-higher smokestacks only serves to waft the problem away from the polluter on the prevailing wind patterns and to dump it unbidden on victims hundreds of miles away: export or die in practice. The quantities are stupendous: Goudie estimates that the sulphur content of global emissions of sulphur dioxide resulting from the burning of fossil fuels has risen from about 3 million tonnes in 1860 to 90 million in 1990. The problem will remain chronic and cumulative even if emissions were merely reduced; ultimate elimination is not feasible.

Acid rain is in many respects the most emotive symbol of humanity's impact on the earth in the twentieth century. We don't actually 'see' ozone depletion or global warming. We most certainly do see the dead trees, waters where we can no longer fish, and the faceless stumps in the alcoves of our churches. The cause lies in the very nature of industrial society, in its success in supplying us with cheap transport, cheap power and an abundance of cheap food and material goods. The prospect for a solution is therefore likely to prove elusive because it is not primarily technical but sociopolitical.

Air, then, deserves to be regarded as a depletable resource of the first order, partly because more and more of us are breathing the less and less of it which is wholesome; and because of what we are doing to the atmosphere of which it is a part. If 'depletable' seems too fanciful a classification, few will disagree that air must be, or once again become, a fully renewable resource and available in adequate quantities. Today, air certainly does not enjoy this status.

So much, then, for one of the three basic elements on our special critical path, for one of the 'inputs', as air might be rather clinically regarded, which are quite indispensable in getting us from now, in 1995, to some point in the third millennium which may serve as a target, as a way of measuring our success in combatting all the other ills we have inflicted upon ourselves – say the year 2050; and quite irrespective, let it be emphasized again, of supply-demand equations for all those rather more mundane commodities not on our critical path. Let us turn now to water.

Water

'Neither Syria nor Iraq can lay claim to Turkey's rivers any more than Ankara could claim their oil... The water is Turkey's, the oil [is] theirs. We don't say we share their oil... and they cannot say they share our water.' Suleyman Demirel, Turkish Prime Minister, quoted in *Water Wars* by Bulloch & Darwish.

The earth is awash with it: seventy percent, and frequently more, of the earth's surface is under water—in parts, up to seven miles deep. However, only about 3% is fresh and most of that is tied up in Arctic and Antarctic icecubes so that from this global bucket only a thimbleful is available for the earth's entire land-based population of flora and fauna, whether for consumption or for processes requiring fresh water. Moreover, this availability is distributed highly erratically and leaves the bulk of Africa and the Middle East, much of Central and eastern Asia, large parts of southern Latin America and western North America and virtually all of Australia parched by chronic water shortage.

In these parts, where there *had* existed an original and permanent ecological compromise of sparse but naturally available water with sustainable indigenous life-forms, the balance can be overturned artificially—and, all too frequently, with unpredictable side-effects—only by importing water, i.e. through irrigation, or by impounding it with dams or by constructing vastly expensive desalinization plants which can operate only where the water is needed, usually because of unsustainable population growth, and the oil is cheap, e.g. the Middle East. It is an irony that just as these plants remove salt from the water in one part of the world, so irrigation should increase salt levels in another through either the evaporation of the imported water and rising salt-rich water tables in the dry areas under irrigation, or by concentrating salinity in the areas from which the irrigation water has been taken. The unplanned side-effects—a term, almost a euphemism, which grossly belittles their impact—of such massive interference with ecological balances will be considered later.

Although floods and droughts have featured in human folklore since before Genesis—and, indeed, irrigation and salt-pans have been part of the landscape since Neolithic times—the notion that water is, in effect, another *depletable* resource rather than merely *scarce*, is a strictly late twentieth-century novelty—simply because it is a phenomenon of our century. Water, like air, had always seemed to be an infinitely abundant resource even though, unlike air, it is unequally distributed over the earth's surface—unlike air, that is, until in the twentieth century when breathable air began to be increasingly poorly distributed. What, then, has happened to put water on to the list of depletables?

The answers are unsurprising: population, and agricultural and industrial pollution. We start with three simple propositions: first, that there is only so much naturally occurring fresh water readily available (and that irregularly distributed) from 'renewable' sources such as rivers, lakes, rainfall and bore-holes plugged into groundwater (although this latter source is of dubious renewability, for the reasons set out below); second, that an unquantifiable part of this total water stock is either inaccessible or unusable or is in the process of natural or artificial recycling; and finally, that demand for water seems to be highly inelastic with respect to either monetary or ecological cost, because either the costs are being incurred but not being recognised and paid, or they are being cross-subsidised which produces similar distortions. The formula for fresh water availability looks something like this:

$$C = (C_{ff} + C_i + C_a + C_{dm}) =/< W - (W_{iu} + W_r + W_d)$$

where C = consumption, ff = fauna and flora, i = industry,
a = agriculture, dm = domestic and municipal, W = total water stock,
iu = inaccessible/unusable, r = recycling, and d = destroyed.

Since W can—by definition—not be increased; since much is being permanently destroyed; and since C is expanding through inexorable population-driven pressure, then only an increase in the rate of r—recycling—would seem to be capable, theoretically, of restoring the equation. And why should it be that if *apparently* prodigal levels of consumption (for example, the United States quaffs water at the rate of over 2 million litres per head per year compared with perhaps 30 thousand litres per head per year in the Third World) *were* reduced, the certainty of an imminent global water crisis would *not* disappear? How has the formula been busted?

The reasons lie partly in the inherent nature of the fresh water stock; partly in entrenched purposes, practices and levels of global water consumption; and, not least, in global abuse of water itself.

Fresh water has been distributed in a highly irregular pattern and with imperfect regard for local demand. While there occur sizeable fluctuations in rainfall from year to year, even in temperate zones, it can be stated as a general guide that there is 'adequate' naturally occurring fresh water, contained in rivers and lakes and—historically at least—in groundwater reserves, in the *Northern Hemisphere* in a band stretching from Alaska the whole way round to the Kamchatka Peninsula across the Bering Straits, south to encompass the eastern half of Canada and the United States, east to include most of Europe and present-day Russia, the Himalayas and a large part of southeast Asia and Japan. The rest of the Northern Hemisphere, i.e. central, western and the extreme southwestern parts of North America, most of central America, most of Africa, the Middle East, much of India and central Asia, have 'inadequate' natural sources of fresh water.

The *Southern Hemisphere* in general is, however, rather poorly watered: this includes much of Andean Latin America, northeast Brazil, Africa excluding the Congo Basin, and most of Australia.

(I surround the words *adequate* and *inadequate* with quotation marks because they are relativistic notions: they have to do with the demands made unilaterally, and upon finite resources, by human activity.)

One very broad conclusion from this highly oversimplified review of global water distribution is that advanced economic development and adequate naturally occurring water resources tend to go together: in statistician's jargon, that there is a strong coefficient of correlation between the two phenomena. Where we see advanced economic development or—and they are not necessarily the same thing—sudden or artificially high standards of living in areas unblessed with abundant water supplies, we will expect to observe either relatively small prosperous populations (frequently but not always of European colonial origin) or a critical dependence on irrigation and pumped-out groundwater, or some combination of both.

The clearest example of *irrigation dependence* is the United States west of the Mississippi, excepting the Pacific Northwest, whose spectacular economic growth and population 'gains' since World War II have relied quite indispensably on massive irrigation schemes including wholesale damming—and that is an appropriate homophone—of rivers like the Colorado; and unsustainable tapping of fossil water such as the Ogallala Aquifer—in effect, a huge underground lake which spans over 500 miles from South Dakota to northern Texas. We shall come back later to this particular distortion of the ecological balance.

A good example of *advanced economic development* in an area *not* blessed with abundant water is southeastern and western Australia, where a transplanted population of largely European origin has contrived to flourish generally within the constraints of water availability, i.e. without resorting to large-scale and destructive irrigation or desalinisation.

High living standards *and* scarce water? The obvious examples are certain statelets bordering the Persian Gulf which have jumped in a generation or two from sustainable nomadic and agricultural subsistence to gross consumer economies utterly dependent on the depletable resource lying beneath the sands—oil—for both their revenue and the means of desalting the seas.

Water differs from the other two depletables, of course, in many respects. For the purposes of this analysis, one key difference is that, unlike oil, it cannot be traded and moved economically from an area of abundance on one side of the world to one of deprivation on the other; towing icebergs from the polar regions to Saudi Arabia is not yet an established trade. For this reason, and for all its seemingly prodigal use of its own water, the United States cannot be indicted for consuming an unfair share of the world's water, as it might be for its gluttony for imported raw materials. Indeed, with cereal exports in 1992 reaching 90,396,000 metric tons out of total world trade of 248,551,000 tons, the USA is actually indirectly subsidising water supplies to much of the rest of the world through the water consumed in producing the grain in the first place and in the moisture content exported.

And water is unlike air, which *does* move freely around the world even if, in so doing, it brings with it unwelcome imports such as acid rain. Water, our second depletable resource, must therefore be examined for the impact which its abundance or scarcity, its pureness or foulness, have on the regions where these factors are observable.

Two broad distinctions can already be made in the differing nature of fresh water pollution around the world. First, the principal causes in the industrialised West and Second World are chemical contamination from agricultural pesticides and fertilisers, from industrial processes and from toxic dumps and landfill sites. By contrast, most water pollution in the Third World stems from the discharge of raw sewage and other household waste into rivers and lakes. However, there is a growing threat of sewage pollution in those countries of the industrialised world where there is under-investment in treatment plants; and, as the Third World embarks on its own chosen journey to industrial happiness, there is little reason for confidence that even the West's inadequately conceived and implemented criteria and operating practices will be transferred along with the technology. Indeed, some industrial multinationals will tend to shift chronic polluting processes from the inconvenient First to the hospitable Third World; and it is unlikely that the epic odyssey of the 'Karin B' in 1988 will prove to be unique in the annals of maritime history. Even as I write, the European Commission has agreed to ban the export of toxic waste to the Third World; but, like the commerce in rhinoceros horns, the illegal nature of the trade will only make it more lucrative, and I am unable to explain why the rigours of supply-and-demand analysis should be so obscure to the armchair bureaucrats in Brussels.

The second distinction is demographic and geographical. We have already remarked a correlation between adequate water supplies and economic development. (They are not, of course, mutually dependent—water is the only independent variable of the two even though economic development itself has now attained the status of an independent force). Third World countries, in many of which there is now industrial development, are generally water have-nots, have exploding populations and exhibit levels of freshwater pollution and an inadequacy of sewage treatment which only stupendous economic development might theoretically generate the capital to redress. And, of course, that very economic development is an intrinsic part of the dilemma posed by corrupting the global water-use formula.

The Third World as a whole has, therefore, to achieve a multiple miracle: in order to avert just the *present* threat and cycle of drought and epidemics, it must clean up its existing polluted water sources, construct dams and reservoirs on a colossal scale, finesse the dilemma posed by the contamination of land and water by the very pesticides and fertilisers which will be needed in ever larger quantities to feed the swelling populations, contain massive quantities of animal waste and build urban and rural sewage systems and industrial treatment plants almost from scratch. But over the next 100 years, Third World population will more than double, to about nine billion, with most of that occurring in cities many of which are already scarcely habitable, and industrialisation will take its toll in water demand and pollution; and I shall consider in Chapter Eight exactly where are to be found all those markets just panting for the goods which are to flood out of the newly industrialised Third World in order to pay for the great clean-up...

There is another dilemma, well exemplified by the Aswan High Dam. This dam, commissioned in 1971, was to have brought to Egypt the benefits of electricity and flood control. In practice, it has been an environmental disaster: the irrigation schemes it has permitted have inevitably raised salinity; the 100 million tons of fertile silt which used to be washed down from the African highlands every year to enrich the lower Nile Delta are now backing up behind the dam, and even threaten to rupture it or divert the Nile itself into the desert; and fertiliser application rates are amongst the highest in the world, as farmers attempt to compensate for the lost natural nutrients. Meanwhile, the anticipated benefits now have to be shared out amongst a population which has doubled since the dam was turned on in 1971.

In their recently published book *Water Wars*, Messrs Bulloch &

Darwish discuss the prospects for armed conflict in the Middle East (defined as encompassing the region from Libya in the west to Iraq in the east, and from Turkey in the north to the Sudan in the south) not least between Arab brother nations, as they contest control of the great international river systems of the area: the Nile, Jordan, Tigris and Euphrates, and of groundwater in the Arabian Peninsula; and they warn of the anomalous and unsustainable nature of Saudi wheat production and of the geopolitical reasons behind it: 'It may be the world's most expensive wheat; it is certainly the most water-costly of all.'[4]

It was interesting to learn that *sharia*, the Arabic word for Islamic law, derives from an Arabic word for water; and to read that [Islamic] 'fundamentalists are using water as a way of involving themselves in other disputes [than water, in order] to install local or national Islamic regimes.'[5] I shall not distract attention from water crises throughout the Third World by focussing too much on the Middle East, which could serve as a proxy for the entire issue of Third World water, but there are two other quotations from this excellent work which merit thought: 'The Middle East is not the only place where water crises and disputes exist, but it is the region in which the potential for conflict over water is at its most extreme, and where a long history of war, as well as of border disputes, plus the presence of oil... gives little confidence that international laws can avert wars in the area'[6] and they conclude: 'Water wars are on the way.'

What of the First World? The Cuyahoga River flows through Cleveland, Ohio, and out into Lake Erie. It flows now but in July 1969 it only oozed; someone threw a match and whoosh! it caught fire, so burdened was it with volatile industrial filth. Perhaps it didn't really matter: the lake was close to death anyway but even this obscenity could not rival that of the wounded innocence of the polluters and some local officials who rallied to their defence.

There are no grounds for complacency, despite a huge expansion of popular awareness of the insupportable demands being made on fresh water supplies through industrial and agricultural processes and discharges from chemical and nuclear waste dumps; and notwithstanding the substantial amount of legislation now being enacted and intended to reverse the steady depletion of fresh water.

Contamination by industry and agriculture will continue—and it is cumulative—as long as the pricing mechanism for so many of the goods and services to which we have become acculturated remains inadequate; and in the final analysis, no amount of water-pricing can increase the absolute availability of water and so redress the equation. Politicians will continue to claim that 'the polluter will pay', but they know, and they aren't saying, that it can only be the consumer of these goods and services who does, in fact, eventually pick up the tab. The First World's economies—all forty or fifty of them—may have high and rising levels of interdependence and integration but their component parts, the businesses and farms, are all subject either to the rigours of domestic and international competition or—and it comes to the same thing—are able to shelter their pricing, their market-shares and their civic responsibility behind modern-day cartels, official or unofficial.

The practical effect in both cases is the same: no industrial company and no farm, other than the organic fringe, is going to peer over the parapet of minimal compliance with the law; and, as we shall explore more fully in later chapters, it is naive to expect government to contemplate the full social and economic implications of an end, effectively, to freshwater pollution.

We'll conclude by revisiting the Ogallala and explaining its significance. For over half a century, this underground lake has been intensively tapped to supply water to an area of the Great Plains almost the size of England. The water goes mainly into irrigation—to support a cereal industry upon whose production much of the world now depends, including many Third World countries which can no longer feed their populations with local produce, or which have acquired a taste for wheat flour. For reasons which are as yet imperfectly understood, grain harvests in the United States dropped in the 1980s, and in 1988 American farmers did not produce enough to feed the nation without drawing on stocks. Whether global warming or ozone depletion or some other man-made phenomenon is the culprit, the fact is that the Ogallala is *not* replenishable and pumping has already been stopped or reduced in certain areas. This depletion certainly means that pumping will continue to decline and, along with it, cereal production. Since the United States in 1992 exported almost 100 million tons of cereals—more than one-third of total world imports—particularly to Third World countries unable to feed their exploding populations, the fate of the Ogallala will have a significance thousands of miles from the Great Plains which are now draining it.

Fresh water has therefore become, for all practical purposes, a depleting resource to be treated as a vital non-renewable commodity—like oil to which we finally turn.

Oil

There can be no certainty about the extent of the world's remaining oil (and gas) reserves until the last half-barrel has been wrung from an exhausted and as yet unknown deposit. That deposit lies in a part of the world which is God-forsaken or blessed wilderness, depending on one's point of view. The cost of extracting it will be astronomical in real terms in today's prices, the technology has not yet been invented, and it will be destined for use in a country which has the financial and military resources to deny its use to rivals.

Despite these uncertainties, it is as well to look at the history of oil consumption and current projections of use and reserves so that we can form a broad appreciation of the scale of new discoveries which will have to be achieved in the next decade or two if the day the oil runs out is to be deferred. In this way we shall have at least a framework for understanding the role oil has played in the twentieth century in bringing unimaginable material comforts to much of mankind— mainly in the West—but also in detaching our culture and our economies from an indefinitely sustainable path, and in subverting Third World societies by bringing them into the Global Village, whose products they neither need nor can afford.

We do not treat natural gas separately in this chapter: *The Global 2000 Report* acknowledges that, unlike with oil, there is no consensus on resources of natural gas.[7] Although gas resources seem likely to exceed those of oil by a modest margin, the present and prospective rates of consumption are similar and it is therefore reasonable for the purposes of this analysis to assume that they will follow *broadly similar* paths to exhaustion; and since oil has a much higher profile in the public awareness, it may serve here as a proxy for natural gas. (The term *exhaustion* is, of course, only relative: oil will remain available for highly specialised, high-value, small-volume purposes in pharmaceuticals and chemistry long after it has ceased to be a fossil fuel.) Chart IV illustrates the scale of the world's oil consumption since the sinking of Drake's Well in 1859 and the level of resources in 1976.

Discussion of the total abundance of any mineral is loaded with both geological and semantic problems. For the US Bureau of Mines *reserves* are a subset of *resources* and consist of 'measured reserves', defined as that quantity whose whereabouts are known and which it is technically and geologically possible to extract at marginal costs which do not exceed the associated revenue (even though as much as 70% of the oil may

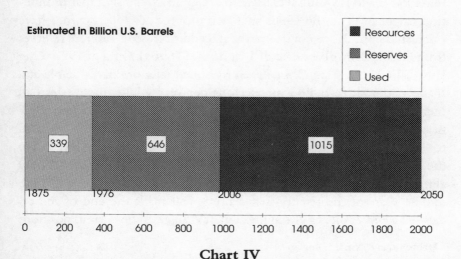

Chart IV
Crude Oil Consumption, Reserves & Resources 1875-2050
Estimated January 1976
Source: Adapted from The Global 2000 Report *p. 188-190*

remain in the field); there then follow two categories of reserves—'indicated' and 'inferred'—which, as the words themselves suggest, represent estimates of declining reliability. The realm of 'resources' is, of course, even more hypothetical. In practice, technology will 'improve' and, quite possibly, operating margins too, which would permit expoitation of hitherto uneconomic deposits. Furthermore, there are several presently unexploited oil 'resources' which do not go into the current supply and demand calculus. These include the Athabasca tar-sands in northern Alberta, oil-shale in Colorado, Wyoming and Utah, the Orinoco tar-belt in Venezuela, so-called condensates found with natural gas, and no doubt other new sources in Asia.

The terms 'measured' and 'resources' are, then, sufficiently rubbery that we might be entitled to regard with some scepticism the conclusion extrapolated in Chart IV, namely that the oil runs out on 31 December 2050. And this scepticism might seem warranted by hindsight: the *Limits to Growth* forecasts of 1972 suggested that exhaustion *could* be reached in between twenty and fifty years, although it must be emphasized in defence of the authors that they were using US Government figures of proven oil reserves and a simple range of consumption growth rates which seemed reasonable at the time (and it was before OPEC struck). However, the *consensus on total resources* in *Global 2000* is

remarkable and it would seem safe to accept its conclusion that production might peak in the 1990s and then proceed to slope down. I have
calculated cumulative consumption and additions to 'measured' reserves
from Global 2000's base date of 1 January 1976 to the end of 1990 using
IEA/OECD statistics. *Consumption* remained extraordinarily stable at a
shade under three billion metric tons per year whilst discoveries had
increased 'measured' reserves by about 50%. Assuming that these additions will merely have been debited to the 'Reserves' box and credited
to 'Resources', and that consumption holds to its consistent level, then
the clear inference to be drawn from the Global 2000 Report from now
almost twenty years ago remains remarkably sound and indicates that the
middle years of the twenty-first century will mark the end of the oil
age—the end of oil as a cheap fuel. Chart V suggests the current position:

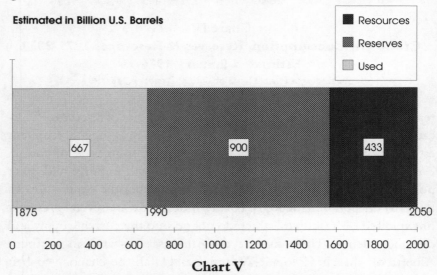

Chart V
Crude Oil Consumption & Reserves—1990 Update
Estimated December 1990
Source: Global 2000 Report *adapted and updated by author*

In *The Next 200 Years*, Herman Kahn cheaply ridicules these forecasts
and somewhat disingenuously cites a US Geological Survey of 1891
reporting '...little or no chance for oil in Texas' and a Department of the
Interior broadcast of 1939 that 'US oil supplies will last only 13 years'[8]
as proof that 'this tendency to underestimate future production [sic] is
so strong that similar mistakes are made over and over again.'[9] However,
Kahn will be seen in the future to have been the worst type of professional optimist and little comfort can be taken from this kind of pseudo-

scientific popularising: 'We have analyzed alternative energy resources in some detail and found that with very little doubt we could expect essentially an eternal abundance of energy, the only requirements being that the sun keep shining and modest technological progress continue for a few years.'[10] Cheap writing, cheap logic.

However, macroeconomic supply-demand equations cannot be left to wrangling between different camps of futurologists whatever the level of the debate. There are major geopolitical considerations which seem likely quite soon to predominate over issues of technology and pricing.

The preceding section was much preoccupied with the Middle East, where two of our depletables—oil and water—don't mix well and seem likely according to some observers, including Arab politicians and officials, to ignite war in the very near future in an improbable chemical reaction. Oil differs from air and water in many obvious respects; but one of the more subtle is that, whereas air circulates automatically around the earth and freshwater doesn't, oil is tankered around it in very large quantities indeed. In 1991 global crude oil production totalled 131 billion barrels, of which the Middle East represented about 29%, but only about one barrel in six stayed there: the rest, some 30 billion barrels, was exported, with over 68% going to OECD countries, i.e. the 'West'. Here are the statistics:

Table II
Sources of OECD Oil imports in 1991—thousands of Metric Tonnes
Source: Oil & Gas Information *IEA/OECD, Paris 1992*

	Middle East	%	Others	%	Total
Europe	240,543	49	254,658	51	495,201
N. America	97,147	29	235,901	71	333,048
Pacific	151,579	72	59,155	28	210,734
All OECD	489,269	47	549,714	53	1,038,983

The West and Japan were therefore in 1991 dependent on the Middle East for 47% of their oil supplies—a figure which is probably misleadingly low because total Middle East exports were currently being affected by an almost complete cessation of contributions from Iraq and Kuwait and a precipitous drop in Iran's share. Whatever the degree of this dependence, it will be the second casualty of the predicted wars when they break out and the oil wells are put to the torch. There will be no simple re-run of the Gulf War of 1991 which had nothing to do with water: whether or not these wars are initially triggered by sectarian forces, they will be fought with irredentist fervour and with the undeclared aim of drawing quite novel lines in the sands. For this reason, putting a date to the day when the earth peacefully yields up that last half-barrel may be a barren exercise. In any event—a conflagration in the Middle East which embroils Turkey and NATO and shatters the maritime oil trade, or a steady decline in oil production in the twenty-first century even as absolute demand increases in response to population growth—it will be as well now to acknowledge the role that oil plays in our culture, and the convulsions which that culture will suffer as the oil runs out and no adequate long-term and environmentally supportable substitutes are devised and phased into the world's economy.

Table III shows the degree of dependence on the five principal sources of energy—coal, oil, natural gas, nuclear and hydroelectricity—of the three OECD groupings of Europe, North America and Pacific (Australia, New Zealand and Japan). Following the figures for oil is shown the contribution to total OECD energy consumption supplied by Middle East OPEC members in 1991, including Iran which might not be expected to remain aloof from the predicted turmoil.

Table III

Total OECD Energy Sources by Type—1973 & 1991 and Contribution from Middle East—all in percentages

Source: Oil & Gas Information *IEA/OECD, Paris 1992*

	Europe			N. America			Pacific		
	1973	1991	Mid. East	1973	1991	Mid. East	1973	1991	Mid. East
Coal	22	22		20	26		21	20	
Oil	63	42	21	47	36	10	74	52	37
Gas	10	18		29	24		2	14	
Nuclear	2	15		1	10		1	11	
Hydro	3	3		3	4		2	3	
Total	100	100		100	100		100	100	

Taken together with Chart V, these two sets of statistics present an extremely forbidding prospect: not only is there a clear indication that the oil-supply curve flattens out in the early twenty-first century, but these disturbing forecasts of demand and supply conceal a dangerous deception by conflating global oil reserves as if they were similar to what economists would call *fungible* goods, that is as if all sources could be poured altruistically into some great global oil-barrel and ladled out to meet global demand. In practice, not only is the Middle East likely to become an ever-more uncertain element in the supply picture, but it would be grossly imprudent to assume that the other major or potential players—Russia and China—will be either able or willing to make up the shortfall. The technological, political and environmental obstacles posed by an unlocking of, for example, Siberian oil deposits—let alone the investment required—are prodigious, and both countries can be expected to give greater priority to domestic demand and—dare it be said?—to conservation.

What of the Third World, which is generally less well-endowed with fossil fuels? Gigantic though the energy crisis will undoubtedly become for these poorest of nations, I have chosen not to treat the Third World separately although, indeed perhaps because, the thesis set out above would only have been further reinforced had I done so. In a later chapter I deal with the dilemma of 'development' as it affects the Third World but, for the time being, it will suffice to point out that all worlds—First, Second and Third—are going to confront the same problem, only with greatly differing survival kits.

This sub-chapter has been all about oil, although the chart below contains information on other sources of energy which, in total at least, exceed the contribution from oil. Why, then, has oil alone been singled out as one of the three 'key' depletables? Why cannot the other energy sources take up the slack as the oil runs out? Table IV provides a synoptic answer:

Table IV
Substitutability of Energy Sources
Source: Adapted by author from IEA

Targets	Oil	Coal	Gas	Nuclear	Hydro.	W&W	Solar	Geoth.
Oil	n/a	Y	T	P	P	P	P	P
Coal	T	n/a	T	P	P	P	P	P
Gas	T	Y	n/a	P	P	P	P	P
Nuclear	T	Y	T	n/a	Y	Y	Y	Y
Hydro	TP	Y	TP	Y	n/a	n/a	n/a	n/a
W&W	n/a	Y	n/a	n/a	n/a	n/a	n/a	n/a
Solar	n/a	Y	n/a	n/a	n/a	n/a	n/a	n/a
Geothermal	n/a	Y	n/a	n/a	n/a	n/a	n/a	n/a

Y = Yes; 'n/a' ('not applicable') predominates in hydro-wave-solar-geothermal, where the presently installed capacity or the current technology or geographical, geological and meteorological conditions do not offer the prospect of early and large-scale substitution, if ever. Leaving aside the all-important matter of technological constraints, 'n/a' refers to the 'non-fungible' nature of energy sources: cod fishermen in Nova Scotia cannot benefit from solar abundance on the steppes of central Asia, any more than Turkic sheep herders will derive comfort from wave power in the western Atlantic—the 'Kirghizistan-Bay of Fundy Syndrome'. To be sure, new sources and fuel economy in one region can affect the *global* energy equation, but the causality is highly indirect and theoretical.

No clarification of T('Temporary only') is needed: it denotes, of course, the non-renewable nature of oil and gas. P('Partly only'), however, most certainly requires elaboration. Note that Oil-Coal-Gas occupy their own tight little highlighted corner of the chart, and that the 'Partly only' pigeon-holes apply uniquely to them. Why? Surely the other sources of energy can combine to provide full and perfect substitutes once the technology is available? This is a question of transcendental importance to humanity and yet it has unaccountably gone unasked. And the answer? The answer is, no—they cannot. And why?

The Carbon Factor

Carbon: they contain no carbon. And whereas carbon in the form of the dioxide is a foul pollutant of the air we breathe and an unwelcome greenhouse gas, carbon *as an element* is an indispensable agent in thousands of industrial processes and a major physical component of most of today's non-metallic products. So starkly does this property of oil, coal and gas—the hydrocarbons—differentiate them from all other forms of energy that I marvelled, as I researched this chapter, that this simple but overwhelmingly important distinction had eluded the attention of the professional energy optimists—the windmill and wave-power aficionados. Our dependence on oil—and to a lesser, extent, gas—as the most convenient source of energy is so central to our economies and has such a high profile in our lives, that the other roles of carbon—as a vital element in practically every aspect of contemporary life—have never reached even the lowest threshold of public awareness. As we shall now see, these other uses of carbon must be made to occupy in the public's perception a prominence at least as great as does our reliance on it as a source of energy.

Until the twentieth century, most human artifacts were fabricated from 'traditional' materials—metal, wood, glass, leather, bone and clay; while paint, oils, medicine, fertilisers and chemicals were derived variously from plants, animals and mineral ores. Friedrich Wohler created the first 'man-made' substance as long ago as 1848 when he synthesized urea, a now widely used intermediate which holds only one carbon atom; but it was not until the early years of this century that chemists and physicists began to learn the arts of molecular engineering. These advances opened up the possibility of creating an infinite array of organic, i.e. carbon-based, compounds, the vast majority of which, though themselves totally useless, provided stepping-stones to a process whereby new and useable materials were hatched in the laboratory in exponentially growing abundance. In the words of Barry Commoner: 'The prewar scientific revolution produced, in modern physics and chemistry, sciences capable of manipulating nature—of creating, for the first time on earth, wholly new forms of matter.'[11]

Today, oil is easily the most important of the hydrocarbons in providing the feedstocks for the organic chemical industry, which produces the intermediate materials for the manufacture of everything from aspirin to polyethylene, rubber to artificial hip-joints, and asphalt to tooth-brushes. As much as 80% of all these organic chemicals are derived from petroleum feedstocks: in 1993 the United States consumed 1 22 *million metric tons* of hydrocarbon feedstocks while world production of plastics and synthetic fibres in 1992 totalled 78 million metric tons. It is in this light that the inevitable exhaustion of oil reserves, probably some time in the twenty-first century, should be assessed because we can't make tarmac and medicines, aviation fuel and plastics out of solar energy or wind power.

Table IV above shows that only coal, alone of the hydrocarbons and alone of what we still unhelpfully lump together as undifferentiated 'energy sources', can—in terms of its chemical properties—substitute *all* the other sources. Furthermore, coal reserves are so much greater than those of oil and gas that the comparative estimates are almost meaningless: Table V borrows the *Limits to Growth* method of illustrating the range in the number of years of reserves, based on static use or exponential growth in use, to yield the following values:

Table V
Hydrocarbon Reserves Expressed in Years
Source: The Limits to Growth

	Static Use	Current Exponential
Oil	31	20
Gas	38	22
Coal	2300	111

Since the likely value for coal would seem to lie somewhere in the upper three- to lower four-figure range, within which some astronomers have predicted the statistical likelihood of an collision involving the earth and a marauding asteroid, a prudent person might be forgiven for choosing to regard coal reserves as—for all practical planning purposes—infinite. Consequently, the issue will turn on the availability of technology, the probable economics and the ecological tolerability of an eventual—in effect, total—replacement of oil and gas by coal for all organic fuels and feedstocks. The Fischer-Tropsch process to convert coal into liquid fuels was used in Germany during World War II; but there are the gravest doubts whether it will be feasible to produce and process coal on a scale adequate to replace present consumption of oil and gas in the second half of the twenty-first century, without even contemplating the *additional* requirements for primary energy and feedstocks which a further five billion people will generate by the year 2050. And there is, of course, the geopolitical angle: the coal is most abundant in the Northern Hemisphere—in North America and Europe, Russia, Ukraine and China; and—in the Southern Hemisphere—principally in Australia, India and southern Africa with only small reserves in Latin America.

Finally, let us return to the first paragraph. As the earth's oil reserves become more and more problematic and production drops even while demand will still be growing, there will be intense financial and military competition for those last barrels; and it is most probable that the theatre for this competition will be the Middle East. The reasons are simple. By that time, probably towards the year 2050, other present or prospective Third World producer-exporting countries in Latin America, West Africa and Southeast Asia will have ceased exporting—perhaps even pumping—and will have diverted what is left to domestic imperatives, and to the carbon equation. Other major producers, such as Russia and China, will probably also have withdrawn from the international oil trade for the same reasons; and it is unimaginable that either of these two giants could be the object of neo-mercantilist incursions and military adventurism by the great oil have-nots of the era, which will be the United States and Canada, Europe and Japan (for the reasons cited above, the Third World will scarcely be in contention).

The present West will be more likely than any others to have begun the inexorable switch to coal, if indeed the immense obstacles alluded to earlier can be overcome; but it is quite unrealistic to expect that progress in such a transition will—by that time—have come anywhere close to compensating for the loss of the comfortable abundance of cheap oil and gas to which the West has become accustomed. And even if the United States and Canada had meanwhile taken the wise precaution of capping all their wells so as to squirrel away reserves for later and less profligate end-uses than burning, the Middle East would still beckon—with the combined attraction and danger of the region's chronic political weakness and military ineptitude.

And, to repeat an earlier question, what of the Third World, poorly endowed not only with oil but also with coal (India is perhaps the main exception), already suffering in 1994 from a near-insoluble crisis in the supply of fuelwood, and unable to cover without insupportable hard-currency debt the cost of importing oil? And without the military option...

★ ★ ★ ★

I have shown in this chapter that three resources critical either to human survival, or to the way of life we have fashioned out of the twentieth century, are rapidly depleting. Beyond presenting some contemporary statistics on oil reserves and consumption, I have not attempted—it is certainly beyond my competence, indeed beyond anybody's—to forecast the approximate dates when the oil will effectively have run out, and the other two depletables will have become inadequate in both quality and quantity to support the projected number of people. But we don't need dates, and my purpose will have been served if even the professional optimists concede that 'we have a problem'; that the task is now to devise better ways of lighting and heating our world, of moving around it, and without overloading it with consumerist dreck. The task is to prevent the cataclysmic social and economic, political and cultural tensions of the early Third Millennium from becoming catastrophic.

The scale and complexity of these challenges dwarf any previously thrown up in all of history. For this reason, they constitute a challenge to history itself.

Interlude One
Footnote to the Environmental Debate

'Towards what ultimate point is society tending by its industrial progress? When the progress ceases, in what condition are we to expect that it will leave mankind?' John Stuart Mill, 1857

IN 1977 PRESIDENT CARTER commissioned Dr Gerald O. Barney to produce a report on the prospect for the world's environment in the year 2000. *The Global 2000 Report to the President* was published in 1980 and its conclusions are summarised on the first page of Volume I.

'If present trends continue, the world in 2000 will be more crowded, more polluted, less stable ecologically, and more vulnerable to disruption than the world we live in now. Serious stresses involving population, resources and environment are clearly visible ahead. Despite greater material output, the world's people will be poorer in many ways than they are today. For hundreds of millions of the desperately poor, the outlook for food and other necessities of life will be no better. For many it will be worse. Barring revolutionary advances in technology, life for most people on earth will be more precarious in 2000 than it is now—unless the nations of the world act decisively to alter current trends.'[1]

Hermann Kahn, whom we have previously encountered, is reported to have said 'baloney' and proceeded with someone called Julian Simon to respond in 1984 with *The Resourceful Earth—a Response to Global 2000*:

'If present trends continue, the world in 2000 will be *less crowded* (though more populated), *less polluted, more stable ecologically* and *less vulnerable to resource-supply disruption* than the world we live in now. Stresses involving population, resources, and environment *will be less in the future than now*... The world's people will be richer in most ways than they are today... The outlook for food and other necessities of life will be *better*... life for most people on earth will be *less precarious* economically than it is now.'[2] [My emphasis, needless to say.]

This is disingenuous parody. Dr Barney states quite clearly at the outset that the Report's conclusions derive from *projections* not *predictions* of current trends. The *Global 2000* study has three major underlying assumptions of which the most important is that 'the projections assume a general continuation around the world of present public

policy relating to population stabilization, natural resource conservation, and environmental protection.' There is no scare-mongering in
Global 2000 and little has happened in the intervening years either to
discredit Barney or to warrant giving Kahn a decent burial.

Let us invite Professor Andrew Goudie to offer a reconciliation
which will allow extreme partisans of either persuasion to sink their
differences and get on with the business of confronting the Third
Millennium in a realistic mood.

'During the 1980s and 1990s the full significance of possible future
environmental changes has become apparent, and national governments
and international institutions have begun to ponder whether the world
is entering a spasm of unparalleled humanly-induced modification. Our
models and predictions are still highly inadequate, and there are great
ranges in some of the values we give for such crucial changes as sea-level
rise and global climatic warming, but the balance of scientific argument
favours the view that change will occur and that change will be substantial. Some of the changes may be advantageous for humans or for particular eco-systems; other will be extremely disadvantageous. But all
change, if it is rapid and of great magnitude, is likely to create uncertainties and instabilities. The study of future events will not only become
a focus for the environmental sciences, but will also become a major
concern for economists, sociologists, lawyers and political scientists.'[3]

Chapter Six

A Simpler Theory of Universal History

'Society is out of control not only in India, but in many other countries as well.' Roy Calne: *Too Many People*

IHAVE IMPLIED THAT Hegel and Marx were probably right 'at the time', and I referred to the view of Marx as a Christian heretic. Marx's view of History as being an end-state of equilibrium reached through a conscious process of struggle and resolution—the dialectic—extending over all of human existence and yielding a stateless condition of perfect equality, seems to be even more romantically Messianic now that the experiment has run its course and failed.

For most people in the West, this view of history has always been too directional and purposeful—in the jargon, too 'teleological'. It may have seemed compellingly obvious to Marx when all around him lay great slabs of apparent evidence, and when events continued to pile up in support of the view. But Marx's views were conditioned by an eclectic reading of history (and, of course, of Hegel himself) and for precise political aims: ideology, like religion, gets in the way of a better understanding of history and how to control it. Even an unreconstructed Eric Hobsbawm can now write, without seeming to shed a tear, 'how superficial the hold of communism proved to be over the enormous area it had conquered more rapidly than any other *ideology* since Islam... it disappeared from one day to the next with the political regimes which had *imposed it.*' [my emphasis][1] We have seen that neither Hegel's nor Toynbee's theories of history have stood the test as *entire, internally consistent systems*; and that Spengler viewed history as a pathological process with no direction except from birth to death. As for the *predictive* properties he quite uncompromisingly claims for the process, we saw that they are not sustainable in any truly utilitarian sense, except as part of an allegedly pessimistic and irreversible philosophy. Bits and pieces of the writing of each man have relevance to the late twentieth century but they cannot be cobbled into a coherent philosophy of history.

My journey in and out of history, and up to the brink of the millennium, has now led me to a much simpler Universal History; and to the recognition that there are certain constant threads running throughout which—taken together—provide the only consistent basis, valid for all time and in all societies, upon which the attempt may be made to construct an approach to Universal History. Its simplicity gives it strength, the absence of the need for revisionism adds to its reliability, and it has no need of ideological or religious props. Let us now construct the theory by reducing human history to a set of *unarguable* observations about human behaviour—as valid in prehistory as they will be at the End of History. Those who wish to embellish it with meta-physics—with the bells and gongs of ideology and religion—are free to do so: what they cannot do is to dislodge it as an unarguable, unswerving characterisation of human behaviour through history.

For most, indeed for all of recorded history, human beings have exercised varying degrees of 'control' over their destiny. Indeed, the very term 'history' might be understood as an account of the process whereby people have sought to increase that control to the point where it may become very substantial and may even, at different times and in different places, approach a level where it might seem that further progress toward absolute control was no longer either possible or worth the effort, where an assurance of self-preservation had been achieved in all important respects.

This 'control' then—always relative and visible in lesser or greater helpings at different times and in different places—reflects the extent to which human beings have succeeded in grappling with the uncertainty and danger—real or imagined—which they perceive surround them.

The uncertainties, the dangers, are infinite in their number and variety and have been part of the human—even hominid—scenery since prehistory. Numerous and disparate as they are, they fall into three broad categories which all bear upon our primordial instinct for self-preservation. I shall call them the Subsistential, Metaphysical and Power drives: they have historically constituted, and remain to this day, humankind's principal sources of anxiety and the focus, albeit often unconsciously, of our consistent behaviour in seeking to maximise 'control'—to eliminate uncertainty.

These drives are, in fact, related almost sequentially and I shall examine each of them in an order of priority as they would have appeared equally to prehistoric man, as they will now to Western man in the 1990's, providing he is ready to strip down to his mesolithic underwear.

The first—Subsistential—is the most physical and elementary. Food and water, warmth and shelter remain as fundamental to human survival now as they were when fore-runners of *homo sapiens* were learning to lean back, to walk on two legs only and to adapt the front pair to more dexterous purposes.

For most people in the developed Western world in the late twentieth century the Subsistential Drive has become almost subliminal as a result of the dislocation and alienation of people from nature brought about by urbanisation. Food comes from look-alike supermarkets with no visible connexion to, or participation in, processes as remote as 'agriculture' or 'fishing'—indeed, some years ago BBC-TV succeeded in gulling enthralled audiences with a programme purporting to show the annual tree-top spaghetti harvest in northern Italy!

Of course, the process of ensuring adequate food supplies has not been a matter of simply awaiting the arrival of the supermarket; nor did prehistoric people simply become bored with being hunters and fishers (or, as modern archaeology suggests, rival scavengers competing—not with invariable success—with the furry competition) and decide to plant seeds and raise cattle.

It was a complex and infinitely protracted process. Climate and geography, zoological and botanical evolution, anthropology, social and political experiment, language, tool-making and natural disaster—all combined fortuitously in the present Middle East and India to enable an infinitesimally slow and interactive transition from nomadism to a more sedentary economy. Indeed, an end to nomadism required that crops be planted and animals domesticated; while nomadism itself was inconsistent with and inimical to the commitment to 'place' which successful agriculture demanded.

Water issues painlessly from taps in the wall in a process linked to the outside world spectrally only once or twice a year when the water bills have to be paid.

Warmth also comes out of the walls, it no longer has even the most tenuous connexion with fuel-gathering, and the remoteness and complexity of its provenance are in deceptively deadly contrast to its easy availability and low price. Shelter, finally, is available in a degree of comfort and at an affordable price to an unprecedented number of people.

No reckoning of the numbers of 'disadvantaged' people in the West, for whom these fundamental physical requisites may still be in inadequate supply, can detract from the generality of these truths. As J.K. Galbraith has remarked in a rather broader context, 'the production problem', i.e. how to satisfy people's aggregate material needs, 'has largely been solved', and that was over thirty years ago.

The Subsistential Drive is—and I am almost tempted to say 'was'—the most important: 'was' because of the process of abstraction referred to earlier. For most people in the West this drive is at most atavistic, and it has long been replaced by less tangible but more enjoyable proxies such as the Seven Deadly Sins or their late second millennium mutations. This physical drive is present throughout the the animal kingdom; indeed it is the only one which generally actuates the rest of the bestiary and, had it not succeeded through the eons, there would have arisen no need for the other drives.

However, even the sex drive may not qualify for inclusion in the Subsistential: the general historical—and even latterday—mystique of sex and widespread ignorance of sexual aetiology may suggest that, for prehistoric people, sex was something you did when you'd finished hunting, chopping wood and lighting the fire, and had rolled the rock across the cave-mouth to keep out the rest of the Subsistentially driven.

We are told that—to this day—Third World people produce numerous offspring as a form of social security for their declining years; people in the West may do so out of social conformity or as a self-gratifying cloning exercise. Whatever the motivation, the sex drive can never be or have been as urgent and undeniable as those identified as Subsistential, whether we speak of Neanderthal Man or his latterday cousins.

The Subsistential Drive, then, is satisfied when the vagaries of hunting and food-gathering give way before the benefits of greater certainty, i.e. *control*, yielded by sedentary agriculture. The new 'farmers'—neolithic—begin to improve their skills and their productivity. This process creates, in turn, the conditions for larger populations, tentative steps towards political organisation and the notion of private property. It is at this point that language will be conscripted to begin to provide the means to formulate and communicate abstract values and concepts by which people can combine into societies. Whatever the stage of political and economic development—whether nomadic or post-nomadic, whether or not the society has graduated from hunting to agriculture—a prehistoric man's attention would be next directed towards the intangible means at his disposal for enhancing the reliability of his Subsistential control. This is the Metaphysical Drive.

The description 'Metaphysical' of the second drive has an appropriate Aristotelian pedigree in following our discussion of the purely *physical* elements in the Subsistential: 'metaphysics' means just *after physics*, and refers simply to the order in which Aristotle chose to treat the tangible and the intangible. The Metaphysical Drive is engaged when the cave- or camp-fire burns low, the Moon glows between eerie-shaped clouds and round the edges of the rock in the door or the tent-flap, ghoulish noises issue from the Subsistentially-deprived outside, and there is a long night's wait to see if the Sun will rise in the morning; and will there be game within a stone's throw during the day or the rain needed to bring forth fresh green shoots in the newly invented bean-patch?

During the night-watch there will be plenty of time for the cave- or tent-dwellers to reflect. And it would not be long before some of those things outside the cave and beyond the circle of tents came to be the object of special veneration inside. The object of veneration would soon become the means of intecession in a world whose mysteries and terrors must be resolved and its spirits—once created—propitiated by their creators for such unashamedly utilitarian purposes as abundant game, a bounteous crop of beans or a murrain on the enemy in the cave across the valley. That line of veneration—a tenuous trickle welling up behind Stonehenge, the cave paintings of Altamira and at Ayers Rock—winds its way down the years and broadens into a spate river of religion and ritual, myth and magic before debouching on to the absorbent sands of scepticism and natural science in the past two centuries.

Still, the Venerated did their job and some are still at it: Shamash and Mithras, Zeus and Jupiter, the Pharaohs and Buddha, Ceres and Mars, Vishnu, Yahveh and Allah, Almighty God, Jesus Christ and the Blessed Virgin. Less celebrated practitioners, whose names have not survived, have provided equally valuable comfort to men in every society and throughout history: shamans, witch-doctors, black-magicians and voodooists, fortune-tellers and snake-oil salesmen, Druids and spiritualists, and so on down to today's psychiatrists and gurus, pop-stars and probation-workers, hallucinogenic drugs and football matches and all the other social paraphernalia which we in the twentieth century use to help us accommodate our mesolithic brains and bodies to the world our science has created. Faust again.

All of this variegated social apparatus, whether delivered in sublime Gothic cathedrals or Shinto shrines, in cheap Bible tracts or cloudy phials, has helped people to calm their apprehensions and, by prescribing ritual and method and authority—*magic* which, as Malinowski shows, can be proved actually to work for the society which practises it—has served to enhance our sense of control over our environment at another level and in a move towards the spiritual realms inhabited by Hegel and Toynbee.

We have arrived, then, at the point where the Subsistential and the Metaphysical Drives are working in harmony. There is, of course, overlap and slippage, reinforcement and conflict. But there is no other tension in the logic and compulsion of this process and it is not conceivable that prehistoric man would one day have emerged into the historic era unless these drives had—quite simply—succeeded; unless, that is, he had begun to assert and achieve control over his environment.

I mentioned earlier the notion of (private) property when discussing the Subsistential Drive. Whether we talk of hunting and fishing rights, reserved to a tribe or some similar grouping, or of fields planted and pasture managed by post-nomadic farmers and graziers, the concept of property would be a prerequisite for emergence into the historic era. Property means 'own-ness', i.e. something appropriated by force or agreement from the rest of the 'society' by a segment of that society for its private and privileged use.

By extension, it may come to include a 'something', newly asserted by one society as belonging to it as a matter of right, against the vigorous dissension to the contrary by another, rival society.

This is the arena of political, economic, ideological, religious, commercial and social rivalry and it is called the Power Drive.

For most of recorded history, it is the very stuff of history: battles, kings and queens, rebellions, plottings and conspiracies, invasions, treason, massacres, religion and idolatry, sieges and embargoes, tyranny and liberty, apostasy, revolution, parliaments and senates, statesmen and generals, mercantilism, Inquisition and the Index Expurgatorius, plagues and famine, strikes and lock-outs, victory and defeat, commercial television and Joseph Goebbels.

All of them have to do with the contest between men for the possession of *property* in its widest possible sense, tangible and intangible: land and natural resources, legislation, justice and taxation, fishing-grounds and trading privileges, patents and licences, slavery, the conscription of armies and, not least, men's minds.

It has to do with *greed* and *intolerance*, *fear* and *cultural arrogance* in varying degrees of malignity—with the wish to deny to others that which they have and wish to keep, and to exercise control by imposing and enforcing all manner of conformity: wars of religion and ideology, multi-national investment and merchandising, propaganda and radio-jamming, foreign aid and missionaries, GATT and CAP, satellite television, metres-kilograms-litres, Celsius, Esperanto and worldspeak, universal electrical plugs, Macdonalds, Coke and all the rest of the levelled geosuburban moonscape.

The Power Drive, and its results, provide the most visible evidence of humanity's tenure of the Earth. The objective of the Subsistential Drive is too elemental to need further embroidery; while the Metaphysical dealt—and I use the past tense advisedly—with human fears and ignorance which modern science and enquiry have now largely banished so that they now afflict only those who wish to cling to unworthy and discredited creeds. I shall leave it to others to sublimate or convert this Metaphysic into a nobler and more philosophical ethic for man's future guidance.

What has the Power Drive achieved? How will the world of 2001 now appear as a result of its operation? Does the Power Drive represent the end-game of human endeavour—the rest of History being now but variations on this theme? Was it inevitable that the Power Drive would deliver man to the very gate of Fukuyama's Promised Land—the liberal democracy practised by most of the West and, if Fukuyama is correct, emulated by most of the rest of the world on the eve of the third millennium? Has third millennium humanity arrived at the end of history, or is there more to do, more to be, somewhere else to go? And if the Power Drive has been so successful in enabling human beings to control their universe, why has the great endeavour now gone sour?

Chapter Seven

Back to the Future with an Historical Discursion

'Joyfully the mobs accepted the name; took up the cry: Simpletons! Yes, yes! I'm a simpleton! Are you a simpleton? We'll build a town and we'll name it Simple Town, because by then all the smart bastards that caused all this, they'll be dead! Simpletons! Let's go! This ought to show 'em! Anybody here not a simpleton? Get the bastard, if there is!' Walter M. Miller Jr: *A Canticle for Leibowitz*

EARLIER I POSED CERTAIN QUESTIONS about history and how various explanations of the forces which have driven it now stood. I then established that a number of aberrations and divergences from the comfortable path of history have arisen since the mid- to late-nineteenth century to the point where they have graduated from having merely nuisance-value status and are now interrogating traditional Western assumptions about progress. Parts of Hegel's and Toynbee's theories were then salvaged for possible later use; but I then proceeded to identify and to examine at some length a number of symbols and consequences of the very success of the Western liberal-democratic system which were now interfering with currently fashionable notions of the End of History. Certainly our reincarnated Hegel has not emerged unblinking and unscathed into the late twentieth century; and although I dismissed Spengler's claim that his system was predictive of history—in the sense of being literally usable for 'historical management'—it seems that much of which he spoke has already come unerringly close to the truth, or seems set to do so.

More awkwardly, did it mean—I wondered—that the tocsins were now sounding over my own preferred theory of Universal History? The reflection of a moment suggests that they remain silent: after all, the Control theory of history elaborated earlier—with its three interrelated Drives—did *not* require that the last of the three, the Power Drive, necessarily *succeed*. In fact, the strength of the Control theory lies very much in the complete absence from it of any notions of destiny, purpose and 'success': it is resolutely descriptive and agnostic. What it *did* say was that the first, the Subsistential, was indispensable while the second, the

Metaphysical, was of only a second order of importance in beckoning human beings out of the cave and inviting them to step into history. The third, the Power Drive, was what they then began to do in their spare time, and that was bound to cause a ruckus.

What can we then say of the Power Drive today? The Power Drive has always been, unlike the other two, measurable and volatile; but although, by its very nature, it would always tend to operate in the direction of continued expansion (because, as Fukuyama says of modern natural sciences, they cannot be forgotten or disinvented), and into areas of historical low-pressure, it is neither equipped with inevitability nor insulated from reversals. Indeed, *reversal* itself implies a deviation from some preordained historical path. Let us take an historical discursion and try to find an example of an extraordinary and cataclysmic historical episode to see whether it and its fallout can tell us anything about the impending tribulations of the very early third millennium.

I rejected some candidates which at first sight seemed promising: the fall of the Roman Empire, for instance, was *not* the single, sudden event which folklore and some book and film titles tend to imply happened when Alaric sacked Rome in 410: the Empire went on creating future instalments of history for a thousand years and it therefore lacks the impact of a precise historical casualty which triggered off a series of after-shocks and reactions. The Great Depression fails for similar reasons: enormous in its destructiveness and complex in its causes but, in the event, too diffuse, and its 'cure' cannot be unravelled from the economic stimulation of World War II. As for the World Wars themselves, they are too close and an inextricably permanent part of the late twentieth century landscape to be viewed apart: they're with us for good. Hernan Cortes' exploits in Mexico come close to qualifying as an isolatable event—and most indisputably one which was catastrophic for the Aztecs—but even the greatest land-grab in history lacks the required symmetry of crisis-and-outcome.

But the Black Death scores on all counts: it has a starting date, it was cataclysmic, it had to be dealt with, people reacted to it, it ran its course, and it ended—to all intents and purposes—at a date which, allowing for the imprecision of much medieval history, is definable. As to its aftermath, it is true that historians will still argue whether it did, in fact, have any aftermath *at all*, since evidence of it lies buried beneath many acre-feet of complex social and economic changes; and it is true that most histories contain remarkably scant discussion of the plague. But it is this very silence which makes the Black Death such a fitting candidate: for how could an event of such monstrousness have been either paltry in its consequences or so easily finessed by medieval society?

The Black Death

None of our world-historians comments on the arrival of the plague in Europe or on its impact on the population of that generation and those which succeeded it. (I can imagine that Hegel would have detected the hand of God at work as He set out first to punish those who had corrupted His Church and then to lay the foundation for the Reformation a century-and-a-half later; however, he might have had trouble explaining why the same punishment should have been meted out to millions of Chinese and Indian infidels several years earlier.)

There is little lengthy or systematic treatment of the cataclysm in most of the standard historical texts; and I am therefore indebted to Philip Ziegler and his splendid book *The Black Death*, first published in 1969, for part of the following narrative, and I shall follow his example in disclaiming any major original research. (Although over half of Ziegler's book has to do with the British Isles, there are good statistical reasons for this, and he makes it clear that the plague seems to have behaved impartially in all but a few isolated parts of Europe.)

The Plague originated around the mountainous lake Issyk-Kul in Kirghizistan where the Black Death bacillus *Pasteurella Pestis* had long parasitized the flea *Xenopsylla Cheopsis* for whom certain rodents were home. Why these hairy hosts decided to leave the lake around 1338 is uncertain; what is clear is that the plague was already raging there when they set off to infest China and India to the east and south while another platoon headed off along the Silk Route to the Crimea where the Plague erupted in 1346. Here, a small colony of Genoese traders had established a fortified trading post named Feodosia in honour of the Emperor Theodosius I, who had made Christianity the official religion of the Eastern Roman Empire a thousand years earlier. For neither the first nor the last time in Europe, this minority was convicted by the indigenous majority—of Tartars—of responsibility for a natural disaster. The besieged Genoese, infected with the cadavers of Plague victims which had been catapulted into their fortress, were forced to flee in their galleys out of the Black Sea and into the Mediterranean.

Here, at Genoa in January 1348, Ziegler quotes a Flemish chronicler:

'Three galleys put in... driven by a fierce wind from the East, horribly infected and laden with a variety of spices and other valuable goods. When the inhabitants of Genoa learnt this, and saw how suddenly and irremediably they infected other people, they were driven forth from that port by burning arrows and divers engines of war... Thus they were scattered from port to port.'[1] Genoa will probably not have been the only or even the first orifice through which the Black Death infiltrated Europe; nor was the black rat the only means of transmission since the flea could itself survive without its host over a lengthy period of time and journey. Nor would primitive medieval medicine immediately have made the connexion between the rodent carrier and the incidence of the disease when rats dead and alive 'no doubt littered the streets and houses... [and were unworthy] of attention at a time when dead human beings were so much more conspicuous.'[2] Furthermore, the Plague came in three varieties—bubonic, pulmonary and septicaemic—which could only add more confusion to such paltry diagnostic skills as might have been available; and rarely did the disease, in whatever form, fail to result in a rapid, agonising and revolting death.

As the Black Death began to spread through the Continent, what was the condition of the victims who lay in its path? The Renaissance of the twelfth and thirteenth centuries was at an end and there were deep-seated social and economic tensions resulting from population growth. A.R. Myers says of England that the financial burden of the Hundred Years' War had already begun to force many great landholders to commute labour dues for rents even though 'the peasant population had apparently been so numerous before the Black Death'[3]; and G.M. Trevelyan makes it clear that this trend was apparent much earlier in the fourteenth century in response to a levelling-off in population growth.[4] Ziegler suggests that by the middle of the thirteenth century 'Europe was becoming uncomfortably over-crowded'[5] and that, by the time of the Plague, these pressures and a string of appalling summers and disastrous harvests had brought about a recession throughout most of Europe. 'Europe... was now suffering the physical and mental malaise which inevitably follows so intemperate a progress [over the previous two-hundred years]... and chronic over-population was rendering intolerable the existence of many, if not a majority of Europeans.'[6] We *may* be seeing the beginning of a tension between town and country: great estates which had begun in the thirteenth century to diversify from mere subsistence farming to producing for the market, as villages were turning into towns, were perhaps now becoming less able to feed both the rural peasantry and growing urban populations drawn from the country by industry. But this argument can be misleading: there seems to be no general proof that over-population produced consequences which would be familiar to us today, i.e. widespread starvation and social dislocation; and Ziegler cites evidence that the social effect of over-population was more likely to be under-employment. He does, however, conclude that malnutrition can quite easily have co-existed with relative abundance and that it would have been a factor in reducing resistance to the Plague.

By 1350, then, virtually all Europe had been reached by the Plague. This was merely the first but incomparably the worst of a succession of pestilential waves which washed across Europe over the following fifty years. Mortality was uneven with rates ranging from a few percent to—in some cases—complete annihilation, but overall it seems that about one person in three would have been felled by the Black Death with a probably higher incidence amongst the elderly. It was otherwise indiscriminate and seems to have thrived in the filth and congestion of the towns, and equally in the country where—in addition to wiping out huge swathes of the peasantry—it fatally weakened the monastic system which sheltered such a large proportion of the nation's literate population; particularly savage also were its effects on the universities of Oxford and Cambridge and on the continent where mortality amongst (generally older) faculty members would have been higher than amongst scholars. In England, the Ordinance and Statute of Labourers passed at the height of the first assault of the pestilence were intended to contain wages between floors and ceilings prescribed by specially appointed judges, and to try to reintroduce stability into a rural economy which was, however, already in flux well before the Plague struck.

It may be melodramatic to try to characterise the mood of the entire fourteenth century populace as it confronted the Black Death: Chaucer paints a frequently prosperous picture of contemporary society but then he was himself a man of cheerful and optimistic disposition. He was also intensely critical of priestly excesses, but at a time when a neo-Augustinian gloom may indeed have cloaked the landscape. Perhaps, but at the risk of tendentiousness, we may agree with Ziegler that, on top of the ordinary person's economic problems, 'The Black Death descended on a people who were drilled by their theological and scientific training into a reaction of apathy and fatalistic resignation.'[7] On the other hand, this evidence of God's power and of His willingness indiscriminately to punish the innocent for the sins of the wicked could have been seen by a resentful populace to highlight the powerlessness of the Church on earth, in the form of its clergy, to offer any protection to the laity: the priesthood was manifestly unable to intercede successfully on behalf of the parishioners. Moreover—and this is where the tensions between landlord and villein, and the villein's incontestable economic and eventual political gains must be seen in parallel—it appears that the rich, for all the protection which high walls might have been expected to afford them, were shown no special mercy by the Plague. Indeed, even more ignominious was the indignity of their deaths. It is therefore not unrealistic to see the late fourteenth century as a time when mighty blows were being delivered on the Establishment; and that although evidence for this is more abundant for England with its unique wealth of contemporary archival material, Ziegler is probably on balance correct in believing that the picture in Europe would not, in the very broadest terms, have been very different. Perhaps the peasants' sense of social injustice was aroused and their expectations not only raised but, indeed, partly gratified; perhaps, however, we are expecting too much of a mainly agrarian population whose masses were illiterate and, lacking historical bearings, rarely looked forward beyond the next harvest and ensuing winter, or backward behind the last village festivity. Viewed in the context of longer-term historical trends and pressures, we can join Ziegler in concluding that 'the Black Death did no more than accelerate, though often violently accelerate, an established and, in the long run, inevitable progress.'[8]

But how could future progress remain possible with a third of the population liquidated—as if no fewer than nineteen million people had gone to their graves in the United Kingdom between 1980 and 1990? After all, the imminent fifteenth century—the Quattrocento—was to be a century of spectacular growth and renaissance throughout Europe and, as we have seen, of the genesis of its conquest by one means or another of the entire world. Did the Renaissance not need people to fuel that expansion?

The answer is, of course, that progress did demand the proper conjunction of talent and opportunity but that it did not require an absolute number of people to make the fourteenth century mass go critical in the fifteenth. We have not located or even identified the trigger to Toynbee's 'challenge-and-response', or to Hegel's 'Spirit' or 'Idea' and we never shall. We can say that there appears to have existed in the fourteenth century, before the events of 1349-50, a degree of over-population which, while not exceeding the capacity of the land to feed, certainly exceeded the powers and the needs of the economy to employ. This meant that there was either a good deal of enforced sloth which the actively engaged economy could subsidise; or a large measure of under-employment—of the type familiar to travellers in Franco's Spain, Brezhnev's USSR or in today's India. The loss of part or all of this possibly less motivated and unproductive element in the population; the longer working-day of the survivors; or the greater incentives which ownership of the same amount of land and capital by a smaller population created—some combination of these forces was the way in which society not only compensated for the loss of mere numbers but, into the bargain, possibly, just possibly, created the elusive spark. Fourteenth-century Europe was a simple, atomised—or certainly a pre-molecular—society. It undoubtedly had its complexities; but there would have been an extremely low level of economic interdependence between villages and hamlets operating at subsistence and isolated from all but their immediate curtilage by poor roads, lack of transport, rules of servitude and—above all—absence of curiosity. Only at the interface of country and the now-expanding towns was this beginning to change and it is this which would become a dynamising feature of the following century.

The Black Death was a holocaust unprecedented in Europe's history and, in the scale of its slaughter, of far greater savagery than any subsequent event until the Great Irish Famine of 1845-52. And yet its horror was not reflected in lasting damage—even the contrary. As I remarked many pages ago, 'there are no redeeming features in population growth' *per se*, and it is clear that the principal—brutal—explanation of the fourteenth century's ability to shrug off the loss of so much of its population is that it simply didn't need them.

This judgement is even more valid in any of today's worlds—First, Second or Third. We simply don't *need* our *present* numbers, let alone the other 5-billion already on the way. Unfortunately, the world has long lost the shielding innocence and simplicity with which Europe responded to the challenge of the Black Death.

Interlude Two
The Machine Age: the View in 1880

THIS BOOK HAS BEEN as much about proportion and speed and quantity, and how humanity has tried to handle their changes since 1875, as anything else. Here is a contemporary view of the Machine from *Everybody's Pocket Cyclopaedia*, published in London around 1880.

The Motive Force of the World.

The Bureau of statistics in Berlin issued in 1877 some interesting information in connexion with this subject. It appears that four-fifths of the engines now working in the world have been constructed during the last 25 years. France owns 49,590 stationary or locomotive boilers, 7,000 locomotives, and 1,850 boats' boilers; Germany has 59,000 boilers, 10,000 locomotives, and 1,700 ships' boilers; Austria 12,000 boilers and 2,800 locomotives. The force equivalent to the working steam-engines represents—in the United States 7,500,000-horse-power, in England 7,000,000 horse-power, in Germany 4,500,000 in France 3,000,000, and in Austria 1,500,000 horse-power. In these figures the motive power of the locomotives is not included, whose number in all the world amounts to 105,000, representing a total of 3,000,000 horse-power. Adding this amount to the other powers we obtain the total of 46,000,000 horse-power. A steam horse-power is equal to three actual horses' power; and a living horse is equal to seven men. The steam engines of the world represent, therefore, approximately the work of 1,000,000,000 men, or more than double the working population of the earth, whose total population amounts to 1,455,923,000 inhabitants. Steam has accordingly trebled man's working power, enabling him to economize his physical strength while attending to his intellectual development.

'Pig awheel' by Andrzej Dworakowski
A fanciful portrayal of the Consumer Economy.
The Pig is gorging himself and hurtling with gathering speed on a
ramshackle vehicle towards an unknown destination.

Chapter Eight

Global Village: Economics in Wonderland

'The Dodo suddenly called out 'The race is over!' and they all crowded round it, panting, and asking, 'But who has won?' This question the Dodo could not answer without a great deal of thought, and it sat for along time with one finger pressed upon its forehead... while the rest waited in silence. At last the Dodo said 'Everybody has won, and all must have prizes.' Lewis Carroll: *Alice's Adventures in Wonderland*

'The cost of human labour cannot, for any length of time, be reduced below the cost of keeping human beings alive at the minimum level regarded as acceptable in their society, or indeed at any level. Human beings are not efficiently designed for a capitalist system of production. The higher the technology, the more expensive the human component of production compared to the mechanical.' Eric Hobsbawm: *Age of Extremes: the Short Twentieth Century 1914-1991*

'Western man has escaped for the moment the poverty which was for so long his all-embracing fate [but]... the affluent country which conducts its affairs with rules of another and poorer age also forgoes opportunities. And in misunderstanding itself, it will, in any time of difficulty, prescribe for itself the wrong remedies.' John Kenneth Galbraith: *The Affluent Society*

UNFORTUNATELY, NOT MANY of those thousand million souls in Interlude Two were, in the event, unshackled from their steam-engines and boilers and set free to pursue their intellectual development, despite the success of the machines in multiplying their numbers in the ensuing century at a rate which exceeded even that of the machine-minders. In this chapter I shall be examining how machine and minder have been faring since then.

In earlier chapters we have ranged over the linked twentieth-century forces of environmental destruction, the depletion of a trio of key natural resources—the only ones that matter indispensably—and exponential population growth—whose scale and seeming intractability now directly contradict certain notions, such as that contained in current End-of-History theory, that the West has triumphantly steered the ship of entire human history into the safe harbour of a liberal democratic economy where—so the credo asserts—all peoples have signified a wish to find a permanent haven. Not only does the theory assert that the entire non-Western world has expressed this wish: contained also in both End-of-History theory and the acts and utterances of governments and international agencies—or, perhaps more eloquently, in their silences—is the assumption that the earth is fully capable of delivering universal levels of Western-style consumption to pullulating numbers even as economic tidal-waves prepare to break over the shores of political humbug and complacency in the third millennium.

The first two of these forces are the direct corollary of the domination of human beings by a form of self-reinforcing economic activity which has long passed out of the control of the governments of the day, by any nation-state, or by that strangely ill-defined and ineffective creation of the late twentieth century, so beloved of the media, the so-called *international community*. The third force—the population explosion—is both a fuel to the process of economic enslavement and a result of it, as technology and the unbridled operation of 'the market' enable growing numbers of people to be sustained—albeit in battery conditions of urban and rural squalor unmatched since the Middle Ages—by gouging unhealable wounds into today's environment and nailing tomorrow's children to a global crucifix of civil strife and deprivation bequeathed by the economic and industrial monstrosities of this century.

The time has come to examine the arena where these forces are now assembling for their final collision: and then—in the last chapter—to review the means we have, or must bolt together, to confront them. The arena is the Economics of Wonderland which the twentieth century has conjured out of a nature which might once have willingly yielded up so much to a less arrogant and nest-fouling species. The forces are economic and are now being driven remorselessly by an imperative whose origin lies in the industrial revolution of the eighteenth and nineteenth centuries but which then found massive reinforcement in Western society's success during the twentieth century in suborning through technology our species from a form of economic activity sustainable in both form and scale.

There is no convenient ideological confessional box here, no absolution: neither today's Western free-marketeers, whose public-relations engineers have so successfully managed to project private consumption and consumer choice as touchstones of democracy, nor advocates of yesterday's centrally planned economies will take much comfort from one of Fukuyama's few acknowledgements of the inimical relationship between industrialisation and the environment: 'Among the most notable products of advanced industrialization are significant levels of pollution and environmental damage... Despite various theories blaming ecological damage either on capitalism or socialism, experience has shown that neither economic system is particularly good for the environment'[1]—an acknowledgement which is both belated and reluctant, as well as minimalist. I use the term 'economics' here as a shorthand to mean the now prevalent form of human economic organisation based upon maximising industrial and agricultural production and consumption through the application of capital, technology and marketing in pursuit of what are—unfortunately— perfectly legitimate private corporate goals. They are, however, goals which have been mutated by government into a set of social aims which include full employment as the norm—yet accompanied contradictorily by targetting continuous 'gains' in productivity (i.e. getting more product out of each unit of labour and capital)—and indefinitely rising standards of living without observance of the elementarily obvious mathematical notion of *limit* when applied to the world's ecology. There's the Faustian bargain: government sanction of untrammelled economic activity which delivers *panem et circenses* to the people who have elected them through the closed loop of democracy. Fukuyama does not do so well here: 'The communist world's truly abysmal environmental record suggests that what is most effective in protecting the environment is neither capitalism nor socialism, but democracy.'[2] There is a fatal flaw in Fukuyama's logic here since he goes on to propose 'A second line of argument explaining why economic development should produce democracy'.[3]

Everything that has gone before and will be adduced in the rest of this chapter constitutes an indictment that must be answered: that if indeed democracy, including accountable and responsible government, and economic development proceed in lock-step—and that this is why the pairing is so attractive to the 'developing world'—then why have they been quite unable as yet to find reconciliation with the environment upon which they gorge themselves? Once merely a Western symptom, the sublimation of economics has now been copycatted throughout most of the contactable rest of the world; but, as we shall see, most of that rest-of-the-world lacks the combination of natural, geographic, climatic and other less tangible resources—all the ingredients of history—with which the West *as a whole* has been blessed and which lies at the heart of Western economic domination.

Hidden away in the undergrowth of Economic Wonderland are the cant and platitudes—recited *ad nauseam*—of a host of politicians, civil servants, diplomats, businessmen, academics, sociologists and international functionaries who have fostered—or, at least, acquiesce in—the notion that today's world is now indeed a neat bourgeois global village economy stretching from Somerset to Somalia, from Massachusetts to Mogadishu all decked out, or eager to do so, in Western garb, just what history had—all along—been contriving it to become: supermarket theosophies and universalised material expectations which political expediency has in its hypocrisy legitimised. We will look at the world's economy as I write this in 1994, and examine a number of major international politico-economic falsehoods and absurdities, perpetrated frequently through the parrotting of slogans for political ends which cloak it and which have gained such destructive currency—more or less since World War II—as to have become icons which only serve to demote the crucial issues which challenge us, and therefore seduce us into denying or deferring the need for a proper response. What is the state of the world's economy? Where is it going? And is anybody running it?

But we must first try to trace the process whereby economics has come centre-stage in motivating seemingly all human political and social activity. When was *homo sapiens* displaced by *homo economicus universalis*? When did economics and economic activity finally succeed in usurping some higher value in human affairs and, cuckoo-like, turf out our historic preoccupation with higher concerns? Or is the very question elitist: did humankind ever have higher concerns and why should our principal concern *not* be the striving for ever greater and more secure material comfort? After all, this is what we earlier called the Subsistential Drive and surely the work of most of humanity has always been essentially materialist in nature; and that same majority has never, it may fairly be argued, been preoccupied with 'higher concerns', the *intellectual development* of Interlude 2—with the creation of art and literature, music and philosophy. As consumers, yes; as creators, no; and even then, only that minority of people with time on their hands.

A remote 'back-marker' to answering this question is the date suggested in Chapter One—1450 or so—when the West set out on its mission to capture history. We then charted the course of that mission as it accelerated towards its triumphalist crescendo in the nineteenth and twentieth centuries. Increasingly as those five hundred years slipped by, we would have noted a phenomenon novel not so much in type but certainly in quantity and influence, namely the emergence, side-by-side with the natural scientists, of a growing number of political philosophers and economists—Mun and Hobbes, John Locke and Adam Smith, David Ricardo and Thomas Malthus, Montesquieu and Thomas Jefferson, Thomas Paine and Robert Owen, Karl Marx and Friedrich Engels, Jeremy Bentham and John Stuart Mill, culminating in the twentieth century in the establishment of the Church of Keynes and the ordination of its celebrants by the thousand who would go forth into the world with the gift of forked tongues; and we witnessed the creation of the (Western) nation-state with its arrogation of economic control and the growing dependence of the state on economic performance for the creation of military power and its outward projection: this is, of course, the third of our historical engines—the Power Drive. At the same time, irresistible gains in the natural sciences; the spread of democratic ideas, aspirations and expectations; industrialisation and urbanisation; communications, universal suffrage, the colonial experience, literacy, banking and demonetised currency, limited liability companies and population growth—all these combined to sweep away non-material ethics—for example, whatever function religion might still have played at the centre of people's view of the world and their role in it—and to subordinate them—to conscript them—in the higher service of economics.

Thomas Malthus' forebodings of 1798 were duly pigeon-holed and the realisation of his worst fears postponed by a combination of three fortuitous and *historically quite unrepeatable* factors: the soaking-up of surplus population by the new industries, emigration to huge and empty lands controlled by the source-country, and a revolution in agricultural technology and practice. Malthus the moralist would still have been horrified at what he would have perceived as the moral depravity and vice of the working-classes (which had anyway always lain at the root of the curate's writings as a demographer and sociologist); and he could not have seen that these three factors, unknowable in 1798, were to combine some time towards the middle of the nineteenth century into the imperative of *economics*, a remorseless treadmill which would now enlist everybody in the aimless circularity of its motion—the speed of its rotation in ever-increasing frenzy as more and more clambered aboard—and so take charge of History as it loomed, now to be written in quite different ways, out of the twentieth century.

Economics, then, had become king and its crown would eventually glitter over a gigantic scatter of social and cultural clues and by-products. Here are just a few: most Western newspapers rarely featured 'business and economics' as a separate topic or section until well into the twentieth century (the London *Economist* was certainly not a business newspaper when founded in 1843, although the novelty of the name must have reflected the perception by its owners of a marketing niche, whilst the *Financial Times* did not appear until 1888 nor the *Wall Street Journal* until 1889); departments of economics were not established at most universities until this century (the London School of Economics and the Harvard Business School were founded as late as 1895 and 1908 respectively). And most jargon now employed in economics does not appear in dictionaries until well after 1900: in vain—at least, with difficulty—will you search for references to even the most commonplace of today's terms such as 'unemployment', 'gross national product', 'balance of trade', 'comparative advantage' and 'free trade' in most dictionaries much earlier than the Great Depression of the 1930's—an approximate dating which, as we have earlier seen and shall later examine, appears to represent a curtain closing on one historical period and opening on another.

Now let us step through Alice's little door and out into the Economics of Wonderland. The first thing we see is that the treadmill of economics seems most incontrovertibly to have done what treadmills are supposed to do: it has been the instrument whereby human effort and energy have been harnessed to convert the seeds of commercial and industrial inventiveness into year-round cornucopias of products and services of unimaginable quantity and variety. Of course, the treadmill analogy is imperfect: it is coal and oil that power it, but it is human ingenuity which set it going in the first place and it is human obedience to it which now seems unlikely or unable to slow it down. Now, I am no Luddite and share no desire to make it stop (many pages ago I said that I would not happily forgo the benefits which industrialisation had brought *me* in place of an otherwise probably more deprived existence; and even Bill McKibben admitted that the system did not make it easy for him to trade down his big house and car even in the interests of fending off his impending End of Nature: like the rest of us, he's boxed in), but I would like to see it slow down—because I want the best bits to survive.

Many chapters ago also, we used some simple algebraic equations to portray the ability of a system—in this case the Earth—to deliver a given quantity of 'product', and the inputs required by the process: there was nothing wrong with a bit of pollution; nothing wrong in consuming raw materials, even chain-sawing a few forests; nothing wrong in having more people. It was all to do with qualities called *balance* and *proportion*, with *sustainability* and *reverence* for the system—for the fine mechanism which James Lovelock calls Gaia. This chapter has to do with what I called 'international falsehoods and absurdities' in the politics of economics; and they, in the final analysis, have to do with words and meanings and the integrity and motives of those who deal in the sloganeering use of them. As long as the words and catch-phrases which slide so glibly off the tongues of politicians and international social engineers—full employment, growth, development, productivity, free trade, closing the North-South divide and a host of others—remain unchallenged, then those who use them will continue to be able to hide behind the superficially noble but, in practice, unrealistic and destructive objectives which the deceitful language conveys; and the problems they mask will remain and suppurate.

Today's economics depend upon the maximisation without limit of production and productivity, and the consumption of the obsolescing products cascading out of this process by the greatest possible number of people at the lowest possible price consistent with an acceptable return on capital invested. I have unearthed no artifact—with perhaps one solitary exception—to evidence that any nation has now, or ever has had, any clear, articulated long-term plan for its evolution beyond the next election, or putsch: the Soviet Union's silly Gosplans used to speak largely in tones of Stakhanovite bombast; whilst the more sinisterly effective operations of Japan's Ministry of Trade & Industry may, if they be that one exceptional artifact, seem rather forlorn and its objectives doomed in the context of the world's economic prospects in the third millennium. And yet, in a bizarre paradox to the short-termism of nations, most transnational corporations commit colossal human and financial resources to ten- and twenty-year 'strategic plans' and corporate 'mission statements' which set goals for the capture of ever greater shares of limitlessly growing global markets.

This neat arrangement requires immense inputs of fuel and raw materials at minimum cost to the process, including the cost of labour and the cost to the environment—the latter cost known to economists by the exciting term 'externalities' and thus well calculated to provoke apathy the world over. However, in order for all of the products produced in the process to clear the market, there must be adequate income (and, therefore, employment) available to exchange for them whilst that income will only be generated, of course, by the employment of huge numbers of people in the production process... and so *ad infinitum*. Such a system long ago became holy writ, but it is replete with internal contradictions and external tensions.

The system has 'got away' with the contradictions and tensions because it delivers nicely packaged things which people have been conditioned to want and because consumerism wins elections in the West: there are not yet any other vote-getters. And envious expectations in much of the rest of the world serve comparable purposes and foreshorten human objectives into politically manageable horizons. Almost nowhere—First World, Second or Third—has there generally survived a non-material competitor for man's allegiance; and where there *may* have, for instance in the Islamic world, there now seethes an Islamic strain of social tension within itself and with the world at its gates. What I have earlier called this *economic imperative* effectively saw off the Malthusian nightmare in the middle of the nineteenth century and not only prevented the collapse of European societies with booming populations but proceeded to create in the West and Japan a consumeristic culture of hitherto inconceivable scale which has now reached into even the most recalcitrant recesses. But a culture, also, of inherent fragility.

Our Western and East Asian populations need the economic imperative for their very survival, whilst the system itself can operate in its own logic only through a total yet dimly perceived commitment to it by people and government and institutions to a degree which, future historians will conclude, borders on statism—however daubed it be with the polychrome of the free-market economy. J.K. Galbraith, writing on affluence, talks of its 'need... to control or plan the environment in which organization functions. Beyond the ability to manage the market behavior of the affluent consumer [is] the need to make his market reaction reliable and thus to make him the instrument of the economic organizations that have been created to serve him.' Galbraith's ruminations rumble on: 'Will these people long be content with the rather mundane goal of ever-increasing affluence which the system espouses as the highest aim of man? Might there not one day be discontent with a society in which there is single-minded concentration on the goal of economic success? Might there not one day be suspicion of leadership and prestige that is so universally associated with economic achievement?'[4]

Galbraith came very near, almost 40 years ago, to fingering the role of language in deceiving people; and even when he wrote these words in 1958, the noble tone of his questions might not have been echoed in equally high-principled answers. And I say this not so much out of despair with the baseness of all my fellow consumers, as from a sense that the process of political bankruptcy—propelled largely by the use of slogans to replace language and the substitution of shibboleths for solutions—was already too far advanced even then to expect a popular uprising. Moreover, Galbraith was writing at a time when none of our the Demons of Chapter Five seems to have rated mention, and there is only the briefest discussion of the issue of population as viewed by Malthus and Ricardo, and that mainly in the context of the repartition of profits and wages to capital and labour. How much more plangent would Galbraith's words have sounded if they had touched upon not only the higher human instincts under siege by the economic imperative, but also on the survivability of the imperative itself? Indeed, he did go on to address some of these issues in *The New Industrial State*.

Let us now venture further into the Economics of Wonderland and try to assess the damage wreaked upon a better popular comprehension of the world's economy and its inherent contradictions by examining the true meaning which lurks behind some of the buzz-words cited earlier and the all too often disastrous practical consequences of their debased use. I shall show that the task of responding to the material challenges of the third millennium—the Demons of Chapter Five—has been rendered immeasurably more intractable by the systematic trivialisation and deliberate corruption of the political lexicon since World War II. George Orwell could have done no better—even with the help of Franz Kafka.

It is the *globalisation* of economics which is largely responsible for the corruption of both the world's individual nation-state economies and the debasement of language employed by politicians, as economists have ceased to be the 'Respectable Professors of the Dismal Science' and have long since moved on to become the 'Shameless Practitioners of Economic Sleight of Hand'. And the blame lies indelibly with the West and with the East Asians, and now increasingly with their emulators: after all, no one ever appears to have seriously proposed copying pariahs like Burkina Faso, North Korea or Burma—and few even the old Soviet Union—as economic exemplars. And the problem began to become serious after World War II with the spreading notion of economic inter-dependence, i.e. the loss, by one nation-state after the other, of *control* of a strategically significant part of its own affairs. This was a violation of the Power Drive (possibly also the Subsistential) and the three culprits were—and are—*free trade* in goods and the export of labour, a policy of indeterminate *growth in production* in pursuit of universal levels of Western-style consumerism, and Third World *'development'* through exporting propelled by intergalactic levels of debt perched on a tottering succession of failed international financial structures. And from the heedless practice and growth of this villainy there flow most of the economic falsehoods and absurdities which now afflict the world.

Let us start with free trade: certainly, *free* is a popular adjective in the West, and *trade* ranks along with motherhood as a virtuous practice. But linked together there is a deadly chemical reaction. For the best part of a half-century leading up to World War I, the practice of 'free-trade'—led largely by an almighty Great Britain—was widely honoured in both the spirit and letter of international trade agreements and, as a consequence, growth in international trade exceeded growth in total output. The following twenty-five years—to the outbreak of World War II—were in stark contrast as the instability of the post-war boom gave way to protectionism (the high-tariff Smoot-Hawley Act was passed in 1930 in the United States) and provoked the Great Depression; and it is axiomatic that the War itself was more effective than any of President Roosevelt's New Deal devices in bringing the Depression to an end through massive Federal spending, and in resolving the Truman admin-istration to avoid a slide-back into the Thirties by concluding duty-cutting trade deals with most of America's trading partners. This trend slowed during the slumbering Eisenhower years of the late 1950s but was reinvigorated with the Kennedy Round of tariff-cutting which was implemented in 1967. In the intervening quarter-century world trade has ballooned to produce the convulsive and compulsive growth depicted in Chart VI opposite.

Clearly, this simple chart tells us nothing about the volumes of trade, nor about the *commodities* being traded nor about *prices* and *inflation*. But more than that, it does not offer a shred of evidence that the wellbeing of humanity has been advanced as the numbers grow; nor does it reveal that, in the case of Latin America, a trading surplus in bookkeeping terms was achieved partly through a brutal reduction in imports in order to generate hard currency for debt service.[5] However, it does show that by far the greatest volume of trade continued over the

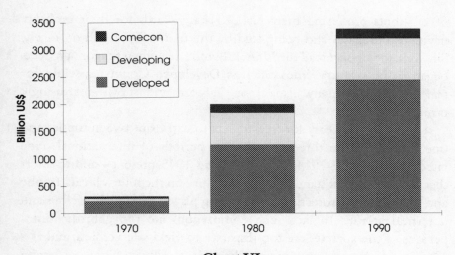

Chart VI
Growth in World Trade 1970–1990
Source: Adapted from UN Statistical Yearbooks, New York

twenty-year period to take place between countries of the First World—a fact long asserted by the Swedish economist Staffan Buren-stam Linder but resolutely ignored by neo-Keynesian Western designers of the Third World. Comecon's share of world trade had declined inexorably; and although the 'developing' world's share *seemed* to have held up, ranging from 18% in 1970 to 29% in 1980 and ending at 23% in 1990, this is mainly through spectacular export growth in East Asia, especially China. By contrast, both volume and growth in most LDCs—Africa, Latin America and India—are extremely low and the trade balances negative or only modestly and erratically positive. And finally, behind these statistics lies an apparently relentless deterioration in the balance of trade of Western Europe, as a whole, and of the United States with the rapidly growing economies of East Asia and Japan.

At the time of the Kennedy Round in the mid-1960s, Lloyd G. Reynolds, a Professor of Economics at Yale, wrote 'Whether there will be a new drive toward further tariff reductions in the 1970s cannot be foreseen. This will depend, among other things, on whether the United States and the United Kingdom are able to overcome the balance-of-payments *difficulties* which plagued them throughout the 1960s.'[6] [my emphasis].

The term *difficulties* may have been an unintentional euphemism. But Reynolds' phrasing reminds me of current advertisements taken out by—ironically—the American Express Company which shows a series of big-shots proffering their AMEX charge-cards for their probably frivolous purchases and being told by the trader: 'That will do nicely, Sir.' Well, for *big-shot* read the USA, UK and later, when the foreign debts began to be run up, almost all Less Developed Countries; while, for *trader*, read Germany, Japan or Taiwan and now—increasingly ominously—China.

It is deceptively easy for free-traders to carry out two autopsies and one biopsy on the three approximate periods of international trade cited above—1870-1914, 1914-1939 and 1945-present—and to assert that the first and last stand as judge-and-jury on the interwar catastrophe and to demonise protectionism as having played a uniquely vicious and determinant role. In fact, such comparisons are too glib; the time-periods of the analyses are too disparate to yield safe verdicts; and as a measure of human happiness, Chart VI is almost bereft of useful meaning except as a set of macroeconomic aggregates of foreign trade, because it tells us nothing of the benefits derived through those countries' participation in it.

These three culprits—the villains which now compromise the world's economy—seem to be almost conspiratorially inteconnected. Let us now look at Third World debt. Here is Professor Reynolds again, writing as far back as 1969: 'Trade and aid policies toward the LDCs are a major issue in international economic relations. The LDCs need large amounts of foreign exchange to import the goods *they are not yet able to produce at home.*' (Hindsight tempts me to add: 'and probably never will be able to produce, anyway.') He goes on: 'The more the LDCs are able to export to us, *the less they will need to borrow.*'[7] ('and, in the event, be unable to repay anyway': hindsight again). I have deliberately chosen to quote and emphasise words written so long ago—and I have no doubt that they were set down with the best of intentions—because they illustrate so well the strain of wrongheadedness which led to the triple madness of Third World debt in the 1970s and 1980s which, together with free trade and the mindless obsession with growth, (e.g. the limitless frenzy to export in order to import with equal frenzy), were soaring out of control and visiting havoc on nations and economies whose governments were too stupid, supine or corrupted by short-termism to look beyond next December.

Although Western and Japanese corporations were, and remain, most often the agents of this trade and growth and the beneficiary of the debt spent by the recipient LDCs, we should not fall into the trap of transnational-bashing so beloved of Western liberals: I am quite content to accept that—the frequent crimes and unethical behaviour of many transnationals notwithstanding—they are private corporations bent on doing what their charters commit them to do: maximising shareholder and director happiness, and that it is for government to control them, where the market cannot or doesn't, within the context of planned national long-term welfare. But more of that later.

In Chart VII below are some data on Third World debt: the actual values themselves are of less interest to us as we seek to understand the Economics of Wonderland, as they are in projecting the enormity of their scale and the speed of their growth, and the criminal mindlessness behind their accumulation:

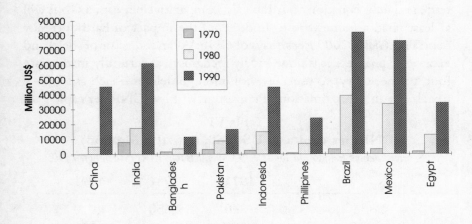

Chart VII
Selected Third World Foreign Debt
Source: UN Statistical Yearbooks & World Tables. World Bank/IBRD Washington DC

These are just nine Third World debtors; almost without exception, most LDCs have *broadly* comparable levels of debt, as do some former Comecon countries (and perfect inability to service such debt), while in recent years the United States has pioneered a novel form of irresponsibility by financing its chronic trade deficits through the great national Bald Eagle Creditcard, and now supports overseas debts which exceed the total of the entire Third World—over a million million dollars and rising, almost $50,000 for every US citizen. Of course, these debts arise from a variety of origins but they are as one in exemplifying the phantasmal character which the world's economy has assumed in just twenty-five years. Before we proceed to investigate the causes and consequences of the underlying instability which Charts VII and VIII illustrate, it will be useful to create a basis to measure the impact of trade and debt on the inhabitants of the First and Third Worlds, and the extent to which Western industrial transnationals and domestic distributors have combined to begin rebuilding profit margins by entrusting to a grateful and, we may imagine, somewhat bemused East Asia the function of manufacturing goods which are then exported back to Western markets, thereby slashing employment in traditional manufacturing sectors and communities, bloating the service sectors and—with no shadow of doubt—making the principal contribution to social deprivation.

Any measure is bound to be imperfect, given the complexity of the trade and debt equations; but Table VI, comparative per capita GNP, will at least yield a framework to understand the impact of hard-currency debt. The *Global 2000 Report* says of GNP: 'As an indicator of social and economic progress, it is now widely recognised as seriously inadequate [but it is necessary] to use a few common guidelines—such as GNP— to achieve an approximation of consistency.'[8] First, GNP per capita:

Table VI
GNP per capita in US Dollars (Atlas Method)
Source: Adapted from World Tables 1993. World Bank/IBRD Washington DC

	1971	1981	1991
World	860	2,650	4,010
OECD	3,290	10,990	20,570
Latin America	640	2,160	2,390
East Asia	140	440	650
China	130	320	370
South Asia	120	270	320
India	110	270	330
Sub-Saharan Africa	190	600	350

Even if we compensate for the inadequacies of GNP per capita, and arbitrarily double the LDC values or halve those of the OECD countries, the figures still point in the same direction: that is to chasms of such breadth between the West and Japan on the one hand, and most of the rest of the world on the other, as to make a nonsense of suggestions by free traders and advocates of external development aid that they are bridgeable if only, that is, Western markets are made fully accessible to exports from the Third World. We shall have more to say about what these hypothetical exports—poised to help redress the imbalance but for the protectionists—might consist of.

And, finally, the switch to foreign-sourced manufactures:

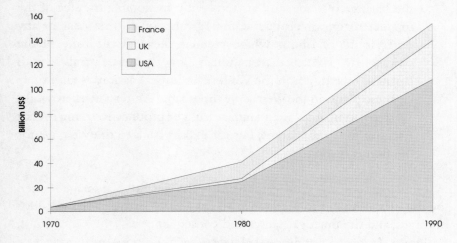

Graph IV
Deficit in Merchandise
Source: UN Trade Yearbooks

All of these statistics point in the same direction:

- an increase in international trade—'free trade'—of scarcely comprehensible proportions and, beyond doubt, of utterly incomprehensible purpose; but, in its mindlessness, a phenomenon which has caused indescribable destruction and social dislocation; a mad export drive to fund imports of frivolous goods without social utility; and, where 'export performance' is inadequate to fund the import of goods, an explosion of foreign debt in order to satisfy rising expectations;

- in a ramshackle international financial structure of terrifying volatility, where no more than 20% of the hundreds of billions of dollars traded *daily* on the foreign exchange markets have anything to do with the financing of trade, a huge and inconceivably repayable debt in most of the Third World stemming from twenty-odd years of accumulation, amounting to double-digit percentages of GNP, with no prospect of breaking the habituation or of permanently improving the terms of trade, there being so few products which are either not primary, or for which the demand is price-elastic, or which have large untapped markets;

- a continuing deterioration in the overall Western balance of payments in manufactured goods and a lumpen determination to do nothing structurally to correct it—the credit-card approach to the balance of trade, and an apparently inexorable transfer of the manufacturing or product-sourcing function to East Asia, or any other fount of labour which seemed cheap at the time of the switch—by *Western* transnationals; any *apparent* parallel with Japanese investment in the Western Industrial nations is false since Japanese plants in the West serve those same Western markets whilst Western companies are manufacturing or product-sourcing in East Asia not for local markets but for export back to the West, i.e. for the home-market.

Now to a scrutiny of the catchwords—the 'deceitful language'—used by the establishment in preference and as an alternative to the need for thought; and the practical causes and consequences.

Free trade means untrammelled access for the goods and services of Nation A into the economies of Nations B to C in order to maximise wealth and employment at home. The rarely stated corollary is that Nations B to C will also maximise *their* wealth and employment by exporting to Nation A. Since the exporters are mainly *private* companies and transnationals making *private* microeconomic trading and investment decisions, the sum of their activities cannot—by definition—be relied upon to complement and support desirable, long-term national government policy such as an approximate balance in external trade, even if such a policy existed. So the response is straightforward: don't have any such policy. To put the conundrum more simply, how can it be assumed that central articles of Nation A's economic faith—such as full employment, stable prices, constant growth and a balance in external trade and capital accounts—will be achieved magically as the net result of—or despite—billions of unintegrated transborder transactions carried out by millions of companies and individuals spread over 200 nations? And it is unlikely that those articles of faith could be inched closer to achievement if government were to replace private enterprise and tailor its policies to the performance of its businesses, since there are so few examples of successful manufacturing and trading enterprises being run by *government*. Why, then, not continue with the present *ad hoc* system?

One practical answer is the thread which runs throughout this book: that is, the unsustainable demand put upon the earth's resources in producing enough exports to pay for all those imports, and the eventual exhaustion of suitable landfill sites for disposing of the broken and obsolete remnants of that frantic trade. Another lies in the contradictory policies pursued by Western governments in their advocacy of free trade overseas combined with full employment at home. Comfortable old notions of comparative advantage have been dealt mortal blows in recent years: as manufactured goods become ever more standardised in their design and methods of production, and constitute an ever larger share of global trade, traditional specialisation based upon favourable factors such as local materials, skills and culture has given way to instant and ephemeral siting and re-siting of the manufacturing function by transnationals using machinery and materials which are identical from Kalamazoo to Kowloon: the only vestige of comparative advantage being labour costs, which are generally supplemented, i.e. distorted, by government inducements.

The Western world long ago abolished controls on the export of capital by transnationals wishing to take advantage of lower labour costs in the Third World, and frequently less onerous occupational and social legislation, by setting up manufacturing plants in less developed countries. In other cases, where such direct investment and foreign control are either not permitted by the host country or are considered too risky, Western transnationals have simply closed down domestic capacity and contracted manufacture out, principally to East Asia. There is no Chinese economic miracle in Shenzhen and Guendong Province: the miracle is that Western governments are too stupid to prevent self-interested transnationals from transferring large sectors of the Western economy and the welfare of the people to a country whose regime would not begin to qualify even as a candidate let alone a signatory of the Helsinki Declaration on Human Rights. At the same time, quotas, tariffs, duties and other impediments to international trade have been knocked aside through bilateral or trading-block arrangements or through collective acts of global madness such as the GATT treaty of 1993 mentioned earlier.

The final lubricant to this international trading machine—lacking after the collapse of the Gold Standard and stalled after World War II by the scarcity or inconvertibility of foreign exchange—was the emergence of the US dollar as the standard global means of financial storage, value and exchange, facilitated by prodigious capital outflows and the slide into an apparently permanent and growing trade deficit. (It is an interesting reflection on the potential stability of the international economic system that the world should have in effect selected as its financial kingpin the currency of the world's greatest spendthrift, with the lowest propensity to prudent fiscal policy.)

These arrangements for free trade and investment, which are now encased in an internationally venerated political reliquary worthy of the Shroud of Turin before it was carbon-dated, have produced consequences which are almost uniformly malignant. Once seen naively as the engine of beneficial growth and employment, free trade must now be indicted for having ravaged the environment; laid waste, by the tens of thousand, traditional manufacturing industries and communities in the West; spawned horrific proletariats of displaced peasants in industrial conurbations in Latin America, Africa and Asia; and created a financial tyranny which scourges mortgagors in Manchester and peons in Paraguay alike through mismanagement in central banks and stock exchanges from Washington and Tokyo to Manila and Brasilia.

And yet the cult of growth goes on: despite ritual recognition at the Rio conference in 1992 of the fact of global warming, and of the threats to biodiversity, GATT was reborn a year later with a fanfare for the 'hundreds of billions of dollars-worth of annual trade which have been saved [sic]' to provide the growth required by the Global Village with its deadly economy. And so do the myths of full employment and endless productivity 'gains': the West flings its doors wide open to a Noahic inundation of imported manufactured goods—in the name, of course, of free trade—and countenances the disappearance of one industry after the other whilst piously assuring the young and the unemployed that vocational retraining and an endless raising of educational levels will create employment and keep the West ahead of the rest of the world. In other words, the West will proceed to raise productivity indefinitely; to increase its absolute output of goods indefinitely; to eliminate present levels of unemployment (which are, therefore, presumed aberrations from some imagined norm); will somehow reverse the present deficit in the work ethic and achieve a permanent educational superiority over a supinely complacent East Asia; and finally, will achieve levels of social welfare which will set standards for the rest of the world to emulate. These delusions are a central part of the Western political apparatus, of right or left, whose implications of some kind of racially sanctioned cultural superiority flourish without challenge.

So much for the West. But what about the poor suburbs of the Global Village—those with the gigantic debts? How were they amassed? Were they *really* for 'development?' Did the recipients duly and obediently develop and what is *development* supposed to mean? If it means, as it seems to—according to bodies such as the World Bank and the United Nations—industrialising for the export markets, is the Third World not simply following the West into an inescapable economic trap? In short, is not *development* a euphemism? And, if it is, then the very term 'developing countries' (which, be it noted, political correctness has now coined to edge out the awkward 'less developed countries' in a chilling example of modern weasel-worded thought-control) is an anomaly.

In light of some of the main conclusions to which this book leads me in Chapter X, and before considering the catastrophe, to borrower and lender alike, of the foreign-debt orgy, we could stage a hypothetical arraignment of today's Western designers of the Third World—and their predecessors of the 1970s and 1980s—and ask what all these new Third World export industries are supposed to achieve, and what the likely consequences may be. The emphasis is, of course, on the export of *manufactured* goods to increase earnings of hard currency, since there are inherent obstacles to expanding exports of *primary* goods, such as foodstuffs; and even these may actually decrease as population growth and desertification impose priority for the home market, or mismanagement reduces exports of commodities such as tropical timber and fishmeal.

Nor is it only Western advocates of Third World industrialisation who have a case to answer: whilst the so-called 'tiger' economies of East Asia—Taiwan, South Korea, Hong Kong, Singapore—have now passed out of the Third World by courtesy of Western markets, the two great imponderables are India and China. Both countries are now determined to emerge into the global trading village, one from ideological isolation, the other from a kind of puritanical purdah. Both are driven by geopolitical fears and, in Paul Kennedy's opinion, 'their ambition to be the regional superpower, in South Asia and East Asia respectively'[9]; and we can therefore offer an answer to the question posed above by examining the implications of the export-driven industrialisation of the two Asian monsters. These seem to me to be four in number: where are their markets? what will they sell? with what benefit? and at what cost?

Their markets will necessarily be—predominantly, at least—the West since nobody else has any money (they are not going to predicate investment on fragile markets in a Third World without hard currency); and they will intend to sell manufactured consumer and capital goods. The Chinese, in particular, have already started. As to the perceived benefits and probable costs, here is the Chilean economist Jacobo

Schatan's view in the mid-1980's: 'It seems that the People's Government is to quadruple both industrial output and per capita income by the year 2000. Given the demographic dimensions involved, a consumption and production expansion of the size foreseen—without discussing its intrinsic merits—will result in a gigantic increment in natural resource utilization; if this is not carried out with proper ecological considerations in mind, China might face environmental upheavals that are similar to those experienced by countries that have already passed through the stage of initial mass industrialization.'[10] There is no reason to suppose that Schatan would have thought differently of India; and it is instructive to recall that he is not one of our Western designers of the Third World intent on making it over in First World image, but— rather—a socialist with a far more sceptical personal viewpoint of the allure of Third World 'development'.

Enough has been written in this book, let alone elsewhere, about environmental mayhem in the twentieth century to make it unnecessary to reinforce Schatan's trepidation that industrialisation on this scale will bring about destruction to their own and the world's physical environment to an extent which the West has already made intolerable and in crisis-need of reversal. Having taken this glimpse of Indian and Chinese plans (perhaps they are exceptions to the short-termism noted earlier, even though they are deeply flawed), let us now revert first and briefly to Table VI on page 148. It is simply inconceivable to imagine how either of these two countries—with populations scheduled to remain at some 33% of the world's growing total even by the year 2025, or around 3 billion—could bring about an industrial transition which would beneficially touch the lives of more than a *small fraction* of their people, newly engaged in manufacture, and thereby begin to bridge the GNP gap for the *entire* population of billions. After all, today's East Asian 'free-market' economies, i.e. Japan, Hong Kong, Singapore, Malaysia, South Korea and Taiwan, are already able to swamp Western markets with consumer goods produced by a population engaged in export manufacturing which cannot exceed some 25 million, Japan included. Nor is there any probability that these already advanced economies will indulge their backward competitors and compliantly mark time while the great Indian and Chinese catch-up proceeds.

Of even more importance, however, in flawing these plans is the already alpine level of consumer satiation in the West. Let us assume that the Western economies as a whole wake up to the social and economic necessity of preserving what will remain by the year 2000 of their present domestic manufacturing sectors, while maintaining existing trading patterns with East Asia. As a consequence, for Chinese and Indian plans for export-based industrial transformation to succeed—in the sense of their multiplying per capita GNP manyfold and generating literally hundreds of millions of jobs in new export-based manufacturing industries—the West will have to contemplate with equanimity Western levels of consumption *several times greater* than the present ability of their own, and the traditional East Asian economies, to satisfy, and with ever greater savaging of Western manufacturing capacity. The prospect is neither persuasive nor comfortable; so much so that future complicity by the West in such Indian and Chinese plans—indispensable for their success—raises enormous ethical implications for both the well-being of our societies and for the global environment.

In a refreshing and largely successful attempt to refute the conventional thinking about debt and development in the Third World—the 'wrongheadedness' I referred to earlier—Jacobo Schatan published *World Debt: Who is to Pay?* in 1987. Schatan has no hang-ups with terminology: for him, there is the *Third World* or the *Periphery*, of which Latin America is part, along with Africa and most of Asia, and there is the *North*, or what I have called the *West*—an interesting instance of differing verbal viewpoints. Anyway, not for him the verbal blandishments and 'honorific category of NIC (Newly Industrialized Country)' status.[11] Schatan's overriding preoccupation is with Latin America, but there is little reason to believe that the causes of the debt and its practical *effects* in that continent are not similar in Africa and much of Asia.

Up until the early 1970's, foreign aid from the First to the Third World took the form predominantly of tied grants of money, foodstuffs and manufactured goods on a bilateral basis, i.e. from government to government, or via the United Nations and its agencies or private charities. A good part of it was about as unaltruistic as the Marshall Plan for Europe after World War II: the United States and the Soviet Union sprayed largesse over their Third World clients as an integral part of Cold War strategy, with goods having a high public-relations profile; whilst for Great Britain and France mixed feelings of moral obligation and commercial advantage found happy resolution in aid to their former colonies.

This fairly harmless pattern began to change in the early Seventies as a response to several parallel pressures: in Western banks, quadrupling oil prices generated huge increases in liquidity with no immediately obvious alternative use; the World Bank and International Monetary Fund, in both their policies and culture, seem to have viewed the Third World as simply a group of 'developing' countries perched merely temporarily at different way-points on a development continuum with the First World beckoning at this end of it; ideological resistance in the South to trading links with the North was probably weakening as import substitution came to be portrayed as a feather-bedding impediment to free trade; and the industrialized world would have found a felicitous solution to its chronic problem of satiated markets through a debt-fed enhancement of Third World purchasing power. The consequence, as illustrated in Chart VII on page 147, was a rise in Third World external debt of almost 1200% between 1970 and 1990.

It is possible to list six major end-uses on which these perching Third World debtors might have spent their new-found hard-currency:

- imports of food for their inevitably exploding populations, aggravated by a Western-induced penchant for things like wheat flour and canned baby-food;
- imports of oil and petrol, aggravated by the exhaustion of local fuel-wood, and abandonment of animal- and human-powered machinery and implements;
- imports of manufactured consumer goods of variable degrees of social utility ranging from pharmaceuticals to cigarettes and Michael Jackson posters;
- imports of military equipment;
- imports of capital equipment, for anything from dams and steel plants to jet aircraft and tourist hotel fixtures;
- finance of government budget deficits.

And cynics would add 'capital flight' as, in effect, an end-use since extremely large amounts of the debt—Schatan quotes an estimate of as much as one-third of the total—undoubtedly were embezzled or misused by government officials, with ex-President Marcos of the Philippines and the national priority of his wife's shoe collection being just the most infamous example.

We have seen from the Reynolds quotation above that foreign indebtedness was—at best—naively once seen to be the route to a closing of the gap between North and South; we now know that, at worst, dollars were parachuted into the slums of the Global Village by 'development experts' under the guise of benign assistance with all the hyperbole of political rhetoric to accompany it. Jacobo Schatan says: 'It is assumed that such external loans will not only produce (through investments made with them) the foreign currency needed to repay the loans, but that they will also contribute to the self-sustained economic growth of the debtor countries, a process that will make further borrowing unnecessary. But reality has proved otherwise. Far from being a temporary phenomenon, foreign indebtedness has become an addiction from which debtor nations have not been capable of escaping.'[11] There are, of course, *technical* reasons why initial levels of borrowing went on to balloon: the loans were no longer fixed-interest and rates sky-rocketed in the 1970's along with devaluation of Third World currencies so that, as demonstrated earlier, domestic US and European interest-rate artillery impacted on innocent targets thousands of miles away; many capital investment projects were aborted or did not generate foreign exchange; commodity prices fluctuated—mainly downward, especially in Africa; and there was capital flight. But even without these complications, the real fallacy lay in the confident assumption that large and permanent foreign-exchange surpluses would be generated through the export of a whole range of new, i.e. non-agricultural, products to the North even as home markets in the Third World would be prised open in the interests of (let us not forget) *free trade*. It is astonishing to realise that these loans were being made by Western bankers who had abandoned all of the lending criteria which they would normally apply to domestic Western borrowers. Schatan again: 'Borrowers must remit resources to pay the interest and amortize the principal; as a result, new loans—bigger than previous ones—must be made available by the lenders, so that a net transfer is created in favour of the borrowers. This requires a continuous increase in the amounts disbursed and the total outstanding debt.'[13]

But central to the foreign debt crisis is a pressing new paradox and a nagging old cultural and ethical dilemma. The *paradox* is simple: it is acknowledged that the debt is unrepayable; that a moratorium would be serious, and a repudiation catastrophic, for borrower and lender alike; and yet, if a write-off could be engineered, there would occur neither a cold-turkey breaking of the debtor's habit, nor a sudden willingness of the lender to resume the flow of funds and so perpetuate an already discredited cycle.

The *dilemma* is much more complex and does not spring from the avoidance of straight language by politicians and development experts, as we have seen in other cases, although it is mightily assisted by it. Back in Chapter One, I traced the growth of the West and its expansion world-wide, which was likened to a high-pressure weather system rolling into and over lower-pressure areas; there, and in later chapters, I identified a number of natural and historical factors which had powered this process. And we saw how an infinitely subtle combination of these factors had propelled the West to unprecedented power and material wealth. This process has engendered in the West a collective mind-set in which the Third World—in all its myriad diversity—is viewed as potentially all-of-a-piece with the West provided only that it is enabled to 'catch up' economically. This is implicit in the incessant recourse by Western political figures to terms we have already censured—the 'international community' and the 'developing nations', all canonized in Fukuyama's End-of-History theory and its eulogy of the Western liberal economy. The very term 'catch up', as applied to the economic position of the Third World in relation to the First, occurs several times in Paul Kennedy's recent guide to the third millennium (*Preparing for the Twenty-first Century*), although his 'pessimistic' subtext leaves us in no doubt of his conclusions.

The West's dilemma springs from an unwillingness to recognise publicly and declare that the world is not a place where God carried out an even-handed distribution job when He handed out the blessings in those first few Genesitic days: just as there are stark differences in the physical and climatic endowments between the regions which comprise Europe and North America, so there are even starker differences— which political correctness would now call 'inequalities'—between the West, as a whole, and a great part of the Third World: just as the Outer Hebrides are not going to 'catch up' economically with Oslo, nor the Peloponnese with Paris, so there is no prospect of Somalia gaining on Sydney, nor Togo closing in on Tokyo. To suggest otherwise is to endorse the litany of errors which have been exposed earlier in this chapter, and so to give encouragement to the doctrine of rising expectations which are neither reasonable not redeemable.

The *cultural* element in the dilemma has long been, and remains, of a missioneering nature and was given fresh impetus in the years covered in this book by the economic imperative. The *ethical* element lies in the West's perception of a collective guilt which can be expiated through 'development'. Jacobo Schatan has no doubt of the corrective course history should take; and I doubt that Vaclav Havel will think it a misappropriation if I use his simple words to deliver a verdict on Economics in Wonderland:

'Many Europeans and Americans today are painfully aware of the fact that the Euro–American civilization has undermined and destroyed the autonomy and singularity of non-European cultures. They feel it was their fault, and thus feel the need to make amends through a kind of emotional identification with others, by accommodating them, by trying to ingratiate themselves, by longing to 'help' them in one way or another.

'To my mind, this is a false way of going about it that can lead to further unhappiness. It contains within itself—albeit in a hidden and somewhat negative fashion—the same familiar feeling of superiority, paternalism and fateful sense of mission to help the 'rest of the world'. It is, again, that feeling of being 'the elect'. It is, in fact, colonialism inside out. It is an intellectual dead end.'[14]

Chapter Nine

Why 2001 Looks the Way it Does

'United Europe will form one major regional entity. There is the United States with all its dependencies; there is the Soviet Union; there is the British Empire and Commonwealth; and there is Europe, with which Great Britain is profoundly blended. Here are the four main pillars of the World Temple of Peace.' Winston Churchill, Albert Hall, London 1947.

'Nobody knew what to do about the vagaries of the world economy or possessed instruments to manage them... government policy, national or internationally coordinated, no longer worked. [These were] the crisis decades... when the national state lost its economic powers... the governments of all states [are] at the mercy of an uncontrollable "world market".' Eric Hobsbawm: *Age of Extremes—the Short Twentieth Century 1914-1991.*

Separating *What* Happened from *Why*

THESE TWO EPIGRAPHS are back- and front-markers to a chasm in human affairs of awesome depth: if we can now perceive but dimly the world of 1945 (a dimness paradoxically enhanced by the mono-chrome photographic records of the age), would our perception *then*, of the distant world of 2001, have been any clearer? I think the image *would* have been clearer, but not in any strictly optical sense: the image would have carried off no prizes for clairvoyance, but it would have been *brighter*, and polychromatic, as befitted an observer peering out with fearful optimism from the wreckage of World War II.

The same observation could be made of the years which separate 1945 from 1900, except that we shall enjoy a better sense of history if we follow Eric Hobsbawm in regarding the period 1914-1945 as an integral historical watershed in its own right—his 'Age of Catastrophe', which acts like a bulkhead between two quite different cargoes of history. And it fits in with the conclusion reached earlier in this book, that it is somewhere in the very early interwar years that we have to seek the more immediate origins of our late twentieth-century malaise; also with the view that the nineteenth century hung on until 1918 and that the history which resumed in 1945 was wholly different from that which preceded it up to 1914, that humanity had stepped across a great 30-year fault-line in history. Yet even so acute an observer as Churchill, who possessed the added advantage of being himself a major participant in history, failed to spot that something had happened in those thirty years, and that the world of 1947 certainly did not conform to the neat, controlled structure which he described and commended to his audience as the way that world would be managed in the future: it was already well on its way to the alternative view suggested by Sir Roy Calne in 1994—of international economic anarchy.

There, somewhere in those years, lies the clue to today's crisis—the mass of political and cultural, economic and ecological flux which constitute a profound transformation in the mood and spirit of humanity at the end of this millennium, and its tremulous view of the next. On the eve of the third millennium, there is a malaise: there is uncertainty, fear, mistrust of institutions, ignorance of the past, contempt for authority, greed, social aimlessness, crime of unprecedented scale and inventiveness. Above all, there is no evidence of enthusiasm for the future except as a short-term extension of the present. It is the task of today's historians to help unlock that clue and so to provide the understanding without which there is no prospect that our society will successfully respond: for the historian's contribution is not merely an academic embellishment, but as central to the process as that of all other observers of the human scene.

Much of the earlier part of this book was concerned with tracing the process whereby the late nineteenth- and twentieth-century phenomena of environmental degradation and resource depletion had complotted with the economic imperative—the new secular theology—to drive humanity to the threshold of a very uncertain new millennium. In fact, they were not all part of a conspiracy but rather, as we saw, mindless mutually reinforcing agencies which both drive, and are driven by, the growth of population which began to exhibit a new, sinister order of increase in the late nineteenth century. I made some play of the dates when parts of this process seemed to have gone critical: they were dates which could only be approximate, and—as tentative as one must be when dealing with subtle shifts in the historical shadows rather than with shafts of sunlight—discrete events; but they had their own significance, as I shall show below.

These, then, were *material* phenomena, visible and measurable; and they had to do with reified changes in people's relationship with the environment, differences in the way they now lived and worked, fed and travelled, thought and hoped and, not least, *where* they did those things as they increasingly became estranged urban animals. Why were the dates, albeit approximate, so important? The answer is that during the period we reviewed, and for perhaps the first time in human history, large sections of humanity began to be able to carry out consciously— or, as we saw, to unleash unwittingly—gigantic historical course-changes, i.e. experiments in *control* of history, which were the direct result of specific scientific, technological and industrial discoveries, applications and processes to which dates and places could be assigned (and therefore the causation established) with far greater precision than history had normally permitted. These 'techno-intellectual events'—the internal combustion engine, inorganic chemicals, synthetics, antibiotics, electricity, the passenger lift, the aeroplane, telephone, radar, semiconductors, DDT, nuclear bombs, robotics, the list is endless—were of a different order of importance from earlier, far more illustrious historical events (crossing the Rubicon and the Crusades, the defeat of the Spanish Armada and the American Civil War) because of the *immediacy* and impersonally *global* nature of their impact. The heroic (frequently military) events of earlier history, even including majestic cerebral exploits by the likes of Newton and Galileo, Leonardo and Descartes, rarely had instant and universal direct or side-effects; the techno-intellectual output of the past century or so, and its impact have, on the contrary, been both profound and instant and indiscriminate.

In this chapter I shall seek to add an understanding of *why* the world is now the way it is, to our earlier perception of what it is, of *what* it has become. Perhaps the *what* is all too obvious—in all its manifestations, noble and evil, sad and comic. The *why* is far less simple, and it is for this reason that we must undertake the task. Nor is the *why* just the sum of all that history—stacks of facts and events, welling up as if in preparation for 2001.

Let us first pause and review where our historical trek has reached. We found a world dominated by the artifacts of five hundred years of West-European-American expansion, but only towards the very end actuated by an all-smothering commitment to economic growth, industrial production and mass consumerism—the *economic imperative*. This had become the universal measure of human activity throughout the world; and it seemed inconceivable that some alternative global vernacular culture would arise naturally to usurp it for something

better. A levelling, a homogenizing of the world's cultural landscape and
its diversity were unavoidable as 'best-practice' manufacturing techniques, managerial criteria, financial systems, advertising and marketing
strategies, communications technology and a host of related factors
colluded to overwhelm or to bypass the subtle frontiers which history
had erected over the preceding centuries, like flood-waters carrying all
before them in a torrent of uprooted trees and breached dykes. Here is
Toynbee enjoying himself: 'In a Modern Western Society that had radiated its influence over the habitable globe, not only the little Orontes
but also the great Ganges and great Yangtse had flowed into the Thames
and the Hudson, while the Danube had reversed its direction and had
deposited a cultural alluvium of Ruman and Serb and Bulgar and Greek
proselytes upstream in an over-filled melting-pot in Vienna.'[1]

The triumph of the West and of 'liberal' democracy, which had
brought unimaginable material blessings to a majority of its own
people, and beckoned the rest of the world with the same blandishments, had not been won without equally unimaginable social and
political upheaval whose viruses then slithered off into the rest of the
world as inseparable cancerous companions to the blessings; nor
without a massive, sustained even if unintentionally malignant assault on
our environment—the thin crust of earth beneath our feet, the oceans
set to rise around our islands, and the few tenuous layers of air and
ozone which lie between us and the black vacuum of space—which has
wrought greater change over most of the earth's surface in a hundred
years than in the ten millennia since the last ice-age.

For 'those of us addicted to diversity in all its forms', there stretched
ahead the narrowest of paths between the flimsiest of brattices, which
separated a comfortable, almost elitist nostalgia for a lost world of
Western privilege and complacency, from the new reality of the fears
and uncertainties now seething in our own industrial societies
(Toynbee's 'internal proletariat'), and equally out there in the rest of the
world clamouring outside the gates.

All of the three theories of history which we interrogated held water,
and were also consistent with each other, as pure *observations* of how
history, at least in its human guise, had worked in practice. But neither
of the two theologically-inspired *mechanisms* worked—or, rather, *worked
any longer* in a secular world; as for the third, it made for disagreeable
company because alongside its more untenable pretensions lay a track-
record in prophecy of laser-like accuracy. But the failure in *method* of all
three theories matters profoundly and not merely out of churlish

academic pique that one favoured esoteric theory or another now appears to be as fatally flawed as the economic imperative. It mattered—and matters—because, as I noted in Chapter One and shall revert to later, an awareness of how history operates—not just the tedious dates and battles and kingly successions—at even the most subliminal level is part of every person's existential equipment, however great their historical illiteracy. Equally important—and even more so for the purposes and argument of this chapter—is the resulting clear choice between two conclusions: if none of these theories any longer stands up to scrutiny in its *entirety*, had this always been the case? Was each of them always flawed right down the middle? Or, more disquietingly, had something happened which was historically so utterly without precedent as to absolve each theoretician from charges of shoddy scholarship? That is the choice: that is the Why.

The final step in my trek was to suggest a more modest and workmanlike view of history. The Control Theory of history bore out the more tenable conclusions of the great theoreticians, but depended on no celestial clockwork. Moreover, because it is essentially humanist in nature, it offered the prospect of a conscious, human-driven project to design an agreeable and sustainable contract with Gaia to replace the deadly inanities of early Genesis; and in so doing, it offers humanity the opportunity—as I shall later show—to regain some of the spirituality and communitarian sense of purpose which has been lost.

And so we come back to the choice: were all these theories to be jettisoned? Or, if not, what had happened to bring down upon us the horrors of the twentieth century and fear of the third millennium after four centuries years of all that glorious human advancement and enlightenment pulsating out of the West? What could we unearth in the political experience and psychological dimensions of the twentieth century which would counterpoint the environmental and cultural crisis at the end of the millennium? In the search, we have to be resolute and determined to resist the modern diseases of reductionism and relativism—the marauding contract-muggers of contemporary independent thinking: not to be obsessed with endless strings of causality, and subatomic particles of truth, not to be fearful of vigorously asserting salient but unpleasant and impolitic truths. There will be leads and lags, dissonance and disharmony; but somewhere out there lies buried the key to that choice.

I thought more and more about that key, as I approached my endview of *what* our world had become. And I became increasingly certain that it lay in the earlier years of the twentieth century, and that not only could we salvage—from our three theoreticians—valuable observations about *how* history operated; but also that we should now ask all three of them actually to help us understand *why*—with old eyes looking freshly at 2001. I remarked earlier that interpretation of history should improve with the passage of time, because there is less uncertainty of fact. Let us, then, requisition some of today's communications technology, call up some of yesterday's spirits, permit them to survey what will be for each of them a novel historical landscape, and—with allowable poetic licence—invite them to help those of us who have followed, to understand why 2001 looks the way it does.

Understanding 2001:
A Symposium for Four Voices

Characters: *Professor G. W. F. Hegel*, Philosopher, University of Berlin.
 Dr Oswald Spengler, Mathematician, University of Munich.
 Professor Arnold Toynbee, Historian, University of London.
 Mr H. G. Wells, Historian, prophet and novelist.

Place: A house in the country near Exmoor, Devon.

Time: The last evening of a long-weekend house-party, February 1995.

Scene: The Library: it is strewn with open books, magazines and journals. There is a television and a video-recorder. *Mr Wells* is narrator and chairman, and introduces the Symposium.

'THE FOUR OF US had met at the invitation of Mr Peter Cruttwell at his house in the West of England. Our purpose was to examine the tide of man's affairs during the many years since we had each laid aside our pens, and to issue what Cruttwell described as a 'sitrep' on humanity as it teeters on the edge of the third millennium. We had also agreed to review the manuscript of his book entitled *History out of Control* and to repay his hospitality by allowing our 'sitrep' to appear towards the end of his book.

'Early in the weekend Hegel, despite fatigue from his long journey, had entertained us with readings from *The Philosophy of History*, a work which he had, of course, never seen since it was his son who had edited it after his father's sudden death in 1830. He was delighted with the book. Frankly, I never much cared for it, but I have to say that its compactness, for want of a better word, made me envious if only because I would love to have been able to take such a simple, uncluttered view of man's ineluctable progress—through history—to Freedom; and to have had the Almighty as tutor would tend to give authority to any historian.

'Toynbee, whom I do not recall having encountered again since a rather strained dinner-party at the Woolfs' in the early 1920's, when I provoked a quite unnecessarily indecorous dispute with him about God's socialist credentials, was thoroughly civil. He could have got his own back on me when Spengler declined to make a presentation of his *The Decline of the West*—stating that he was not disposed to 'vulgar academic competition'—but instead he saved the day by giving the company a splendid *tour d'horizon* of his *A Study of History*, which had run to only two or three volumes when I died in 1945. (He later confided to me that Spengler's behaviour was consistent with his own earlier impressions of a man whose 'method is to set up a metaphor and then proceed to argue from it as if it were a law based on observed phenomena.')[2]

'Cruttwell gave us an astounding account—perforce highly compressed—of events since the end of the War (I mean the first German War, of course) and he made use of some extraordinary new cinematographic equipment. He has a strongly held view, which he advocates with great vigour, that something has gone very wrong with man's relationship with what I learnt has come to be known as the 'environment' in the later twentieth century, and he has a closely related general theory of history which I feel is very persuasive. Hegel was shattered, Toynbee looked unutterably sad, and I felt strangely but uncomfortably redeemed when I reflected on some of my last writings such as *Mind at the End of Its Tether*. Spengler just looked smug.

'For the rest of the weekend we were engrossed in acquainting ourselves with the world of 1995 by liberal use of the library and, in particular, in assessing commercial and trading developments throughout the world, and the role of government in the later twentieth century—these promising to be the principal subjects on the agenda for our last evening. We met in informal seminars of two or three to exchange views and interpretation of what we had seen and read in order to try to produce a synthesized verdict on the twentieth century. We were free to order our thoughts by means of brisk walks on the

Moor; and partook of a lunch at a moorland inn to which I am sure no ploughman ever aspired. Initially, Spengler remained rather aloof, while the three of us took the air, and said that nothing he might hear or read could do other than simply confirm what 'it had been ordained that he would predict' eighty years ago! He sometimes makes me uncomfortable, but I do not actively dislike him, as I believe both Hegel and Toynbee did, at least at the beginning. (Mind you, I do recall Hegel saying that it was not necessary for anyone to question his own theories since he had already proved them!) Nevertheless, Spengler seemed rapidly to warm to our project; our party has been enthusiastic and the atmosphere conducive to the successful accomplishment of our task.

'Hegel and Toynbee went to the parish church of St Michael & All Angels this morning, while I heard Cruttwell arranging for Spengler to visit an atomic electricity generating station on the Somerset coast. I busied myself with preparations for this evening, which I decided would take the form of a symposium. At dinner, I was relieved to find that Spengler was in unaccountably high spirits—at least, relatively speaking—after his excursion, and he even made a rather ponderous attempt at a joke when he informed us that the manager of the electricity station was named 'Frost' and that he—Spengler—had suggested to the bemused gentleman that a minor exchange of letters would produce 'Faust'—a far more appropriate name for a man living in such close daily communion with the devil! He also told me that he had enjoyed *The War of the Worlds* and *The War in the Air*, which he thought to be typical examples of Anglo-American culture at its best. What a strange man!

'In the following account of the evening's proceedings, which were conducted in a variety of linguistic styles, I have taken the liberty of conforming the dialogue to a modern-day standard.'

The Symposium

Wells: 'Gentlemen, welcome to our Symposium. Please be seated. This is our last evening together and, if we are ever to meet again, it will be in a new millennium. Since I cannot favour Dr Spengler with special dispensation, I shall say that none of us here tonight can imagine how *that* future world might look; but I suspect we might have felt more confident in our historian's power of prophecy had we not spent these last few extraordinary days together. We have seen evidence of quite remarkable transformation in the human condition in *this* world of the late twentieth century. We have seen unimaginable levels of wealth and private consumption, but no accompanying sense of public well-being. On the contrary, there is a global malaise and there is no appetite for the twenty-first century; and it is our task tonight to present our analysis of the political and psychological changes which have brought it about.

Each of us—it is not immodest of me to say—has left his mark on the writing of history, and has invested the effort of a lifetime in fashioning a way of interpreting history as a conscious process. But I ask you, as you consider the task we have undertaken for our host, to lay aside your own prejudices—for we all have our share of them—and to assess the century not as a vindication of your own work but rather, if I do not ask too much, to be as willing to acknowledge its weaknesses as I shall be to praise its strengths.

May I enquire whether you have reached a common verdict, Gentlemen? What is your verdict and who will speak first?

Hegel: That honour, Mr Chairman, has been graciously accorded to me by my companions, and I am to present our findings.

In the few days allotted to us to perform our task, it was clear that we should behold such a profusion of events—as normally would require three lifetimes of ordering and analysis—that we must impose on ourselves a discipline, as upon a glutton at a feast. Moreover, we are each of us separated from 1995 by such unequal time and space, that we resolved that we must seek an explanation of the environmental, political and cultural malaise of the late twentieth century through agreement on no more than three, perhaps four, interrelated phenomena of this century which most incontrovertibly distinguish it from the previous century—the nineteenth, with which the three of us are most closely bound through birth or work or influence—and from which we can view this twentieth century with dispassion. All else, all other observations, are at best contributory factors; at worst, distractions.

We have identified these interrelated phenomena and each of us will now present our findings. They are:

- The collapse of the system of independent nations, and the new international anarchy;
- The triumph of liberal democracy and the economic imperative;
- The failure of political institutions and their replacement by the system of transnational corporations.

If we were to suggest a single term or phrase to characterize what has happened in the twentieth century and which embraces these linked phenomena, it is *loss of control* by humanity over its affairs; and in that respect we entirely endorse the conclusions reached by Mr Cruttwell in his new book. It is clear that the corrective historical mechanisms, which both Professor Toynbee and I proposed in our life's work, have yet to operate or seem to have become strangely suspended; and that unless and until they do, Dr Spengler's views will continue to receive the confirmation of history.

Wells: You are, then, not united in your verdict?

Hegel: For reasons which will become apparent, Mr Chairman, we each continue to hold to our personal philosophy of history; but we are unanimous in our verdict on the twentieth century, and are each of us able to confirm it within his own philosophy. There has been no compromise.

We shall not recapitulate our host's conclusions respecting the physical assault made upon the earth by human numbers and technology: we accept them as given. We have sought explanations of the political and—in the widest sense—cultural conditions whose change in such a short period of time has permitted the world to appear as it now does.

Each of us will now present one phenomenon; and we shall then discuss them. I first ask Dr Spengler to discuss our findings on the decline of the nation-state.'

Act One
The collapse of the system of independent nations, and the new international anarchy

'This pacific and inevitable struggle [the Great War] was undertaken in the reign of His Good and Memorable Majesty King George V and it was the cause of nowadays and the end of History.'
Sellars & Yeatman: *1066 And All That*

Spengler: 'Thank you, Professor Hegel.

The world up to 1914 exhibited a degree of stability—of certainty—which is now quite lost—possibly irretrievably. That stability was based on a system of great and independent nations, referred to nowadays rather disapprovingly as 'nation-states'. This system of five or six European empires and a new imperial America had been perfected in the late nineteenth century, so that it now controlled the world and, allowing for occasional minor friction at the margins, there thus existed an almost familial compromise which favoured international good order, whatever the underlying tensions. The system was seen by the ruling elites to be generally beneficial and we shall not dwell on the origins of the Great War, nor on the blame we should attach to the Treaty of Versailles, and the Washington Conference, for the catastrophes which have followed: these were *political* failures which will shortly be discussed by Professor Toynbee.

The nation-state originated, of course, through the spreading outwards of central political authority, which absorbed or amalgamated communities hitherto partly or largely autonomous. Despite our common detestation of gigantism, we do *not* argue that this process was—by definition—*wholly* undesirable, although, as we shall later show, the malaise of the twentieth century may be attributed in major part to the weakening of the community and of communities in favour of the centre. With this weakening there has come about a loss which we are all three content to call *spiritual*; and there is in our host's prescription for the ills of what is still called 'society', an appeal for a spiritual element—one which will enlist a newly revived sense of community purpose. We *do* argue that the nation and the system of nation-states represented itself a type of community; that the nation-states were the political expression of a cultural and linguistic integrity which permitted the citizen, now estranged from a closer community, still to relate his identity to that of a society, albeit now more impersonal as had been made inevitable by urbanization; and to perceive that society operating through the nation in its relationship to the rest of the world.

However, four years later (by 1918), as a result of that war, all of these great empires—except the American—had either utterly collapsed (Prussia, Austro-Hungary and Russia), or had been irreparably and terminally weakened (France and Great Britain) and a great political vacuum was created in their wake; and this weekend we have now been able to see that the process of imperial dismantlement would be complete just a generation or so later. 1918 was therefore the beginning of the end not only of the nation-state—a demise which Professor Hegel might applaud—but the symbolic and utter end of the vestigial system of communities which had gone before. Deference to the Chairman's wishes impeaches claims by any of us that this war was foreseen; and I shall therefore remark merely that, although we all three believe in the eventual *probability* of that war, we equally believe that it might have been postponed indefinitely had the vacuum I have referred to been filled promptly. But it was not; and, as a consequence, the fact of the vacuum when it was created is of profound significance to our analysis of the ensuing decades. Yes, Professor Toynbee?

Toynbee: Mr Chairman, may I say that Professor Hegel and I differ from Dr Spengler, of course, in regarding 1918 as merely an historical accident which precipitated or hastened the gigantism of the twentieth century, but which was implicit in his scheme of history. But these are purely philosophical differences which do not prevent our agreement that 1918 represented the final crushing of the human scale in human affairs; and that a recognition of what Dr Spengler has called a vacuum, in the widest cultural sense, is vital to a proper understanding of the rest of the century.

Wells: Thank you, Professor Toynbee, that is a most useful endorsement. But Dr Spengler, in what respect can you possibly assert that the system of nations has collapsed? Surely, we now have a world of some two hundred independent nations?

Spengler: I have noted from your own writings in 1920, Mr Chairman, that you fully shared—even indeed, anticipated—this perception of collapse: that the Great War was so shattering in both the military and the politico-cultural sense, that a new order was needed to replace all that had been destroyed by 1918. I have to say that the *idea*, at least, of the League of Nations shows how wide was the awareness that something had been lost in the mud; and that the new democracy which emerged from that mud must never again let loose on mankind the weapons of the equally new technology.

As to the independence of two hundred nations, No! True political and economic independence came to an end there, in the mud, along with the death of any lingering spirit of human commonalty; the vacuum was, to mix our metaphors, all-embracing: the nineteenth century ended then, and the victors were completely unequipped to retrieve an old and flawed world or to design a new and better one; or to carry on managing the old world. And with the disappearance—real if not apparent—of what community the nation-state still offered in 1914, there began the process whereby the citizen's estrangement from an independent and culturally integral unit would be perfected—social and economic nomads cut adrift from a defining belongingness. And, as I think Professor Hegel will show, the new partnership of democracy and the economic imperative was to prove a false substitute.

Hegel: Do you not call America a victor, Herr Doctor, and did she not fill the vacuum?

Spengler: It is known to me that Germany was not to win that war, even without America's entry. She would probably not quite have lost it and there would have developed a stalemate of mutual prostration, but let there be no doubt that our vacuum would have been created anyway. America was a victor, as we now know, in emerging as a creditor from a war she entered as a debtor. A type of victory. But America's imperial credentials have never been beyond question, never impeccable, never entirely trustworthy; and where neither Great Britain nor France was now able to fill our vacuum or, more charitably, did not perceive its presence, America failed to do so through a combination of Jeffersonian high principles (how does it go? 'Peace, commerce, and honest friend-ship with all nations—entangling alliances with none') on the one hand, and the same strain of unpredictability and inconsistency which, as we have seen, has persisted to the end of the twentieth century, on the other; so that the world could not look to America to preserve what-ever remnants of orderly international community might have survived.

Wells: Therefore, Dr Spengler, by 1918 the system of nation-states had collapsed (or was in fatal decline), and with it had gone the final remem-brance of community, albeit community on an already vast scale; and it had not been—or never would be—replaced by something better. And the vacuum in history persists? The League of Nations was a failure?

Spengler: Precisely, but even more than a failure: the League gave a danger-ous illusion of new order, and at just the moment —insofar as we can attribute exact dates to historical turning-points—when entirely new demands began to be made, or should have been made, on political insti-tutions by the exigencies of the new economics, the new technologies and the rupture of humanity's contract with nature. The United Nations has failed in so far as its founders believed, as you may have Mr Chairman, that it was embryonic world government; and the prolifera-tion of 'global' and 'world' supranational organizations gives a merely cosmetic impression that competent international management of man's affairs truly exists and has satisfactorily replaced the nation-state.

Wells: Is this not, Dr Spengler, a highly theoretical view of the world seventy-five years ago? Did the world, and its nations, not in fact tend to its wounds and was not greater democracy to be one of the great gains in the years which have followed? And has not the spread of democracy compensated for the losses you describe?

Hegel: May I interject? We do not think it theoretical in the slightest. The system of nation-states had itself only just completed the final suppression of community—after centuries when power was being drawn to the centre—but had yet to replace it with human-scale cultural and political alternatives. But no sooner had this process ended than the nation-state and the system of nation-states were themselves literally smashed abruptly and no new world-order or new authority was then created, or has been since, to resolve the tensions which would then follow with increasing speed and severity. It is but one lifetime ago; and the uncertainties created by that vacuum, which may have once seemed to be so esoteric, have percolated into the psychology of late twentieth-century humanity.

Toynbee: My companions are correct; and I must confess that it was only in my own very late work that I belatedly allowed there to emerge serious doubts whether democracy and what I called 'social harmony' could adequately replace more traditional community systems; and then survive to respond to the challenges of environmental dislocation which I was only just then beginning to observe.

Spengler: Thank you, Gentlemen, but I know our Chairman speaks as *advocatus diaboli*, as his own later writing reveals. No, an appreciation of today's human malaise internalized, as I believe the expression has it, by most individuals must begin with a clear understanding of all of the institutional arrangements which people create to manage their affairs and—in the matter we are now discussing—of the defects in those arrangements, even their very absence.

Toynbee: Professor Hegel is quite right: the vacuum of 1918, is not esoteric, and neither the League of Nations nor the United Nations nor, as I once had hoped, the United States has filled it. It persists to this day and impedes humanity in the formulation of a proper response to the stupendous challenges it now faces.

Wells: And I suppose the Soviet Union was never a contender—never a candidate for the role of world-leader?

Spengler: If I may speak personally for just a moment, my own work was to have included a chapter on Russia's position in my scheme; but, for various reasons, I did not do so. I wrote also that America is 'neither a real nation nor a real State' and that it is rather too similar to Bolshevik Russia in being 'organized exclusively from the economic side'. Indeed, is it not a paradox that we see in America the greatest materialist culture side-by-side with some of the most extreme democratic arrangements and pretensions? Besides which, one society *is* and the other *was* in its gigantism a denial of the possibility of community whose demise was already signalled in the cotton-mills and furnaces of northern England, and their deracinated servants.

Hegel: I had also never included Russia in my own scheme; and I have now seen that my own students' appropriation of my teachings was even more corrupted by Russia's Marxists; and that the striving for Freedom which is at the root of my philosophy was quite inconceivable in the Soviet Union, and has simply been commuted in the West into a loss of spirituality and community and a bondage to consumerism. As for America, I was of course always an optimist, and that is where I saw the future of the West, in which a host of true communities existed on the new frontiers. I agree that it has not, or not yet, become a nation; and yet (or perhaps because it never did become one), it made the leap from the naive republican optimism of the nineteenth century to world supremacy in 1918 too quickly and without the necessary political maturity and conviction. It was a feat of economics liberated by the anarchy of a democracy without social goals.

Wells: Dr Spengler, what are the practical consequences today of the collapse of the nation-state system so many years ago?

Spengler: The true cultural symptoms of collectivisation—the various industrial revolutions—had not been fully worked through even by 1918 when this second massive assault on the human spirit was launched. That process of disintegration is even now incomplete even though it has proceeded apace. And it is this enduring myth of national sovereignty pasted on to a cultivated folk-memory of village life which, combined with the imposition of conjured-up creations such as the

European Union, make for such popular confusion, insecurity and hostility to political institutions.

I know that Professor Hegel will shortly be expounding our conclusions about what our host has called the 'economic imperative'. When I spoke earlier of the 'minor frictions' which existed between the old empire-states, I could not deny that these included serious commercial rivalries; and certainly there were trading tensions developing between Great Britain, Germany, Japan and the United States. But we do not believe that they were indispensable elements in creating the war.

What clearly emerged, however, from the rubble of the Great War was a new type of political economy radiating out of the United States and eagerly embraced by the rest of the West and Japan. It relied upon the dislocation of enormous numbers of rural workers to the town and economies of scale which would rapidly complete the process already begun in old Europe whereby mass-produced goods would crush cottage-industries and the communities which they constituted. It was laissez-faire; it did not respect national boundaries, as can be seen from the growth of American exports and direct foreign investment; it was technically very efficient and productive; and it exemplified a characteristic ebullience of America and of Americans which was irresistibly attractive to the new generation of Europeans now separated and safely emancipated from the nineteenth century, but about to be re-enslaved to a new and comfortable tyranny. This was, as I believe Professor Hegel will demonstrate, the beginning of the eventual hegemony of economics: it began to act as a rival, in directing human affairs, to the traditional role of politics or religion or the community as the major equilibrating mechanisms in society. And because the nation-state system had collapsed, there were no longer any effective political constraints to the expansionary process whereby economics filled that vacuum.

Wells: Thank you, Dr Spengler. That is an excellent introduction to Professor Hegel's discussion of the domination of economics. But surely, in the midst of this vacuum, have there then been *no* examples where these enfeebled and failing nation-states *did* manage to respond to challenge, individually or in concert?

Spengler: Perhaps Professor Toynbee can comment more authoritatively than I.

Toynbee: Yes, there have been collective responses but they have been exceptional—the Great Depression, the Second World War are instances. And, in the event, the grand irony is that these international catastrophes—whether or not they go unchallenged—are themselves the direct result of the vacuum, and so there is a tragic circularity. For example, my readings tell me that the Great Depression was not, as is popularly supposed, the result of protectionism but, rather, of anarchic trading practices in a world where the old nation-states could no longer control their own affairs, but had not set up adequate replacement mechanisms. As for the Second World War, neither Great Britain nor France was, in fact, equipped to declare and wage war on Germany in 1939 but were goaded into doing so by some galvanic spark of national resolve still flickering in the embers of the nation-state, which had so grossly failed its duty earlier in the 1930's. By contrast, by far the century's greatest crisis—the environmental-economic trap—has so far met with virtually no concerted response.

I believe that Professor Hegel will have something similar to say on the matter of the inadequacy of *response*—because of the absence of national and international political authority—when he discusses economics and democracy in relation to the world's environmental crisis.

Wells: Thank you, Gentlemen. We have, then, a world whose great nation-states—themselves forged over centuries from atomised communities—have collapsed in a virtual instant of history and where no satisfactory international political substitutes have been created despite the passage of two generations when the need for them was to become of critical importance to man's very survival in a culturally recognisable form. Put differently, the powers and responsibilities of the nation-state are no longer of equal length or cover similar areas. And that is the background for some new overwhelming force to emerge and to usurp the nation-state. Professor Hegel: your address, please, on democracy and economics.'

Act Two
The triumph of liberal democracy and
the economic imperative

'The paradox of... secular liberalism is that excessive freedom leads inexorably to anarchy.' Sir Roy Calne

'Was man liebt, asphaltiert man doch nicht.' (What man loves, he shouldn't cover with asphalt) Gerhard Polt in *Grün Kaputt*.

Hegel: 'Mr Chairman, at one level we three feared that, unlike the matter of community and the nation-state, these linked subjects of democracy and economics *might* defy common agreement—principally because we have widely differing views on the merits of democracy in general, and in particular therefore of its adequacy as a political system in the twenty-first century. For me ideally, democracy meant and means *republicanism*, as it burst forth when I was a child at the time of the American and French revolutions, even though I always favoured an oligarchic system of government until such time as we could have trust in a republic. For Dr Spengler, democracy has little merit in any manifestation; whilst, for Professor Toynbee, democracy means or includes, at least, the highest degree of popular participation, as we see in today's system of universal suffrage, even though he reserves a special role for the dominant minority.

As a consequence of these differences, we doubtless hold different views as to the long-term objective of the entire human experiment, as I might call it. Mine—and Professor Toynbee's—remain bound inseparably to God's will and to the achievement of Freedom. Dr Spengler's scheme admits of no higher purpose, since it is of a preordained history with its own cycle from birth to death. However, we were able to agree without compromise first upon the destructive role of Mr Cruttwell's *economic imperative* in the twentieth century—probably the worst example of loss of control by the community and the greater nation-state. But Dr Spengler then proceeded to propose an elegant and robust solution to what threatened to be a serious obstacle to our arriving at a unanimous position on democracy; and I should like to ask him to put forward what is now our common ground as it pertains to the role of politics, democracy and government in today's environmental and economic crisis.

Spengler: Yes: the resolution is, in fact, simple. We are at one on the evil of the dominance of what I used to call 'money', now known as economics in the world to which we are visitors. As to democracy, although our disagreements are, indeed, fundamental, they are quite irrelevant to the issue of democracy and its role in economics and environmental destruction. For my two colleagues, *social* democracy is failing to respond to these challenges, as Professor Toynbee describes the process, so that new and extraordinary responses may be required unless democracy can redeem itself; while for me, democracy—social or liberal—would have been inadequate and ineffectual, anyway, so that those same responses would always have needed to be deployed, whatever the consequences for democracy.

Finally—and in support of this conclusion, and of whatever it may betoken for democracy—we have all three of us laid profound importance in our writings on the paramount need history has of unique and superhuman figures to be present at moments of historical crisis, even to precipitate them: for my two colleagues, so as to re-direct history; for me to propel it along its predetermined course.

Wells: Thank you, Dr Spengler. I presume that you are, then, all agreed that the twenty-first century must deliver up great figures for the furtherance of history, whether or not it is preordained; and regardless of the consequences for either brand of democracy—social or liberal?

Hegel: Your first presumption is correct. The second fills Professor Toynbee and me with alarm even as it lends support to Dr Spengler's views. It seems to challenge my philosophy of history as a process, not unlike that advocated by Professor Toynbee, whereby steady progress would be made irreversibly to Freedom within a republican framework.

I am very conscious of the use which has been made of my own work, since my death, in the service of Marxism and the construction of two monstrous tyrannies in this century. One of the principal lies employed by both was the notion of 'the dictatorship of the proletariat'. This was, of course, a slogan with neither substance nor promise of fulfilment. I had always said that *republicanism*, that is the *democracy* we are here discussing, was an ideal form of government but that, pending its perfection, enlightened government by an altruistic oligarchy was in the better interests of the people.

I am also aware that, much more recently, my work has been adapted so as to lend support to the view currently held or urged by many influential observers, that democracy—usually nowadays qualified as *liberal* democracy—is now the preferred worldwide form of political arrangement because it has provided immeasurable material comfort in West-Europe-America; in sum, that mass economic activity and liberal democracy are mutually supportive. We have no doubt that this type of economic activity requires a liberal political structure in which to flourish; and that democracy may thrive on material well-being. But we are equally in no doubt that a paradox of economic freedom is that it must be controlled. The alternative is anarchy.

Wells: This is the *economic imperative*, which depends for its prosperity on democratic institutions?

Hegel: Well, it does indeed seem to be quite unarguable that the greatest success in the matter of economic activity began in a country touched by the first stirrings, however faltering and tentative, of democratic ideals, that is Great Britain; and that this extraordinary duality has spread with incredible rapidity and irresistible force throughout West-Europe-America and now to the four corners of the world in this century. Yes, in that restricted sense limitless economic expansion and democratic notions have travelled together. But ultimately, they are irreconcilable— they are antinomic—and what we are now seeing is not the global consummation of their marriage but the beginnings of the end-game in the latent struggle between the two. It is a doomed duopoly.

But clearly, they were *not* linked in many parts of the world histori-cally outside that West-Europe-America orbit, where they have been artificially transplanted most frequently at the initiative of West-Europe-America, which provides the markets, capital and expertise. At least, neither of the two giant Marxist states (by no means nation-states, by the way, and far from being so) exhibited the same duality, nor have most of the other countries which had never become nation-states.

Wells: So, if I understand you correctly, the preconditions for the economic imperative to 'succeed' are the replacement of community by the nation-state, followed hard-on-its-heels with its being usurped by the *liberal* brand of democracy?

Hegel: Yes, but the experience of this twentieth century suggests that it is a poisoned chalice because...

Toynbee: Loss of control?

Hegel: Yes, precisely. As long as the nation-state remained the standard political arrangement (and I mean, of course, the international system which survived—with all its imperfections—until 1918), that form of polity could control with great precision the most important elements in the nation's economic structure and operation. This is not to deny— rather, in fact, it is to admit and recognise that a consequence of purely *national* political and economic control would be the occasional, even frequent, denial to the citizenry of the products of certain types of economic activity: for example, because they are ecologically destructive, or they jeopardise domestic employment, or are beyond the nation's capacity to afford.

Spengler: Meaning, then, the exercise of discretionary powers by your oligarchy, or Professor Toynbee's dominant minority for the greater good of the masses?

Hegel: Again, yes. The nation-state does not—did not—*guarantee* that all decisions of its government, duly elected, would always be popular, or even that they would be correct decisions. What it did mean, and I fear we must now use the past tense, is that at least decisions would be taken and policies adopted and followed within what I may call a *manageable cultural curtilage*, that is a political unit with which the citizen could still feel at ease, of which he could still feel part even though there had already been much loss of community. It should mean in addition that the nation-state would resist enacting the kind of legislation to attain social and economic objectives which clearly lie beyond its capacity— without, that is, either entering into unrepayable piles of foreign indebtedness; or constructing manufacturing industries which depend on undependable foreign markets and the consumption of wasting raw materials to deliver ephemeral benefits. Those who conceived and formulated social democracy—Athenians, disaffected American colonists, French and English thinkers—were not challenged by the twentieth century by-products of its liberal-economic mutation.

Wells: You seem, Professor Hegel, to have made a very strong *personal* identification with the crisis of the twenty-first century.

Hegel: I am—not unnaturally—saddened, as a human being, by the plight in which our host and his generation now seem to be enmeshed. More than that, I am also deeply disturbed, as an historian, that my philosophy of history seems to have been flawed or, at least, that I was unable to foresee as clearly as Dr Spengler what might, indeed would, supervene to devalue it.

Toynbee: I think, Mr Chairman, that Professor Hegel must be quite exonerated. My own performance as a prophet, writing a century and more later, is sadly defective; and I call to mind an interesting aphorism of Mr Cruttwell when he remarks that 'When Hegel was writing, history as we now know it, had not even started' or words to that effect.

Spengler: It is not my wish to disturb the great harmony of views which we have developed during our seminars; but, even as I sympathise with my colleagues in their academic distress, I am bound to observe most respectfully that each may have to reconcile the role which was reserved to the Divine in their philosophies, with the reality of His abandonment of humanity in this century.

Wells: Um…I think that we had best defer for a moment discussion of the spiritual dimension of the crisis. May I finally ask you, Professor Hegel, before inviting Professor Toynbee to address us, whether the weight of evidence suggests that the economic imperative destroyed the nation-state, or was it the destruction of the nation-state which permitted the economic imperative to fill the vacuum? After all, you have established that there is a close synchronism between the two phenomena.

Hegel: Yes, there is; and it is a matter which has engaged our attention this weekend. Professor Toynbee and I take the view that the causality is too fine and the two phenomena, as you usefully call them, too intricately bound and mutually reinforcing for there to be a simple answer. However, one could argue that the nation-state has merely followed the community to the same grave in yielding to the twin forces of science and economics. Dear Dr Spengler, of course, holds that cause-and-effect has played no role whatsoever, and never has in history at large.

What I can say—as a kind of response—is that both the question and any answer to it are probably now quite irrelevant: certainly we all three believe that both the problem and the solution are political—and cultural—not economic.

Wells: Thank you, Professor Hegel. In summary, then, a largely harmonious system of nation-states formed from smaller communities, and able to determine their own destinies and historical direction, has collapsed in the twentieth century, so that even as democracy has vanquished both communism and fascism, political and cultural authority have everywhere been put in thrall to unsustainably destructive economic activity—the economic imperative. Professor Toynbee, would you now please conclude your task by setting our two phenomena—our nearly-complete explanation of the world's current malaise—in today's political and cultural context?'

Act Three
The failure of political institutions and their replacement by the system of transnational corporations

'Capitalism is the exploitation by man of man—Communism is quite the reverse.' Warsaw taxi-driver, 1985.

Toynbee: 'Thank you, Mr Chairman. Professor Hegel has referred to the practice by governments the world over—since the passing of the system of nation-states—of enacting what I may call 'declarative' legislation in the pursuit of unattainable socio-economic objectives: goals which may in themselves be noble and desirable but which are, in the very jargon of economists, 'uncosted' or beyond the national capacity. To the obverse of this political coinage I would add the reverse which, in an atmosphere of opportunism and short-term expediency, is the practice of declining to contemplate legislation which is perceived to be what I have read as 'electorally dysfunctional'. It is a practice which seems us to be a central feature of liberal democracy and of the politics of the later twentieth century and to have originated partly in the politician's fear of universal suffrage and partly in the intensity of ideological competition—no longer, if indeed ever, between the great global ideologies of democracy, fascism and communism, but within democracy itself. And it is in the arena of economics and of material consumerism, that the sordid political battle-lines are now drawn up. More particularly, we believe that those lines now clearly divide democracy itself into two opposing wings—liberal and social.

There is another dichotomy: throughout the West since the Second World War, except in the United States, there has developed the concept and practice of the welfare state. But it seems that not even today's economies, with their tremendous generation of tax revenue, can support the burden of welfare-state funding—partly through actuarial incompetence, partly through fraud but largely through opportunistic politics—and this has become a constant theme of social discontent and therefore of distrust of government. An excellent, that is to say an appalling example is the United States where short-term political calculation has produced a level of national indebtedness which will, within a predictable period, consume the entire Federal tax revenue in interest and repayment of principal. It is precisely matched by a comparable mound of private foreign debt resulting largely from grossly irresponsible trading practices. This is loss of control and of political will at its most extreme, but it is symptomatic of all government.

Wells: Is it not a legitimate duty of government to seek to maximise the material well-being of the people; and is it not right that the people support that form of democracy—liberal or social—which seems most likely to be able to deliver that well-being?

Toynbee: Most certainly. Yes, to maximise or, rather, to *optimise* national well-being but in other than a merely material sense and, as we have insisted, in strict accordance with the constraints of national resources. As to those electoral proclamations, the impact of this practice is enormously enhanced by the cheapness of mass electronic communications, which are almost invariably organized in the furtherance of commercial purposes. They also now stretch across national boundaries and therefore exert a levelling and homogenizing effect on peoples throughout the world, even as they encourage envy, resentment, undeliverable expectations and—in the worst examples—extreme retaliation by fundamental religionists who feel culturally blasphemed. In the process, just as identical *material* goods are being manufactured and marketed throughout the world, so also are the socio-economic aspirations I mentioned earlier.

Wells: Are these governments not, in fact, the 'altruistic oligarchs' of Professor Hegel, or your own favoured 'dominant minorities'? Is government not, by definition, always the function of a minority?

Toynbee: Well, they are certainly not 'altruistic', even where they are not inherently despotic; and, yes, they are oligarchic and dominant albeit, as in any form of electoral democracy, ephemeral. However, even this ephemeral character is illusory since the liberal-economic form of democratic government in the West shows little sign of being replaced by something more enlightened, and it is uncertain that social democracy will have practical and politically marketable solutions to the crisis. But we must come back to how government is functioning now, at the end of the millennium, and how politicians interpret their purpose. In this respect, we agree with an opinion expressed to us by our host: namely, that neither today's politicians nor the political institutions in which they operate are inherently inferior to paradigms of the past. It is simply that, for the reasons already set out, the theology of production and consumption have usurped the higher purposes of government; and the economic imperative has become both the lowest common denominator and the highest common factor as measures of human activity.

Spengler: Will you explain, Professor Toynbee, how the insecurity and opportunism we have seen in so much of contemporary society—short-termism is a popular synonym—are expressed and aggravated through this obsession with economics?

Toynbee: I suppose I can best offer that explanation by means of some examples, which all have to do with the deadly belief in limitless and costless growth in production and consumption. (I recall your warnings, Dr Spengler, that *limitlessness* and *gigantism* would be curses of the twentieth and twenty-first centuries.) Economic activity—I could almost say *human* activity—today is measured by statistics, which are never in themselves descriptive of the benefits which that activity is deemed to bring to mankind. Thus, deviations from some statistically measurable aspect of economic activity are *ipso facto* causes of insecurity. Successive governments in many countries have committed themselves through addiction to the declarative, *aspirational* kind of legislation to concepts such as 'full employment', or the abolition of 'protectionism' in foreign trade; and are convulsed in a quasi-religious frenzy by parables from the GATT priesthood. The people are invited to believe these to be wholly 'good' things when in fact they make individuals and society hostage to massively destructive international forces over which the legislature has no control. There is a military analogy:

Where nation-state government had once been able to ensure, with a measurable degree of confidence, its 'territorial integrity' through military preparedness, its ability to control its economic affairs, which have been wilfully made 'interdependent' on two hundred or more other equally uncontrollable economies, has been frittered away in pursuit of utterly undefined objectives. As a consequence, the theoretical commitment by so-called 'national' government to this or that socio-economic policy or objective has become meaningless; and it is unable significantly to control inflation, unemployment, interest rates and—most seriously for the long-term well-being of its people—the global environmental degradation which uncontrolled, unplanned and uncosted economic 'development' has inflicted on the twentieth century.

The intrinsic powerlessness of government can only be papered over with weasel-words. But the people see through the sham, and hence the contempt felt for politicians and political institutions.

Wells: Do you say, then, that there no effective supra-national organizations? no arrangements for the detection and elimination of the problems you describe?

Toynbee: There is only one effective supra-national form of organization in a late twentieth-century world otherwise littered with public international institutions of myriad purpose and dubious effectiveness. But we have found that, ironically, some of the most powerful and august of such bodies—examples are the World Bank and International Monetary Fund, the United Nations Commission on Trade & Development, and the General Agreement on Tariffs and Trade (shortly to be renamed the World Trade Organization)—are major contributors to and supporters of the growth and internationalization of the economic imperative. They are the *public* guardians of *private* privilege, as I shall show.

Parallel with the erosion—now almost complete—of the authority and effectiveness of the nation-state, and its putative replacement by the type of unaccountable bureaucracies we have cited, there has arisen a form of concentrated private international economic power which transcends both the remnants of the nation-state system *and* the international bureaucracies and which, even though they may operate for the most part in perfect conformity with the law, remain virtually unaccountable to any higher authority. This is the only effective supra-national form of organization: it is the transnational corporation.

Wells: I should be grateful if you would describe it and explain your assertion that it has supplanted the nation-state.

Toynbee: We can say of West-Europe-America that the locus and exercise of power had traditionally resided in Four Estates: parliament and presidency, priesthood and press. We have sufficiently examined the eclipse of the first three. The last, along with its electronic extensions, is now part of the culture of transnational corporatism.

The transnational corporation derives its overweening power from an oxymoron: its *public* nature—in the mass employment it provides, the products and services it lavishes on the world it has homogenized, and government dependence on it for tax revenue; its *private* nature—in its exemption from democratic constraints, its unaccountability, except in a narrow bookkeeping sense, and its purpose, namely the enrichment of those who own and operate it. In addition it is, unlike government, immortal.

Wells: And will this unaccountability invariably work against the interests of the people? Do you say that the transnational corporation is inherently evil in its effect and intention? That it differs from the great commercial baronies of the nineteenth century?

Toynbee: A single answer: No, not invariably, but the very fact of unaccountability is itself a potential force for evil. Whilst our research has shown many examples of illegal or anti-social behaviour, we do *not* say that the transnational corporation is *inherently* evil in all its works; indeed, there are innumerable instances of the material benefits which are most cost-effectively brought to society by large, well-run businesses, not to mention the huge direct and indirect employment it creates in a world where labour and employment have become self-fulfilling and self-reinforcing necessities but with no social purpose.

But we *do* say that the transnational corporation is now the dominant force in economic activity and that, since the economic imperative is the all-consuming preoccupation of those vestiges of national government which remain, the orderly exercise of political power has quite literally been surrendered not by proxy but by default to the transnational corporate culture.

Do you not find it a strange irony, Mr Chairman, that Corporatism, which was both feared and advocated in the nineteenth century—but which did not, in the event, come to pass—should now have utterly triumphed through a by-passing of the political control which was to have been so central to it.

Wells: And is the law equally as impotent as government?

Spengler: It is not the duty of the law to plan and direct economic activity. The law will tend to be reactive—rarely prophetic, never proactive. Besides, in a regime of free-for-all economics, it is inconceivable that the countless millions of daily decisions and transactions could ever be monitored—controlled—or that, in the absence of that control, their sum could miraculously be beneficial or value-neutral. It seems to us vital for a dialectical understanding of the twentieth century to recognise that the global surrender by government of *economic* control has not been sanctified by a formal transfer to the transnational corporate establishment of *political* control. But the practical location of that control is no longer in doubt, as I foresaw many years ago and...

Wells: Yes, Dr Spengler, but let us stick to our theme. Professor Toynbee, you wish to comment?

Toynbee: Thank you, Mr Chairman. To develop Dr Spengler's point, we emphasize again that we are not asserting an ethical, and certainly not a moral, view of the transnational corporate culture; we have merely described the practical consequences of the subordination of civil society to the economic imperative seen in its most overwhelming form.

Central problems presented by the transnational corporation—not an inherently evil institution—are first, that it is largely free not so much of *political*, but of *societary* control. It is organized not for the intrinsic welfare of the community but—legally, and by definition—for the enrichment of its shareholders, management and perhaps its employees. Thus, in the absence of clearly formulated consensual community purpose, the global sum of all the transnational corporations' activities and strategies acts as a kind of surrogate global government. Put another way, society's—the world's, if you wish—macroeconomics are the sum of the microeconomics of a thousand transnational corporations.

Second, what we may call the *ethic* of the transnational is endless growth, undifferentiated as to value. In other words, quantity has displaced quality in almost exactly the same way that *development* and *growth* have become meaningless synonyms for each other, so that the debasement of language now adds a metaphysical complication to the material fact of environmental destruction. And it is strange that endless growth, to which this culture has committed itself, is a phenomenon which simple observation of nature—or of human societies in history—shows has never happened or has ever been possible. In this respect, we are both at one with Dr Spengler in his pathology.

Third, and by no means last, there seems to be no evidence whatever that this endless growth upon which the transnational culture must depend, yields even a linear increase in human happiness: on the contrary, that the two curves intersected some decades ago so that as the *growth* curve now strides ever upward, the *happiness* curve has at best flattened, and at worst is now pitching down towards the x-axis.

Spengler: Yes. But yet, of course, our host's world will need the transnational corporation's active participation—even its leadership, certainly its partnership—in responding to the challenges it has itself largely created and which threaten its own existence. Self-interest may thus serve selflessness.

Wells: Your prophecy has been proved correct then, Dr Spengler?

Spengler: Thank you, Mr Wells, but no: you will recall my confession that I have served only to expound 'history and the philosophy of destiny', and I take no credit if I have seen little cause to change my views.

Wells: You wished to add something in conclusion, Professor Toynbee?

Toynbee: Yes, Mr Chairman, may I briefly comment on an earlier remark of Dr Spengler. It is perfectly true to say that the three of us have reached a position of unanimity in identifying the three *causes*—if Dr Spengler will not object to my use of the word—of the environmental and cultural crisis of 2001. Nevertheless, Professor Hegel and I are, and remain, Christians and we therefore believe in good and evil. Evil has, in the main, prevailed over good in this century; and already in the 1960s and 1970s—towards the end of my life—I was having to reconcile growing inconsistencies between my own view of God's purpose being expressed in history, and the reality of evil and religious apathy in this century. It is for this reason that I added a twelfth volume to my work and entitled it *Reconsiderations*. You may perhaps not have read it.

The fact that the evil has been utterly indiscriminate between peoples—that war and environmental destruction, for example, have been so to speak ecumenical in selecting their human targets—has convinced me that both my faith and my Christian despair were too narrow. I do not know, and in the circumstances may never know, whether my God and my faith are ultimately the same as that shared by all other peoples but under strange and different names. But I am certain that alongside the environmental and cultural crisis of 2001, there lies a spiritual crisis—indeed, that they are linked in a way similar to the link we have explored between the decline of the nation-state and the supremacy of the economic imperative.

I have had to abandon the arrogance which once would have seen me advocating a last-minute capitulation to my (Christian) God as His condition for aiding humanity in his solution of the crisis; but I firmly believe that a sense of spiritual rebirth will be vital in energizing people's response to the imminent challenge, however 'secular' that spirituality may be.

Wells: Thank you, Gentlemen. I shall now acquaint our host with the results of your deliberations. I thank you all and bid you goodnight and farewell.'

Chapter Ten

Towards a Political Resolution

'The power of [pastoral fables] to move us derives from the magnitude of the protean conflict figured by the machine's increasing domination of the visible world... The machine's sudden entrance into the garden presents a problem that ultimately belongs not to art but to politics.' Leo Marx: *The Machine in the Garden*

'The larger and more centralised our institutions, the more resistant will they be to change—and the more catastrophic will be any change when it comes... [We need] different social structures, starting with the dismantling of the nation state and all other forms of gigantism, and ending with the restoration of community.' Maurice Ash: *Journey into the Eye of a Needle*

Using Theories of History

IN MY INTRODUCTION, I said that I was setting out on a single-scull journey of exploration into the future of history, and that I did not know where it would lead me. I didn't; but I have now traversed three major theories of history—including one from the 1820s which has recently been dusted off, skilfully adapted and repackaged for the 1990s—and I have found each of them wanting—for quite different reasons. Still, two of them have yielded up some implements which may possibly prove useful in grappling with imminent history; the third—all its blemishes notwithstanding—seems sufficiently prophetic even eighty years on so as to make the need for such a grappling a future historical probability, even though the variant fourth posits that history need seek no further advances beyond today's liberal democracy and free-market economics.

We cannot indict Hegel for having misread the then current drift of history of which his obscure Prussia was but a small and as yet unimportant part. Why not? The simple but startling answer is the very substance of this book: history, as we now know and see it, *hadn't even started* when Hegel was writing. I had earlier shown that it had always been random; but that it was not to be until the twentieth century that history would attain a perverse form of directionality imposed upon humanity through its own works. As for Oswald Spengler, his historical instincts were not so much surer than Hegel's, simply more reflective of the ominous clouds lowering on the horizon of 1914: by then, history most certainly *had* started. Moreover, Spengler had a special historical insight through his horror at the notion of *limitlessness*—which we have seen in the form of the excesses of the twentieth century—even though this horror extended as much to the sublimeness of Gothic cathedrals with spires of limitless vertical ambition and Bach fugues and inventions, as to to the banality of infinite bank credit.

But where Spengler was a visionary, Hegel's God had not endowed him with the same gifts; and Toynbee was unaccountably purblinded by his religion to the evidence of political and economic malaise which was already beginning to foam up around him when he took up his pen. We can never know whether Hegel and Toynbee would have developed their theories as they did—or, indeed, whether they would even have embarked on the enterprise in the first place—had it not been for the sense each had that their God's will was being worked out in history. Perhaps we can only repeat that Hegel would have been aghast at the course history was to follow after his century; whilst Toynbee must have felt sufficiently disconcerted by the events which paralleled his thirty-year labour that he went on to write a revisionist twelfth volume entitled *Reconsiderations* some years before his death. Toynbee makes it clear that God's precise purpose had, by then, become considerably less unambiguous.

I also remarked in my opening pages that the book was not yet another addition to the ecological canon; but that changes in the relationship of human beings to their environment, as we went on to investigate, had been so colossal in the twentieth century that not only would history and theories of history need to be rewritten, but—far more importantly—humankind's very survival in its *traditional* environment would become problematical in the early third millennium. The word is emphasised because, as Bill McKibben had shown in *The End of Nature*, survival in some *unaccustomed* environment—a kind of global life-support system—may be perfectly possible, even if decidedly ghoulish. McKibben's *The End of Nature* and Fukuyama's *The End of History* appeared within a couple of years of each other and yet their conclusions—reached from starting-points which we might expect them to have shared in objectivity—suggest that their authors were gazing across at each other from different planets.

The pestilence of insupportably growing numbers, destruction of the environment and the wasting of three indispensable natural resources were shown to be inseparably connected and self-reinforcing; and I then went on to peer into the cauldron where the menaces are brewing and boiling towards the brim: this is the wired-up world of global-village economics which has become the arena where these forces will collide and touch the everyday lives of people in a far more immediate way than the still somewhat abstract 'warnings' about the environment.

There is a legion of exceedingly important issues which I have either ignored or given the shortest of shrifts. They include—and I will certainly have forgotten several other worthy candidates which might merit the attention of a more encyclopaedic work—nuclear war and proliferation; mass migration for economic, political or environmental reasons; disintegration of the United States and eruption of China; equality of (and for) women; extreme expressions of racism; biotech farming; genetic engineering; (even greater) thought-control; robots and automation; urban nuclear terrorism; bulging Internets and empty fishing-nets; ageing populations in the Northern hemisphere; biodiversity; information superhighways; and AIDS. The justification for these omissions, apart from considerations of time and space, is very simple: none of them individually—and, conceivably, even in combination—adds up to as great a challenge as *any single one* of my three core menaces—overpopulation and the Demons of Chapter Five—but I have, by way of atonement, cited Paul Kennedy's recent Guide, as he calls it, to the Twenty-first Century where he discusses several of these issues and comes to a number of conclusions which are both perceptive and sombre.

Having set these characters against a set of props—theories of history—and found that they were no longer appropriate, as *complete systems*, to the drama, I proceeded to formulate a far more humble and agnostic but more robust theory: that from earliest prehistory humankind as a whole, or in given societies, has simply passed through a number of phases characterized by *Drives*—Subsistential, Metaphysical and finally Power. Such a workaday theory is perfectly consistent with the more *mechanical* elements of Hegel and Toynbee—the concepts of recurrent tension and resolution in Hegel and of challenge-and-response in Toynbee—but it rejects any notion of pre-direction and purpose, divine or otherwise. It is also consistent with all three theories where they unite in their theory of history as a process of birth, growth, maturity and decline (in fact, this aspect can scarcely merit the term 'theory' since it is so obviously observable in every recess of human history); and it supports the theme that history needs exceptional individuals to energize it. Finally, although I could not swallow Spengler's claim of predictive qualities for his theory—'the venture of predetermining history'—I have defended him against the meaningless chorus of 'pessimist!' which has rung down the years to and beyond such blatherskites as Herman Kahn.

Human beings had to all intents and purposes solved the more purely *technical* problems of producing enough food and warmth, shelter and manufactured goods fairly early in the present century. Certainly there remained the issues of their equitable distribution, of the threat of war and of natural disasters; but it seemed to many that 'liberal' democracy had emerged in the second half of the century as the form of political and economic organization which would best promise to ease our passage from the trials of ten millennia of history and on into Fukuyama's Promised Land: 'Just as a modern economist does not try to define a product's 'utility' or 'value' in itself, but rather accepts the marketplace's valuation of it as expressed in a price, so one would accept the judgement of the 'marketplace' of world history... if there do not appear to be viable alternatives to liberal democracy, and if people living in liberal democracies express no radical discontent with their lives, we can say that the dialogue has reached a final and definitive conclusion.'[1]

In *economics*, this radical market-orientation of the 1980s has been unmasked as a false god; whilst, in *history*, what Fukuyama saw as mere 'problems' remaining to be solved, were not limited to his odd little list of 'serious [sic] ones like budget deficits, inflation, crime or drugs', but were first and foremost overpopulation, environmental destruction and resource depletion which had colluded to become an obstinate *contradiction* to the End-of-History success of liberal democracy; and one which, as I have shown, Fukuyama has not recognised as having become 'so serious that it not only cannot be solved *within the system*, but corrodes the legitimacy of the system itself such that the latter collapses under its own weight.' [my italics][2]

An impartial reading of the impending collisions discussed in this book leaves none of us in any doubt that humanity, having come close to mastering nature in the last one hundred years or so, is now losing control of history. We shall, therefore, now put forward a syncretized theory of history, drawing on contributions from our survey, and apply it to the task of helping humanity to reverse the excesses of the twentieth century and thereby to create a sustainable basis for successful survival in the twenty-first and beyond.

From remotest prehistory, human beings had sought to increase their *control* of their time-and-space environment. They did this by resolving tensions and contradictions and proceeding to ever-higher orders of conflict resolution (Hegel), and through responding successfully to challenges (Toynbee). Their means of *Subsistence* had been effectively ensured by the turn of this century; their *Metaphysical* needs had been commuted—or were at least commutable—into knowledge by the advance of natural science; and in the attainment of both of these drives, superhistorical individuals deployed the *Power* drive. Western liberal democracy, tracing back to Fifth-century Athens and slowly maturing over the past half-millennium, had vanquished two mortal enemies in this century; had brought about a large measure of personal freedom for its citizens through their willingness to allow the state to arbitrate in areas of social confrontation; and had created such wealth as to make it the most powerful and potentially benign force in a world—one which most of its people wish to sign up to.

This syncretic theory of history is based purely upon the observation that this is the way that history has, in fact, operated; it allows for no role whatsoever for a *divine* element—except, of course, for the role the *idea* of the divine has played as a force in motivating some of the creators of history; nor have I found room for any suggestion of *direction*, except in the sense of the irreversibility of the sum of acquired human knowledge. My journey has yielded no idea of how and why the Demons got loose, and I do not imagine that there is any way of rebottling them: new quart genies don't easily fit back into old pint bottles. Here, perhaps, lies the flaw in God's creation—that spark which arced from His finger-tip to Adam's in Michelangelo's painting, the same one which compromised Faust with Mephistopheles, and which was to produce Spengler's vision of the fate of humanity starting some two hundred years after Napoleon's death in 1821. Anyway, it is the one which we are left with for better or worse, and the very same one we have to use to extricate ourselves creatively from the destructive consequences of its use over the last century—to fashion a resolution using this simple theory of history.

My journey is finished: I now know where history has deposited me—and my five-and-a-half billion fellow-travellers—on the eve of the third millennium. Our history is going out of control; there is little time, and only the resources listed earlier, to decide where we go from here.

The End of History: Changing the Destination

The resolution must involve *change;* and change means deliberately opting for something which we have identified as an end-state which is more desirable than the one in which we find ourselves today because it is sustainable, not simply 'more sustainable' in the current jargon—a steady state and possibly something closer to a true end-of-history state. There is a choice here: theoretically, that steady state could be one we revert to, i.e. some time-space we *think*, at least, we remember collectively and used to inhabit—like people sitting round a campfire listening to blind Homer reciting tales of times of which they really had no personal knowledge; or it might be a newly-fashioned world which will have to be hewn out of the organized chaos of today, that is to say one which lies well beyond Fukuyama's cherished buffer-stop to history.

But one thing that end-state will have nothing to do with is what I referred to some time earlier as 'bottle-bank' environmentalism—a form of do-goodery which only serves to divert attention from the political and economic roots of our crisis—nor, indeed, will it have to do primarily with traditional notions of environmentalism. Here is a representative list of what our Resolution will *not* be all about: 'Recycle aluminium; segregate jam-jars from tin cans; lag hotwater tanks; use fluorescent light bulbs; stuff your freezer with newspapers; turn off the lights; build cavity walls'—all excerpted from the more mundane parts of '5000 Days to Save the World'.[3] These are, at their best, simple commonsense house-keeping practices and, at their worst, just handy forms of ritual absolution which we can all do whilst James Lovelock's Gaia shrugs us off with all the insouciance of a bull flicking flies off his sore rump.

The first choice—some old comfortable time-space—is no longer on offer: we cannot disremember it; but neither can we dismantle science and technology; nor can we pour the oil back into the ground or re-fix the carbon dioxide or top up the Ogalalla; we cannot undo the history which started a few decades after Hegel; we can only try to head off the vision which Spengler has scheduled to begin in the first decades of the twenty-first century, and siphon it off into a kind of historical landfill site. It has to be a newly-fashioned world—one which will have been purged of the sicknesses which afflict the old one—where human beings can regain control of the history now slipping out of their grasp:

the Resolution is not environmental, but political and economic and therefore, above all, social and cultural.

A new world order will reject the Economics of Wonderland, which we nailed in the last chapter as the cause of environmental destruction, resource depletion and, at the same time, the main cause-and-effect of the population explosion. Here again, there is a theoretical choice: shall we see what can be salvaged from today's shambles? shall we seek to create a centralised world government? or do we strike out in a completely new direction? For we cannot afford the time to give *today's* world another chance, having spent a large part of around two hundred pages enumerating its fatal contradictions. Let us look briefly to our world-historians and at recent and current proposals for deliberately-engineered forms of supranational government to see if they are credible candidates to confront the challenges and offer the solutions we shall require in the new millennium.

Hegel thought that although republicanism was the superior form of government in a more perfect world, the moral condition of the people did not yet allow of it and that therefore it would be a safer bet to continue to depend on the benign rule of a traditional strong oligarchy, pending a significant improvement in the manners of the populace. Whilst he was speaking of Prussia, there is no reason to suppose that he would have thought differently of forms of government elsewhere, nor that he would have recommended a different model for America, where he saw history moving. If Hegel was not thinking explicitly in *global* terms, it is only because for him Prussia-Europe-America *was* the world, history had always moved in a westerly direction (having gone through its Oriental and Graeco-Roman phases) and would one day have to stop only when it reached the Pacific. When Hegel was writing, neither political nor economic gigantism was yet a phenomenon of human history: and we can therefore only conjecture idly how he would have had his republican oligarchs handle the gigantism whose birth Spengler dates to shortly before Hegel's death in 1830.

Spengler was similarly lukewarm towards the notion of democracy (hence his veneration of Caesar and Napoleon); and he could even detect a linkage between plutocracy and democracy—almost a trail of Fukuyama's later announcement of the triumph of liberal democracy and the economic imperative. But, in any event, since history was preordained, Spengler could hardly allow himself to engage in speculation about the merits of alternative political systems—national or supranational—and their adequacy in a confrontation with novel challenges.

There is no menu in prewritten history, no choice.

As for Toynbee, by Volume X he had come to believe that a form of world government, run—it mattered little—by either the United States or the Soviet Union, or split between the two American and Soviet 'demi-mundane dispensations', would be the best approach 'towards a future world order', with her generosity, commitment to the federal principle and her very reluctance to play the role at all tending to favour the United States. The United Nations 'was evidently incapable of becoming the embryo of a world government… [because of] the unrealistic principle of "one state, one vote".'[4] If some new form of world order commended itself to Toynbee in the simpler days of the 1950s, how much more imperative would it now have seemed to him in 1995? But there is no evidence that there have, since Toynbee wrote, arisen new candidates to govern the world where the United Nations is, to paraphrase Senator Patrick Moynihan, 'an even more dangerous place to be', and where the sole other contender is compromised by political self-doubt and economic malaise.

H.G. Wells had a go at world government in the last nine pages of his 760-page *Outline of History*, published in 1920. Today, they seem extraordinarily naive—viewed through lenses distorted by the disappointments and cynicism of the following seventy-five years—but Wells felt that the end of the Great War was a turning-point in history, and many must have shared his belief that 'the world-wide outbreak of faith and hope in President Wilson, before he began to wilt and fail us, was a very significant thing indeed for the future of mankind.'[5] Some of Wells' musings on the League of Nations are worth reciting as a gloss on the political and strategic powerlessness of today's United Nations and the persistence of the nation-state, albeit it in feeble condition:

'There are few intimations of… enthusiasm for the League at the present time. The League does not even seem to know how to talk to common men. It has gone into official buildings, and comparatively few people in the world understand or care what it is doing there. It may be that the League is no more than a first project of union, exemplary only in its dangers and deficiencies… The League is at present a mere partial league of governments and states. It emphasizes nationality; it defers to sovereignty. What the world needs is no such league of nations as this nor even a mere league of peoples, but a *world league of men*.'[6] An early plea for communitarianism?

Wells goes on to pass in review the forces which seemed to be propelling 1920s man towards his Federal World State:

'The increasing destructiveness and intolerableness of war waged with the new powers of science... The inevitable fusion of the world's economic affairs into one system [requiring] world control of very considerable authority and *powers of enforcement*... Equalization of labour conditions... and some minimum standard of education for everyone.'[7] [my italics]

And he trails some of the features of that Federal World State:

'A common world religion... and universal education... no armies, no navies and no classes of unemployed people, wealthy or poor. The world's political organization will be democratic... and responsive to the general thought of the educated whole population... and its economic organization will be an exploitation of all natural wealth and every fresh possibility science reveals [while] private enterprise will be... no longer the robber master of the commonweal.'[8]

Not much wrong with all that. But I have in front of me a copy of Wells' last book—an oddity entitled *Mind at the End of its Tether*, written twenty-five years later in 1945 when both Wells and his world were very sick indeed. Certainly, the League of Nations had long since foundered; and I have no doubt that Wells, had he been writing another half-century later, would have felt rather differently about progress either to his Federal World State through the United Nations, or to a successful diminution of the role of the nation-state.

Wells, the Fabian socialist, was rather ambivalent about *empire* and *imperialism*; and it is ironic that the collapse of many of the great European empires in World War I and the rest a generation later, and the resulting global profusion of new 'nations'—few of them, be it noted, true nation-states—with little prospect of true economic independence, might have put an end to any liberal notion that some form of multi-imperial fusion might provide the basis for a unitary government of much of the world. Perhaps the very idea was as will-o'-the-wispish as all the other advocacies of world government; but here is Wells again, writing of the British Empire: 'It was and is a quite unique political combination... It is impossible to say whether this unprecedented imperialism will obstruct or help forward that final unification of the world's affairs towards which all history is pointing.'[9] That was Wells writing in 1920; and one is bound to think that he did so in a first flush or afterglow of wish-fulfilment following the end of the war.

Given Wells' despair at the end of the next one just twenty-five years later, we are entitled to doubt whether he then still harboured that same historicist heresy—the view that history was heading somewhere with indeflectible purpose; nor can we suppose that he would have persisted in his belief that world government was the agency by which it would reach its destination.

May we then compromise? Is not the so-called European Union, for example, a subset of world government, a prototype, a pilot-scheme, the first bold stride towards a new world order? There is yet little agreement on the precise direction and probable evolution of this Procrustean organization except, perhaps, amongst its most extreme advocates and opponents. What began as the ECSC—a coal-and-steel club—has metamorphosed through EEC to EC and now to a notional union administered by oligarchs of uncertain benignity; and its smokestack origins now lie under a political mulch of indeterminate fragrance and composition. All that seems certain about it today is an absence of popular passion in its support; its commitment to economic gigantism; and the very blend of political dislocation and ambiguity which our historians unearthed in their Symposium. Now, in 1995, what was called—but never was—a *community*, is yet to become a union; and even assuming that such a hydra-headed creature were desirable, the difficulties its advocates are experiencing in forging a true union amongst peoples closely linked by history and race, suggest that replication on a global level will require human engineering of an ingenuity yet to be devised.

And so we had better look elsewhere for our new world order.

Autarky:
A Way for the Third Millennium

'All the world is not Greenwich, Connecticut.' David Rockefeller, Chairman of Chase Manhattan Bank, to the author in Geneva, Switzerland, 1980.

'It makes sense to incorporate everyone into the global economy on the grounds that it will expand trade... Inequalities grow despite the claim that the global market is the panacea for all ills.' François Mitterand, President of France, *The Guardian*, 5 July 1994.

This book would have failed completely if it had not dripped large drops of introspection into the veins of at least some of the less bigoted of the business-as-usual salon, whether they are queueing at the gates of Fukuyama's Promised Land at *his* End of History; or eagerly contemplating an ever-accelerating race on to the broad sunlit consumerist uplands beyond. And it will have reinforced the convictions of those in the opposing salon who know that the political economy of today's Global Village cannot be sustained, and never could have been. In between lies a majority of people for whom these problems have remained subliminal but which are now poised to crash through the roof and into their lives in the next century. Those who have 'heard it all before' and demand that a date and a description be put to some finite point where unsustainability is reached, are either seeking to discredit what is probably now the opinion of the informed and moderate majority who have rumbled the Global Village for the deadly sham it is; or, more innocently, they simply misgauge both the surreptitiousness and yet the malevolence of the menaces confronting us. The polarization of these two positions into 'salons' is a potential disaster for the human race; but those who occupy the second salon, notwithstanding all its imperfections and imprecision, could draw some comfort if there were growing acceptance of at least the *principle* set out in the Global Equation of Chapter Four, namely that an indefinite increase in consumption out of a fixed supply of resources by indefinitely growing numbers is, *ipso facto*, illogical and impossible. For the vast majority of people who can articulate it—and certainly for virtually all politicians, most of whom *cannot*—this is the ultimate human conundrum with which this book has been chiefly concerned: the pure logic of the principle is overpowering and inescapable, but the conundrum is so disagreeable that a response to the challenge it poses is perhaps best be deferred to a future generation... Alternatively, the very technology whose ethical neutrality has enabled us to inflict such terrors on ourselves and our living-space will somehow purge itself of its capacity for evil and, in a miraculous *coup de théatre*, will be co-opted by us to re-focus its power on solving rather than creating problems. Even H.G. Wells at his most optimistic could only conclude that 'Human history becomes more and more a race between education and catastrophe.'[10]

If there is one word which we might single out to characterise the twentieth century and to distinguish it from its predecessors—a word whose appropriate ugliness will be exceeded only by its incontestable accuracy—it is surely *globalisation*, with all its cognates and synonyms. It is this century which invented *total* war and has gone on to stage two *global* examples so far; we have *global* communications and *global* pollution;

multi- and *trans*-national corporations; there are bureaucracies like the *World* Health Organization, *World* Bank and *United* Nations; there is *Earth*watch and the *World* Wildlife Fund; the *global* media frequently reports the outrage felt by *the international community* at some atrocity, even though nobody has the remotest idea what the community is or where it has its address; there are *World* football cups (and the anomalously named *World* baseball series); and of course, last but not least, there is the *Global* Village and the global economic imperative. All in all, enough to give *universal* man *Welt*schmerz.

Globalisation has operated to substitute economic activity and its relentless and directionless growth for any other measure of human dignity, purpose and happiness. Economic growth, resource depletion and environmental destruction are twentieth century phenomena which are inseparable from each other, co-carcinogens which feed off and at the same time contribute to an exploding global population. Their relationship might be called *symbiotic*, were it benign: it is, in fact, malign and a more usefully honest epithet which I shall coin as more properly descriptive of its impact on humankind, is *synthanatic*. Since there exists this collusive relationship, where each phenomenon is indispensable to the entirety of the process, it follows that it is in the reduction or elimination of any one of them—but preferably all—that the beginnings of a resolution of our crisis will be found.

Unfortunately, it is not a simple matter of mechanically reversing the process; or, as we saw earlier, of attempting to revert to some imagined former pristine state: imagined or not, it is not an option and—even if it were—I do not advocate puritanism as the cure for our ills, any more than Bill McKibben in Chapter Three and later, with his impeccable green credentials, was happy to turn in his big car and move into a log cabin.

One of the great ironies of the history of the century or so with which this book has been concerned, is that it operated until yesterday on a binary system of opposing ideologies—capitalism and communism—each of which, whilst appearing to offer the political 'consumer' a clear choice—always assuming, of course, that it was a choice which could be freely exercised—promised a commitment to the same unsustainable economic imperative; and the fact that the communist command system of economic management failed, through its ideological disdain for the mechanism of prices and markets, in no way detracts from that commitment. For when Nikita Khruschev took off his peasant boot and banged that table in Vienna in 1961, his threat that 'communism would bury capitalism' was not military, but economic. And we saw that even Fukuyama had to steel himself to acknowledge ruefully that 'neither economic system is particularly good for the environment'.[11] Neither capitalism nor communism foresaw what physical despoliation their industrial exploits would create. But yet we must be wary of latterday smugness in our having discovered these truths so late in the millennium: neither system set out deliberately to create the conditions for its own eventual failure and destruction; and, indeed, a central preoccupation of this book has been to locate an approximate symbolic point where an industrial system, which had been so uniquely successful in delivering unimaginable material comfort to so many people, first began to go wrong. That point, originating of course from earlier wellsprings, seems to have arisen somewhere early between the two World Wars (Chapter Three passim), when what had previously seemed to be purely a collection of individual *quantitative* changes and excesses coalesced to become a *qualitative* critical mass and presaged the pivot on which control of history would be lost.

Nor, even when the evidence began to turn up in one case after another, was either system willing spontaneously to confront the hidden costs of the nature and culture of its operations—the 'externalities'— and to pass them on for absorption by the final consumer. Neither was government—not only in the West, but even more especially in the old Comecon—prepared to lead from the front in modifying the economic culture in the long-term interest of its own survival. Probably the best that can be said of one system is that it began to be forced, from back in the 1960s, grudgingly to develop and to exercise a greater social responsibility in the conduct of its affairs; whilst the other was to collapse before it could graduate into the truly big league of consumerist lunacy.

Communism-Marxism was an academically constructed creation which was to be corrupted, betrayed and forfeited long before any initial promise it *might* have held, had even the chance of offering a proven alternate economic and political system; capitalism was the happenstantial result of a set of favourable geographical, political and even religious circumstances driven by the radical thinking of an unbroken series of advocates and apologists from Mun, Ricardo and Smith to Darwin, Friedman and von Hayek. In the event, the consequences—mindless globalisation—would have been the same. Now, one system has evaporated and any virtues it might have offered are too irretrievably buried in historical sludge to expect any early rehabilitation; and the other—the survivor—shiftily averts its gaze from the evidence that it must itself now adapt if it is to avoid *its* end of history. Totally new political machinery is now needed if the inherent tensions and incompatibility between (social) democracy and the free private market economy are to be resolved so that a human culture can survive and prosper in the third millennium.

Since today's organised global anarchy—it certainly does not deserve the term 'system'—won't work much longer, and there should seem little prospect of relief on the horizon in the form of H.G. Wells' (or anybody else's) *Federal World State*, there is only the third option of creating a quite different world order which will yet hold out some remaining promise of resolving *simultaneously*, albeit over many dangerous and painful decades of turmoil and readjustment, the linked menaces of environmental destruction, resource depletion, population explosion and the economic madness which binds them all together. The solution must overarch these menaces: it must go far beyond the well-meaning but ineffectual tinkering which sees humanity's salvation in a list of technical fixes ranging from catalytic converters and recycled paper to organic potatoes and dolphin-friendly fishing nets. Thomas More called his, rather Wellsian, ideal world Utopia (literally 'Nowhere'), first published in English in 1551. I shall call humankind's last shot at a sustainable world order: Autarky.

Let us start with a definition. Aristotle first coined the term *Autarkeia* (autarky = self-sufficiency) with reference to the ideal *size* and *condition* of the *polis*, the city-state which was the political and economic unit of fifth- and fourth-century Greece. By *polis*, Aristotle meant a body-politic with the 'possession of such material resources, and such moral incentives, as make a full human development possible, without any dependence on help from outside, material or moral.'[12] That was close to a realistically attainable ideal in Aristotle's time because the *polis* was a unit whose strength lay in its simplicity and an intuitive philosophical commitment to proportion and moderation. But tomorrow's Autarky will not be so stark—indeed, it cannot be because of the irreversibility of technology. And yet it will offer the promise of the benefits which were so apparent to Aristotle. So I shall now say what I mean, and do *not* mean, by Autarky; and I shall start by stating the objective behind Autarky.

That objective of Autarky is the regaining by the nation-state, or other given unit of community, of effective control over its affairs through the deliberate elevation of the interests and wellbeing of its people over—and in place of—the sectional priorities of national and transnational corporations and organisations, of whatever nature. Behind this key objective lies the determination to create a civil society whose nature reflects in full measure optimal use of its natural assets and liabilities in a process unstressed by extraneous factors over which the nation-state has now lost control—and lost, be it noted, to a set of forces over which humankind, as a whole, does not now pretend to exercise the slightest control at either a local or global level.

I am well aware that the *nation-state* does not enjoy an unblemished image. As a political phenomenon it is of recent vintage, having reached its apogee in Europe of the early twentieth century and—with a few major exceptions such as Japan—not having been widely or successfully paralleled or copied. That it has generally not been imitated elsewhere is due less to a lack of enthusiasm than to the escape of uncontrollable forces which have destroyed both the nation-state system in Europe itself, and virtually all other politically even less resilient entities in the rest of the world.

The image is now hopelessly and indelibly smudged partly by language decay: nation-state=Nationalsozialismus=Nazism; and partly by the conflation of nation-state with latterday *government*, which is popularly and rightly perceived to have failed almost everywhere it leaves its footprints. I shall frequently use the term 'nation-state' but, in doing so, I am not advocating a return specifically or only to the old nation-state as the basic or optimum unit of community. I intend the term to be used for two reasons and in two senses.

First, I use the term as shorthand to denote any culturally homogeneous unit of a size that is manageable by a true community of men and women; in this respect, then, it serves in the broadest way to differentiate such a unit from the gigantist and anarchic global contraptions we see today. This is how Maurice Ash puts it: 'We have to achieve government on a human scale. Such a scale is one in which democracy is… a reality—not the hypocritical farce of elective dictatorship which it now inevitably passes for. The very problem of environment seems to have arisen with the growing scale of our activities',[13] by which he means both economic and political.

The second use of the term is more literal and procedural. For many observers 'Small is indeed beautiful', and I have no argument with this view, quite to the contrary, except to point out that however small 'Small' is to be, these new communities can arise only through a conscious strategy which must almost certainly involve the nation-state. Earlier, in the Symposium, our world-historians showed that the nation-state system had collapsed but that it had not been replaced by something better. In fact, even worse, there was now international anarchy in the most literal meaning of the term of an 'absence of rule and order', other than that provided by the parastatal transnational corporation. If government *is* to become smaller, including the disaggregation of today's polities into county-size or smaller communities, there must first be a repossession by today's titular nation-states of the power now wafting aimlessly but dangerously around the world along with the CFCs; only then can there be a further devolvement from the centre. In other words, we must pass back to, through, and beyond the nation-state.

The implementation of Autarky means the formulation, adoption and pursuance by the nation-state (comprising the resulting smaller communities) of policies to achieve national self-sufficiency in foodstuffs, fuel, manufactured products and services supplemented, *where necessary*, by supplies acquired from exterior sources and funded by offsetting exports, all within the framework of a true balance of payments assisted, as necessary, by barter and multilateral clearing arrangements. It means the abandonment of the follies of modern development theory with its symbolic credo that the gap between Chad and Connecticut is an aberration which can be bridged through a bit of development in the former, and a junking of the second or third car in the latter. It means a reversion to a system of national political economies which observe natural and national advantages and constraints; and in a society governed by and for its people on a scale and in a manner which does not become blurred and vitiated by the international economic hooliganism which has alienated us from both nature and our fellow human beings.

Autarky does *not* mean, nor will it seek to encourage, a deliberate policy of economic or cultural isolationism or beggar-my-neighbour xenophobia. To the contrary: we shall see that it can only promote greater international harmony by relegating today's 'system' of political and economic distortions, tensions and absurdities to that historical landfill site. And it will not mean any reduction in international collaboration to respond to challenges which are not confinable to national frontiers, such as pollution, terrorism, nuclear proliferation and mass migration. All of these phenomena of the twentieth century—and many others—are the results of the loss to international anarchy of 'national or community air-space', and of the ease with which they can be internationalised.

Let us see how Autarky will lead us away from the end of history: in the process we shall come to recognise that it represents not only the best but, in fact, probably the only realistic prospect for humanity to parlay its condition in 2001 from imminent catastrophe, as depicted and even closely dated by Spengler, to a condition of indefinite and comfortable survivability for an infinitely smaller and happier world population by the year 2099. It will require in great measure the qualities and processes we salvaged from Toynbee and Hegel: successful responses to a never-ending phalanx of challenges as successive contradictions and tensions are met and resolved; and the recruitment of great leaders to the effort—all to the reassertion by a humbler humanity of *control* over its own behaviour within the environment to a degree and in a manner which reflect the lessons drawn from our hideous century. In this process, we must cease to regard the environment as an offshore object separate from ourselves—as something 'out there' in the words of Maurice Ash[14]—to be ministered to rather in the way you make a contribution to your favourite charity or help an old lady across a busy street. Of course, the very etymology of the word 'environment' gives the game away: it means 'aroundness' and so leaves no doubt of its anthropocentric nature.

Not the least of those challenges will be that to democracy itself, that is, the very form of political economy which is menaced and which we wish to save. But that particular challenge, and the certain issue of coercion of the passive majority by the dominant minority—which, let us recall, was expressly permitted by all three of our world historians—are inevitable whether we confide our future to the blandishments now being dangled before us by the snake-oil peddlers of the End-of-History scenario or, instead, seize the initiative and pursue the option of Autarky in the confidence that, with all its disagreeable disciplines, indeed because of them, it offers even odds on a resolution.

Now, deconstruct the first epigraph above, rearrange the words, and you can begin to see what Mr Rockefeller was probably getting at: then apply it in support of Autarky.

Throughout this book I have laid great emphasis on the naturally unequal global distribution of resources of every kind—God was tiring towards the end of that first difficult week; on the distortions that have been allowed to arise through the untrammelled pursuit of economic growth and the mirage of material equality amongst nations; and on the now deadly damage that has been wreaked on innocent people through attempts to bulldoze aside these natural inequalities in the name of free trade and the worldwide evangelization of Western-style liberal democracy—as if they were preordained by history as in some of Hegel's and Toynbee's more fanciful imaginings. The world is an inherently unequal and randomly hostile place, as uneven and capricious in the distribution of its amenities as its geography suggests. Autarky accepts this inequality as a natural condition but it rejects sticking-plaster 'development' surgery and demands that this inequality be given open and honest recognition so that each political unit—the nation-state or local community—can chart its natural unstressed course in that unequal world with the best chance of endurance within its means and in harmony with its neighbours.

Autarky will demand long-term planning by each nation-state and therefore a national commitment—a consensus—to support it to a distant horizon: today's adversarial party politics do us all a disservice. But it will not mean a reversion to Soviet-style Gosplans whose assumptions of eternal costless growth in industrial and agricultural production were as flawed as their counterparts in Western corporate boardrooms and trade ministries. It will require political courage and innovation, consistency and constancy in place of the opportunistic party politics which make vital long-term decisions incompatible with the greater short-term imperative of winning tomorrow's election.

Paul Kennedy writes: 'Even if the autonomy and functions of the [nation] state have been eroded by transnational trends, no adequate substitute has yet emerged to replace it as the key unit in *responding to change*.' [my emphasis][15] The central objective of Autarky shall be for each nation-state, and eventually smaller communities, to achieve equilibrium in its external trading accounts with the rest of the world; and for each nation-state to reassert control over inward and outward capital transactions. It is now beyond argument that it is the furious drive to manufacture and to export in order to finance imports, in a mindless vortex quite unrelated to any conscious national purpose, which is responsible for environmental destruction and resource depletion; and it is these distortions of the natural state which are largely responsible for fuelling the population explosion and for the seismic uprooting and urbanization of people by the billion around the world as they seek to respond with mesolithic brains and bodies to the twin imperatives of economics and technology.

For the First World, Autarky will—without any question—entail over the course of the twenty-first century a systematic decrease in the *perceived* material standard of living of the majority of its national populations, as calibrated by the squalid consumerist criteria which are presently used to measure the tinsel success of our Economic Wonderland. Each nation, each community, will negotiate trading treaties with all those with which it still needs to trade—in order to ensure supplies of commodities and services in which it is deficient—and always in the context of a balanced external trading account. Structural imbalances, where bilateral equivalence in trade cannot be achieved over the long term, will be remedied through multilateral clearing arrangements of the type which worked satisfactorily between the Western and Comecon nations up until the 1980s. It will mean a progressive drop in the sheer quantity and variety of consumer goods—but also ever-lessening obsolescence—as our bauble-bloated societies adjust to a form of political economy which is not at permanent war with the thin crust of raw materials, water and air upon which all depends; and as nation-states reassert control over their own economies so that employment in domestic industries is, in the interests of the nation as a whole, protected from the anarchic operation of the international economic imperative. It is clear that, over the new units of economy as a whole, the true costs of consumption are likely to increase as the culture of economies of scale and comparative advantage are replaced by consideration of more narrowly defined societary and ecological interest. In response to changes in technology, and changes in trading patterns brought about through Autarky, total national employment will adapt with expansion in one sector and contraction in another (it is a sinister feature of the progressive debasement of our language by jargon that, whereas jobs are 'created' in one industry, they are never 'destroyed' in another—only 'lost'); but neither individual lives nor the health of nations must any longer be permitted to be buffetted about by uncontrollable transnational convulsions in the name of privately directed economic growth driven by calculation of marginal costs.

It is self-evident that, at the macroeconomic level, any country which operates chronic balance of payments deficits in goods and services will benefit from a systematic move to full and permanent balance, with a reassertion of control over its national economy. Those who counter that the world's trading economy could not survive a sobered-up US economy—with a hundred-billion dollars' worth of annual purchasing power, i.e. the current typical trade deficit, eventually eliminated by Autarky, as well a progressive reduction in the service by the US of its million-million dollar pile of external debts run up through profligate consumption—would be well advised to reconsider the corrupt nature of the system they are implicitly advocating. It is quite hostile to all the precepts and axioms of prudent private and corporate financial management: after all, in a truly global or federal world political system—which has proved to be, and will no doubt remain, elusive—such massively destructive violations of fiscal prudence would be impossible, just as they are between regions of today's nominal nation-states. But Autarky is equally relevant to all other nations—whether in chronic deficit or surplus—whose economic sovereignty, and the implicit duty of care of government to the people, is compromised by extraneous events and forces over which it has relinquished control.

Autarky is not a single-issue, economics-only system for the future; rather, it is a coherent skein into which are woven equally strong political, moral, social and ecological elements. To illustrate, there is one recent example of governmental microeconomic mismanagement of such monumental and breathtaking stupidity, which I shall present because it will so brilliantly portray the benefits of Autarky and, coincidentally, tie in with the Carbon Factor of Chapter Five. The example is British, but I have no doubt that it can be easily replicated the world over, as well as in this country.

Great Britain, like most other countries, had since World War II reduced its dependence on coal (domestically produced) as a fuel, source of energy, and chemical feedstock. But even as late as the 1980s British Coal, the state-owned producer, routinely ran advertisements directed at selling to existing and potential industrial and domestic users the strategic advantages of a fuel whose reliability was not vulnerable to foreign disruption, and of which there were 300 years and more of reserves. Now, there is no doubt that oil is more flexible and versatile than coal; may have higher thermal efficiencies, i.e. cost advantages depending on current prices and, where applicable, freight rates; and has traditionally come in large measure from sources with the comfort of a high British profile (even before the North Sea): all good reasons for using oil. But it is equally true that, unlike most of its trading competitors, Great Britain had, in addition to its huge coal reserves, several other assets integral to a healthy coal industry—namely, a highly developed mining-equipment design and manufacturing sector, sophisticated mining technology, and a skilled and well-motivated workforce: all good arguments for coal.

Commonsense should have dictated that this country—blessed, as few others, with abundant coal, oil and gas—develop an integrated long-range national policy for something as fundamental as its energy supplies. In practice, not only are there not even the beginnings of such a policy but, for reasons of both political spite and ideological stupidity, the British coal industry has been flung out of the keystone position it should occupy not as a monopoly, but balanced in the energy equation as the only ultimate long-term domestic source of fossil fuel. As it is, in the 10 years between 1980 and 1990 the contribution of British coal to total British energy supplies declined by one-third and the decline continues apace; production and employment have collapsed; the mines are flooded and leak toxic chemicals into the rivers; and the longterm prospects for not only the mining-equipment industry but also for the even more important effort to research more efficient and cleaner methods of using coal, have been ravaged. Coal is, as demonstrated in The Carbon Factor, the only ultimate source of the mineral carbon which is of literally radical importance. The government's only defence of its failure to consult and to further the national interest is that British industry must have the cheapest sources of energy—in order, of course, to nourish the economic imperative: longer-term considerations of quite crucial importance to the nation subordinated to the economic imperative. Autarky will spring this trap.

So much for the First World. For a substantial portion of the Third World, the problem is made doubly intractable by the kind of wrong-headed nonsense exemplified in the second epigraph above: two mutually contradictory assertions made in successive paragraphs by a man of unquestioned good intentions. For this World, at least for those parts of it with an intelligentsia and deep reserves of social discipline or author-itarian traditions—Autarky can only be a good thing as barriers are erected to the import of products which are trivial and even socially injurious, and certainly ecologically malign: this World, at least, has no need to squander its limited hard-currency earnings on Michael Jackson posters, substitutes for mother's milk and Marlboro cigarettes. In place of the conditioned compulsion to extract, slash and burn and to export to pay for such tawdriness; to tolerate the social convulsions it provokes; and to service the foreign debt which has served these countries so ill, there will be a gradual reversion to a dignified sense of nationhood and to a sustainable practice of self-reliance. In any event, there will have to be found in the fairly near future the means to extricate both borrower and lender finally from the morass of hard-currency debt which rolled up in the 1970s and 1980s, and there can be scant likelihood that either party would happily contemplate a renewal of the relationship. Autarky will therefore be almost self-imposed.

At the international level, the economic culture gap which must be bridged is chasmic. Over there, in the green corner, is Jacobo Schatan on import substitution: 'Latin American countries are in a position to develop suitable capital-goods industries that can produce both the machines... and the finished essential goods that are required. If, in addition, an aggressive import substitution policy is pursued... Latin America could become economically self-sufficient and politically sovereign.'[16] And here, in the red corner, is Francis Fukuyama—also on import substitution: 'It became common practice in Latin America to use state power to advance the economic interests of the upper classes. These elites were protected by their own governments from international competition through import-substitution policies adopted by many Latin American governments... local producers could not realize potential economies of scale; the cost of producing an automobile in Brazil, Argentina, or Mexico, for example, ran from 60 to 150 percent higher than in the United States.'[17]

Well, Schatan is not a noted member of the cosseted automobile-producing upper class in Chile; and Fukuyama's blinkered view of the virtues of free trade is well illustrated by this piece of bathos—the example of the cost of producing a wretched automobile as a surrogate for a deeper analysis of the cultural and macroeconomic implications of free trade between such ill-matched trading partners. Perhaps the gap is indeed unbridgeable, perhaps this example may illustrate all too well and prophetically the monstrous cultural and political obstacles which lie in the path of Autarky—the gap symbolized by the irreconcilability of views of an introspective patriotic socialist economist, and of a cosmopolitan liberal democrat free-trader. But we must not forget that Chile is Schatan's country, not Fukuyama's; and that this is merely one vignette amongst millions which illustrate life at the receiving end of Western expansionism—often, no doubt, of a naively well-intentioned nature—which I chronicled in Chapter One, and which drives the Economics of Wonderland.

For much of the rest of the Third World—and I am bound to think of much of Africa and of parts of south Asia, the Middle East and the Western Hemisphere, particularly where population growth is so rampant—the very notion of Autarky as a conscious political choice will be a cruel illusion because the distortive malignity of the economic imperative has already pushed these regions beyond the point of self-redemption. Or rather, if it is not an illusion—that is to say, if these benighted territories are to submit to the stringencies of Autarky—then there arise ethical issues which our televisual view of the world forces nightly on to Western consciences stretched by either genuine compassion or atavistic guilt. Compassion or guilt, there is a moral dilemma for the First World; but fortunately the solution of Autarky is the same, and it is one which has the great advantage of being in the self-interest of the Firstworlders, as we shall see later.

An orderly decline in production and consumption, a deliberate decrease in foreign trade, and an intentionally contrived drop in living standards: to say that these are not the planks of successful election platforms is a modest understatement. However, they will undoubtedly be central elements and measures of our success in converting, through the first decades of the new millennium, today's Juggernaut economy into a mechanism which serves rather than enslaves humankind; in recapturing the control of history which seemed to be ours as the nineteenth century progressed; and, finally, in disciplining and subordinating technology. The survival, then, of the best features of social and liberal democracy should be in itself sufficient commendation for most people today to enlist in responding to the challenge: we are, after all, talking of a younger generation whose children and grandchildren they will expect to live to see out the twenty-first century.

But what will be the practical consequences of Autarky? Although there can be no simple reversion to some lost age of preindustrial innocence—nor do I advocate it—it is certain that achievement of Autarky will involve a lengthy process which, despite all its discomforts and dislocation, will be seen to be far less harrowing and stressful an experience for the vast mass of humankind than has been the horrific litany of war, social convulsion and technology-driven degradation which has brought us through the twentieth century to a conjuncture which none but the most optimistic neo-liberal would describe as a promising threshold for the third millennium. Moreover, in a world which seems now to lack even the vestige of any common human purpose, Autarky has the inestimable advantage of being an objective with clear social utility and purpose: a world consciously redesigned for human survival and welfare, in place of the chaos, selfishness, myopia and organised anarchy which have dominated human history in the age of the economic imperative. In the pursuit of that objective—of rediscovering community—there is plenty of room for an energizing spiritual element to replace the inanities of today's lumpen consumerism.

We now understand that there is no absolute virtue or intrinsic value in having a huge and still burgeoning human population unless, that is, it is for the purpose of ensuring ever-greater economies of scale in manufacturing for mass consumer markets. Even the so-called 'pro-lifers' in the current abortion furore are not, as I understand it, in some unholy collusion with transnational consumer-goods manufacturers. Autarky will both require and bring about a progressive decline in population, not only in the Third World but equally in the grossly over-populated First, in a process which will be the major single contributor to ecological repair. The population's age distribution will change as fertility rates drop below the replacement rate; and there will be funda-mental changes to present assumptions and practices as they bear on lifetime employment expectations and leisure-time. There will eventu-ally be a progressively smaller amount of work needing to be done, as nationally- and subnationally-managed companies and community units reclaim their sovereignty out of today's anarchy and resume responsibility for manufacturing and service functions which produce less and less for fewer and happier people working shorter hours.

The required population decreases—and we are looking at decre-ments of the order of perhaps 50% to 75% of present numbers, or broadly equivalent to the inevitable 'losses' which our present lunacies will otherwise surely bring about in the twenty-first and twenty-second centuries in conditions of unimaginable barbarity and inhumanness—will be brought about, it is to be hoped, through a change in popular perception of many so-called inalienable individual rights: in this case, the one which is invoked to justify the spawning of families of any size making unilateral demands narrowly on the charity of the state and, more broadly on the patience of the earth itself. Without such a change, there are otherwise only the prospects of either benign coercion through legal and fiscal sanctions, or of the barbarous alternative already clamouring in the faces of the future unborn billions.

There will arise the gravest and most profound challenges to our ethical and moral systems, and to our Western values and notions of personal liberty, as I shall note in the Epilogue. To take just one contentious example, compulsory sterilisation in all Worlds after the age of, say, twenty-five may well come to be regarded as no longer an unthinkable practice, inconsistent with notions of inalienable civil liberty in societies North and South, East and West, whose very excesses have made them quite incompatible with their own survival in any worthwhile form of human dignity. However, these values were culti-vated over centuries of thought, and of social and political experimen-tation and experience, and they could hardly have prepared us for the ironic possibility that the very enlightenment brought about in this long process might, through the unfettered development of applied technology, one late day call for forms and degrees of coercion and even an abridgement of those liberties so hardly won in that same enlightenment. In fact, what may seem like abridgements of personal liberty in today's democractic anarchy must come to be internalized as vital expressions of commitment to higher community purposes.

But Autarky will not in any way not diminish free and expanding cultural exchange between autarkic nations and communities in the new world order: on the contrary, as the role of consumption and the race to provide production to feed it diminish from the dominance they exert in the affairs of humanity today and, with the necessary economic functions shared out more equitably and sustainably between human beings and in national and local enterprises of human scale, people will find more natural release and recreation in cultural activities of the widest range both within the community and in its relationship with the rest of Autarky.

Meanwhile, there remains the Third World and the dilemma it will continue to pose equally for either the conscience or self-interest of the First World. Whatever the motivation, the dilemma remains the same: these countries, these regions, are entrapped in a vortex from which there is seemingly no escape as their exploding populations have served to chain them to a global economy which doesn't need their products— or enough of them, at any rate—to pay for their imports, whether of frivolities or of goods upon which they have become dependent. Since the latter now include foodstuffs and fuel for populations which have outstripped the ability of their living-space to provide, as well as medicines, the First World has an elegant choice: it must now most forcefully reject as an unequivocal failure the diet of foreign loans and 'aid' for half-baked development, and all the other cross-border investment and contractual paraphernalia designed purely to increase foreign trade in pursuit of some mirage of attainable global equality. These policies and practices are a curse upon the receiving country and on the rest of the world's economic and ecological health. So does the First World acknowledge that special arrangements should—for reasons of egoism or altruism—be engineered for countries which are presently or prospectively in permanent bankruptcy? Or does it simply cast these people adrift, as many have suggested, fully prepared to see their populations repeat in millions the pattern of a Rwanda a thousand times over, knowing that, in the healing fullness of time, history will employ benign neglect to produce final solutions?

From the midst of what is now set to become one of the world's greatest dilemmas, both moral and practical, and as the First World gets on, as it now must, with the design and implementation of Autarky, it seems that an exception must be made of the probably growing number of 'no-hopers' of the Third World, and I use the term not in a pejorative sense but to re-emphasize once more that the way of the West is neither sustainable where it has taken hold, nor achievable where its seeds are being sown. Once the First World accepts that harsh but realistic judgement, and has rid itself of the twin, grim notions of 'development' and 'developing nations', it can set about the task of caring for those regions for which there really is no hope—except, ironically, of being spared the false hope of Western-style bounty through industrialization. It is in the interests of the First World also to prevent rampaging migration— economic tourism, in the jargon—as well as further despoliation of the environments of the Third World. With the abandonment of the fetish of 'development', as well as its own adoption of Autarky, the First World can brazen out charges of neo-colonialism and enter into trusteeship arrangements with much of the Third World. The intention will be to stabilise their economies in ways as close to traditional sustainability as possible in return for adequate lifelong welfare as part of the compact of trusteeship. This will be, in effect, the North-South transfer advocated so widely, but without all the usual cant about economic development.

There will be something zoo-like in some such arrangements: but we must remember that one function of enlightened zoos is to preserve and protect species for which the quondam natural environment is no longer an option. What is incontestable is that there is no longer any justification—on the ground of either sentiment or hard-nosed reality—for continued 'aid' without conditions; the only alternatives are a continuation of the present multilaterally destructive madness, or the ruthless tossing aside of a large part of superfluous humanity—their abandonment to a catastrophe which would be no respecter of Third World borders.

Autarky for the First, Second and Third Worlds; trusteeship and subsistence support for the utterly hopeless. These policies, implemented in the first years of the third millennium, will provide the chance of unique and simultaneous equations for successful solutions to the interrelated menaces of pestilential human numbers, environmental destruction, resource depletion and the depredations of consumerism. It is a paradox that the very technology which has driven us towards the end of history will be required to redeem itself by providing many of the *material* solutions which Autarky will require. It remains only to consider whether we can make the cultural transition and overcome the global political thrombosis which now stands between ourselves and a resumption of history.

Epilogue:

Prologue to the Rest of History

'History is, once again, producing its list of winners and losers...
[we must ask] whether today's global forces for change are not
moving us beyond our traditional guidelines into a remarkable
new set of circumstances—one in which human social organizations may be unequal to the challenges posed by overpopulation,
environmental damage, and technology-driven revolutions. We
may have to think about the future on a far broader scale than has
characterized thinking about international politics in the past.' Paul
Kennedy: *Preparing for the Twenty-first Century*

To HAVE ANY PROSPECT of success, the Resolution will require
substantial changes in the relationship between the citizen and the
new forms of government, whether nation-state or city-state—changes
which, at first sight, may seem to cut across the grain of contemporary
liberal democratic culture. I am very conscious how hard-won and
fragile are our liberties and values; that we have thought and fought for
them in an erratic pattern of triumph and failure stretching back to
Fifth-century Athens; and that more than a thousand years of darkening
imperialist and barbarian brutishness in much of Europe separate the
civic enlightenment of Cicero from the modest promise of Magna
Carta. Although the entire process has needed over 2400 years to
mature, it is notable that much of its most emblematic success has, in
fact, been secured in only the last one hundred and fifty years or so. Here
are some of the more obviously important social achievements of the
West as a whole during the period:

- abolition of slavery
- legalisation of trades unions
- universal suffrage
- free education and health-care
- abolition of capital punishment
- welfare legislation
- adult literacy
- desegregation
- freedom of speech and association

None of these, and there are countless others, has a price if you don't enjoy them; and we cannot take lightly the prospect of curtailment of any one of them or a piecemeal infringement of the principles which lie behind them as a canon of Western culture. But the history which has occupied the last two hundred and more years—and pages—is now prodding us to recognition of the gross economic contradictions and tensions which now clearly threaten to destroy in the twenty-first century the very culture which rests on these principles. And it prompts me to flag the following historical coincidence, and to ask whether it is merely ironic or if there is a more causal connexion:

The social achievements cited above—deriving, though they indisputably do, from centuries of deep and slow-moving historical currents—have been bolted down into our culture precisely during the period after Napoleon Bonaparte's death in 1821 (when, according to Spengler, the West *peaked*) since when we have witnessed the elevation of the economic imperative to the pinnacle of human preoccupation. Now, is that just ironic coincidence or is there cause-and-effect at work? This book is not the place to draw a conclusion as to the truth of one proposition or the other—to argue for example that, if the case for the second proposition *were* proven, then we should promptly move to dismantle the whole social and economic infrastructure. But Francis Fukuyama is not alone in detecting a symbiosis of democracy and economic development; nor shall I hesitate to reiterate—with great reluctance—that the cure for our ills may indeed entail some abridgement of what we have become accustomed to regard as non-negotiable civil liberties, all as part of the 'price' of redeeming our pledges and restoring our lost community.

Overpopulation is the area where such an abridgement may best illustrate the choices—or, more truthfully, the absence of choice—which lie before us; and the case for abridgement is all the more powerful in tackling that *one single factor* which has been indicted as the *sine qua non* cause of our crisis, without which none of the others would menace the future of humankind. And here there are high stakes in what seems at first sight to be a zero-sum game: in a continuing regime of *laissez procréer*, the growth in numbers already programmed into the twenty-first century will impose its own mindless form of political repression on the First and Third Worlds; whilst deliberate interference by the state in what is still regarded archaically—certainly anomalously—as the inalienable right to produce unlimited numbers of human beings, will appear to many as a form of coercion inconsistent with our civil liberties.

But put it as starkly as this, and it is not a zero-sum game; it becomes a choice between indubitably losing our control of history in a chaos of extraneously imposed and involuntary social and political repression; or regaining that control through the orderly and humane but urgent adoption of stringent and, if they don't work, coercive legal, fiscal and social measures to reverse population growth. The sense of coercion must be replaced by an internalised sense of the personal and communal benefits which will result from population reduction. There is no longer room for pseudo-liberal fudging.

In many parts of this book I have contested Francis Fukuyama's announcement that the triumph of liberal economic democracy has delivered humankind at the End of History—to the very gates of his Promised Land. The untenability of his thesis has been one of my main themes, and its practical bankruptcy is evident throughout the world as small human advances are overwhelmed by massive inhuman reversals. As I reflect on the institutional and cultural obstacles which Autarky will have to vanquish, and relate those obstacles to the now proven role of liberal economic democracy in contributing to our crisis, I am reminded of some further words of Sir Roy Calne:

'The paradox of religion and secular liberalism is that excessive freedom leads inexorably to anarchy, and religious fundamentalism opposed to birth control results in population increase, with the danger of holy war and eventual anarchy. A crucial question... is whether it is possible to reconcile human nature, dependent as it is on the DNA we receive from our parents, with a peaceful coexistence with the rest of the planet. Looking back at history and viewing contemporary events, the outlook is bleak.'[1]

I would like Fukuyama to have been right about liberal democracy. But he isn't—he's dead wrong. Only in the very last paragraph of his splendid book does Fukuyama allow a hint of uncertainty to surface when he likens the course of humankind in History to a string of wagons plodding through immense adversity forward to a common destination: 'Nor can we in the final analysis know, provided a majority of the wagons eventually reach the same town, whether their occupants, having looked around a bit at their new surroundings, will not find them inadequate and set their eyes on a new and more distant journey.'[2]

The experience of researching and writing my book should perhaps have taught me better; but the temptation persists not to second-guess my own theory, which is the one certain product of my efforts, but to speculate on whether Autarky—the course I have shown to offer one sure solution to the forebodings of Kennedy and Calne and thousands like them—is likely to be adopted: that is, whether it will itself become the end of history. The question is, in fact, *political*, as an earlier quotation from Leo Marx suggests [p.193], and as even those not sold on Autarky will concede, unless they deny the need for *any* political changes whatsoever in the early third millennium. Having rejected the notion of *predirection* in history, I can hardly argue that Autarky is history in its finished state; but I can ponder the prospects for political change.

Paul Kennedy remarks: 'Since most politicians... have risen to the top through a process of compromise, making deals and alliances, and taking care not to annoy powerful interests, they are hardly prepared to endorse controversial policies now for purported benefits twenty years away.'[3] But he concludes that because there is such a dire need for a conscious and courageous response to the challenges of the twenty-first century, 'it may still be possible for intelligent men and women to lead their societies through the complex task of preparing for the century ahead.'[4] Some may say that this is not, in fact, an especially helpful conclusion since there is no definition of 'the complex task'. But if that complex task were to be anything as radical as a global embrace of Autarky before it's too late, then I would have to say that my profound confidence in Autarky on the one hand, and my uneasy scepticism of human beings' collective political courage, on the other, are in very very fine balance; and the utmost discipline and disinterest are required when sifting through the evidence for signs that the balance may one day shift for the better.

There *are* signs of political change: changes in the way ordinary people view government and how they interpret their own role in political processes. But it is far too early either to claim with conviction that these changes are truly systemic—for nothing less will do—or simply to concede that the numerous contemporary examples of a newly-awoken political activism are generally isolated campaigns in favour of *this* and against *that*, rather than surface ripples from some deeper-flowing radical undertow. But it is indisputable that in the West as a whole we are seeing more and more cases of direct action, referendums and direct participation, voting on special propositions at local and regional level, and agitation for the devolution of power from the centre; and that there is popular revulsion at the confrontational and adversarial nature of the legislature, and contempt for those who sustain the practice. The great dilemmas and issues which have been presented in this book do not deserve and cannot be solved by mediocre party-political pork-barrelling. As power is redeemed from global limbo, drawn back to the nation-state and on down into smaller polities, we shall see that we no longer enjoy the luxury—or is it that we can no longer afford the waste?—of spitefully competitive and narrowly self-interested solutions to problems which have but one solution. It is time for new forms of community and consensus.

There never was a golden era of good government when our kings, paramount chiefs and Caesars, our parliaments, senates and national assemblies were paradigms of probity and courage, of vision and charisma who would lead from the front and carry the people with them through challenges of the scale and complexity which now confront us. Like most historical romantics, I have a scrapbook of favourite historical vignettes—places and periods, acts and ages—which, give or take a few inconveniences and always assuming that I would have been born on the right side of the tracks, seem to have been 'good times to be around'. I recognise that the attractiveness of the vignette may be inversely proportional to a truly honest historical appraisal of it, but mine include:

• Fifth-century Athens
• Rome under Augustus
• Byzantium under Justinian
• The Quattrocento
• Eighteenth-century England
• America or England 1850-1914

I might have been tempted to add 'almost anywhere else than in the twenty-first century' were it not for a firm belief in the practicality of Autarky if only the *people* can translate the wish into political action. Common to all these vignettes is an almost remembered sense of order and progress, security and excitement, discovery and harmony, spirit and community which all now seem to be such remote virtues. If this is so, it is not because it is our particular misfortune to be governed in the embers of the twentieth century by men and women of unprecedented stupidity, selfishness, incompetence and dishonesty: today's breed possesses these human qualities in good measure but in no more than historically average quotas.

None of the issues which confronted all governments until the earlier years of this century were of the complexity—perhaps intractability—of those which beset us today. There were greater certainties and less public opinion to be cosseted; most of today's Demons were still in the larval stage; and most of the 'discovered' world was safe in the hands of a network of mutually supportive and tolerant European empire-states and their outposts in North America. Hegel and Marx, the Christian heretic, were probably right in their views—at the time—of Universal History. All the evidence, when they wrote in the first half of the nineteenth century, suggested that History was indeed an inexorable, conscious, human- or God-driven process towards a state of perfect harmony from which there would be no need for further development. They differed significantly only in their precise vision of the end-product of history: Hegel saw the destination as unequal *freedom* in the service of God, while Marx saw the state disappearing with the attainment of complete equality.

All that had changed with 1918. The larvae had begun to pupate; the popularly-imagined benign political giants—which we now need to square up to an increasingly dangerous and complex world in which the speed of change which our very ingenuity has created, has now begun to outrun the rate at which the same mesolithic brain can operate to contain it—all seemed to have gone to earth. Malign giants sprang up in Hitler and Stalin and Mao and hastened the loss of control of history even as they created stupendously hideous passages of it. But today's leaders have probably fared and performed no worse than their predecessors; and those who have been true giants of their time were largely single-issue operators—Churchill and Gandhi, Roosevelt and de Gaulle, Martin Luther King and Nelson Mandela—who might have been no more effective than the perceived dwarfs of today in recognising that a new history has started and that we have little more than stone-age tools to manage it. We *will* need the giant personalities of history, of which Hegel and Spengler and Toynbee all spoke, and the people will need to form their own conclusions about the nature of history and what they want to do with it.

Everything I have written proves that there are no quick fixes; maybe there are no slow ones, either. Autarky is not a fix at *any* speed: it's a condition, an attitude, it is the vision of a unique stable state which still beckons us from the future and holds out the prospect of humanity's regaining control of history, or what is left of it, if only the people *collectively* recognise the challenge and respond to it. This must be the Resolution—this alone will allow humankind to compound its fate with Gaia and her self-healing properties—'how she has coped with many accidents and diseases'.

Citation Index

Full publication details of the original works from which the following quotations are taken will be found in the Bibliography.

Chapter 1: Theories of Universal History
Oswald Spengler
Volumes I & II.
1 I.16-17; 2 I.3; 3 I.46; 4 I.47; 5 I.22; 6 I.4; 7 I.25-26; 8 II.32; 9 I.120-121; 10 I.353; 11 I.293; 12 I.43-44; 13 I.30; 14 I.xiv; 15 I.39; 16 I.160; 17 II.90; 18 I.39; 19 II.100; 20 II.416; 21 II.428-429; 22 II.431-432; 23 Table III—I. following p. 428; 24 II.454; 25 II.435; 26 II.421; 27 I.36; 28 I.42-43; 29 II.323; 30 II.99; 31 I.32; 32 I.44; 33 II.431; 34 II.502-503; 35 II.503.

Georg Wilhelm Friedrich Hegel
1 86; 2 99; 3 86; 4 86; 5 10; 6 15; 7 17-18; 8 (Parsons) 93; 9 1; 10 3; 11 6; 12 9; 13 13; 14 10; 15 456; 16 72; 17 73; 18 47; 19 74; 20 75; 21 341; 22 21; 23 (Spengler): I.22; 24 30; 25 31; 26 32; 27 45; 28 109; 29 449; 30 103; 31 19; 32 86; 33 Fukuyama: 3; 34 ibid. 65; 35 Hegel: 74; 36 Fukuyama: 67.

Arnold Joseph Toynbee
By kind permission of Oxford University Press.
Volumes I & II.
1 I.8; 2 I.7; 3 I.49; 4 I.49; 5 I.49; 6 I.53; 7 I.54; 8 I.55; 9 I.57; 10 I.60; 11 I.63; 12 I.67; 13 I.248; 14 I.211; 15 I.211; 16 I.548; 17 (V.G. Childe) I.69; 18 I.70; 19 (H.J. Spinden) I.75; 20 I.75; 21 I.98; 22 I.99; 23 I.549; 24 I.244; 25 I.553; 26 I.553; 27 I.245; 28 II.303-306; 29 II.306; 30 II.342; 31 II.338; 32 II.326-329; 33 II.314; 34 II.314; 35 I.129.

Chapter 3: Sowing the Seeds
1 Lovelock: 154; 2 McKibben: 156; 3 ibid.: 188; 4 Lovelock: 165; 5 McKibben: 3; 6 Greenpeace leaflet.

Chapter 4: No Pollution but People
1 *Limits to Growth*: 21; 2 Bulloch & Darwish: passim; 3 *Earth Report* 2: 8; 4 Malthus: Book I, 6; 5 ibid.: 5; 6 ibid.: 5; 7 ibid.: 6.

Chapter 5: Demons of the Third Millennium
1 Georgius Agricola: 214; 2 Goudie: 47; 3 Lovelock: 168; 4 Bulloch &
Darwish: 156; 5 ibid. 179; 6 ibid. 199; 7 Global 2000: 191; 8 Kahn: 94; 9
ibid.: 93; 10 ibid.: 89; 11 Commoner: 132.

Interlude 1: Footnote to the Environmental Debate
1 Barney: 1; 2 Simon & Kahn: 1; 3 Goudie: 350.

Chapter 6: A Simpler Theory of History
1 Hobsbawm: 495.

Chapter 7: Back to the Future with an Historical Discursion
1 Ziegler: 6; 2 ibid.: 27; 3 Myers: 47; 4 Trevelyan: 9-11; 5 Ziegler: 20; 6
ibid.: 22; 7 ibid.: 26; 8 ibid.: 196;

Chapter 8: Global Village: Economics in Wonderland
1 Fukuyama: 114; 2 ibid.: 114; 3 ibid.: 115; 4 Galbraith: Introduction
xxxi-xxxii; 5 Schatan: 15; 6 Reynolds: 679; 7 ibid.: 680; 8 Barney: Vol.
2, p.39; 9 Kennedy: 177; 10 Schatan: 68; 11 ibid.: 3; 12 ibid.: 26; 13 ibid.:
27; 14 Vaclav Havel: 'Needed: a new spirit for a new world'. The Globe
and Mail, Vancouver, 28 February 1994.

Chapter 9: Why 2001 Looks the Way it Does
1 Toynbee: II.222; 2 ibid.: I.248

Chapter 10: Towards a Political Resolution
1 Fukuyama: 136-7; 2 ibid.: 136; 3 Goldsmith & al. 275; 4 Toynbee:
II.326-331; 5 Wells: 752; 6 ibid.: 753-4; 7 ibid.: 754; 8 ibid.: 688-90; 9
ibid.: 758; 10 ibid.: 114; 11 Fukuyama 758; 12 Barker: 439; 13 Ash 75;
14 Ash passim; 15 Kennedy: 134; 16 Schatan: 115; 17 Fukuyama: 104.

Epilogue
1 Calne: 71; 2 Fukuyama: 339; 3 Kennedy: 345; 4 ibid.: 349.

A Note on the Statistics

This book is not intended as a major or even a minor source of economic and social statistics. However, statistics necessary to the book's purpose are presented, and some explanatory notes will therefore be useful.

The purpose of these selective statistics is to convey the immense scale and speed of change in the human condition since the late nineteenth century—1875 is my base year—a period of change without precedent in history. For this reason, I decided to minimise the use of tables—which are light on dramatic content—in favour of charts and graphs. For the same reason, I have also avoided as far as possible the presentation of actual statistical values, in favour of simply showing growth expressed as a rising percentage of the value 100 which I set at 1995/2001. The effect of this decision is to spare the reader from a surfeit of individually meaningless numbers and equally meaningless dates, and so to simplify and yet enhance graphic impact.

The late nineteenth and early twentieth century sources are all too often fragmentary, sometimes unreliable and in no case do they form part of a consistent series extending to the present day. Mulhall's *Dictionary of Statistics* of 1909-11 and Baron G. Fr. Kolb's *The Condition of Nations* of 1880 are vital sources for this early period and make wonderful reading even today. For the later period from 1937, the early United Nations Yearbooks are excellent, and they are then supplemented by other sources such as the OECD, IEA, FAO and B. R. Mitchell's *International Historical Statistics*. Because of the absence throughout the period from 1875 of uniform statistics and the consequent need to consult various sources, I have as far as possible included the same major countries in each statistic so that, between them, they represent 80%-90%, or more, of the universe. Some statistics, such as population and crude oil production, are 100%. In any event, incompleteness does not detract from the message conveyed by the statistics: in fact, quite to the contrary since, were they complete, the signal would only be that much stronger.

Bibliography

1. *The End of History and the Last Man.* Francis Fukuyama. Penguin Books, London. 1992.

2. *The Decline of the West.* Oswald Spengler. Tr. C.F. Atkinson. 2 Volumes. George Allen & Unwin Ltd. London, 1926 & 1928.

3. *The Philosophy of History.* Georg W.F. Hegel. Tr. J. Sibree. Prometheus Books, New York City, 1991.

4. *A Study of History.* Arnold J. Toynbee. Oxford University Press. 10 Volumes 1934-1955. Abridged by D.C. Somervell in 2 Volumes. Readers Union, London, 1960.

5. *Gaia: The Practical Science of Planetary Medicine.* James Lovelock. Gaia Books Limited, London, 1991.

6. *The End of Nature.* Bill McKibben. Viking, London, 1990.

7. *International Historical Statistics.* B.R. Mitchell. Stockton Press, New York.

8. *The Condition of Nations.* Baron G. Fr. Kolb. Tr. Mrs Brewer. G. Bell & Sons, London 1880.

9. *Dictionary of Statistics.* Michael G. Mulhall. Routledge, London 1909. Rev. Augustus D. Webb, 1911.

10. *Man and Nature.* G.P. Marsh. Ed. D. Lowenthal. Belknap Press, Cambridge, Mass, 1965.

11. *Silent Spring.* Rachel Carson. Alfred A. Knopf Inc., New York, 1962.

12. *The Closing Circle.* Barry Commoner. Alfred A. Knopf Inc., New York, 1971.

13. *Limits to Growth*. Meadows, Randers & Behrens. Signet, New York, 1972.

14. *The Earth Report 2*. Goldsmith & Hildyard. Mitchell Beazley International Limited, London, 1990.

15. *The Global 2000 Report to the President*. Dr Gerald O. Barney, Study Director. Penguin Books Ltd., London, 1982.

16. *The Machine in the Garden*. Leo Marx. Oxford University Press Inc., New York, 1964.

17. *Essay on the Principle of Population*. Thomas Malthus. J.M. Dent & Sons Ltd., London, 1970.

18. *A Geography of Population: World Patterns*. Glenn T. Trewartha. John Wiley & Sons Inc., N.Y., 1969.

19. *Water Wars*. John Bulloch & Adel Darwish. Gollancz, London, 1993.

20. *Future Shock*. Alvin Toffler. Pan Books Ltd., London, 1971.

21. *De Re Metallica*. Georgius Agricola. Herbert Clark Hoover and Lou Henry Hoover, translators. Dover Publications Inc., New York, 1950.

22. *The Next 200 Years*. Herman Kahn et al. Associated Business Programmes Ltd., London. 1977.

23. *Oil & Gas Information*. IEA/OECD, Paris, 1992.

24. *FAO Yearbook*—Trade Vol. 46, 1992.

25. UN Statistical Yearbooks.

26. *The Earth as Transformed by Human Action*. B.L. Turner, R.W. Kates. Cambridge University Press, Cambridge.

27. *Mineral Commodity Summaries 1994*. United States Department of the Interior. Washington DC, 1994.

28. *Oxford Economic Atlas of the World*. Oxford University Press, London, 1972.

29. *Atlas of the Environment*. Lean, Hinrichsen & Markham. Random Century Ltd., London, 1990.

30. *Theories of Society*. Ed. Talcott Parsons et al. The Free Press, New York, 1961.

31. *World Land and Water Resources*. Martin Duddin & Alister Hendrie. Edward Arnold, London, 1988.

32. *5000 Days to save the Planet*. Goldsmith, Hildyard, Bunyard & McCully. Paul Hamlyn Publishing, London, 1990.

33. *The Human Impact on the Natural Environment*. Andrew Goudie. Blackwell Publishers, Oxford, 1993.

34. *Earth*. Anne H. Ehrlich and Paul R. Ehrlich. Methuen London Ltd., London, 1987.

35. *A Handbook of Marxism*. Emile Burns, ed. Victor Gollancz Ltd., London, 1935.

36. *The Black Death*. Philip Ziegler. Alan Sutton Publishing Ltd, Stroud, 1991.

37. *English Social History*. G.M. Trevelyan. Longmans, London, 1945.

38. *England in the Late Middle Ages*. A.R. Myers. Pelican Books, London, 1956.

39. *The Resourceful Earth: a response to Global 2000*. Julian L. Simon & Herman Kahn. Basil Blackwell Publishers Ltd., Oxford, 1984.

40. *The Pocket Encyclopaedia*. London, ca. 1880.

41. *Economics*. Lloyd G. Reynolds. Ralph D. Irwin Inc. Homewood, Ill., 1969.

42. *The Affluent Society.* J.K. Galbraith. Hamish Hamilton, London, 1958.

43. *World Debt—Who is to Pay?* Jacobo Schatan. Zed Books Ltd., London, 1987.

44. *Outline of History.* H.G. Wells. 2 Vols. George Newnes Limited. London, 1920.

45. *Preparing for the Twenty-first Century.* Paul Kennedy. HarperCollins Publishers Ltd., London, 1993.

46. *Too Many People.* Sir Roy Calne. Calder Publications Limited, London, 1994.

47. *Space, Time and Man.* Grahame Clark. Cambridge University Press, 1992.

48. *Age of Extremes: the Short Twentieth Century 1914-1991.* Eric Hobsbawm. Michael Joseph, London, 1994.

49. *The Politics of Aristotle.* Tr. Ernest Barker. Oxford University Press, Oxford 1948.

50. *The Fabric of the World.* Maurice Ash. Green Books, Dartington, 1992.

Index